D0773666

REFORMATTED

Reformatted

*Code, Networks, and the Transformation
of the Music Industry*

ANDREW LEYSHON

OXFORD
UNIVERSITY PRESS

OXFORD

UNIVERSITY PRESS

Great Clarendon Street, Oxford, OX2 6DP,
United Kingdom

Oxford University Press is a department of the University of Oxford.
It furthers the University's objective of excellence in research, scholarship,
and education by publishing worldwide. Oxford is a registered trade mark of
Oxford University Press in the UK and in certain other countries

First Edition published in 2014

Impression: 1

Published in the United States of America by Oxford University Press
198 Madison Avenue, New York, NY 10016, United States of America

British Library Cataloguing in Publication Data

Data available

Library of Congress Control Number: 2014933807

ISBN 978–0–19–957241–0

Printed and bound by
CPI Group (UK) Ltd, Croydon, CR0 4YY

For Linda, Sophie, and Tom

Preface

In his book about the history of the music industry, *Appetite for Self-Destruction*, music journalist Steve Knopper (2009) describes an international music convention called to address the wide-reaching implications of a new digital technological development that had the potential to transform the musical economy. The advocates of this new technology made big claims, arguing that it was likely to have a significant impact on the record business as it would be very popular with music consumers and lead to an unprecedented era of growth and expansion. Its supporters, who were mainly based in technology companies, were keen that record companies should be converted to its merits and promote the conversion of music catalogues to the new format so that record labels and technology companies alike would be able to share in the coming bonanza. However, the technology company executive that had been deputed to make the case for the new format found it hard to get through to his audience of senior record company executives. Indeed, Knopper reports how they rounded on him, arguing forcefully against the technology, insisting that it would not drive revenues up but, rather, would actually lose them money. As far as the record companies were concerned, the new format would merely facilitate what the industry described as 'piracy', or the generation of illegal copies of copyrighted material. In addition, all the record companies had considerable sunk costs invested in capital equipment within manufacturing facilities, which would now be forgone, and the costs of adjustment would be considerable. The technology company rep was taken aback: 'I was fortunate there weren't any rotten tomatoes in the room ... [or] they would have thrown them at me' (quoted in Knopper, 2009: 23).

The revolutionary new format being pitched to the music industry was not, as you might reasonably expect, MP3 in the mid to late 1990s but rather the compact disc in the early 1980s—at the 1981 International Music Industry Conference in Athens to be precise. In hindsight, the opposition to the introduction of the CD by record companies seems absurd. The digital reformatting of the industry ushered in a golden era for industry as per capita expenditure

Preface

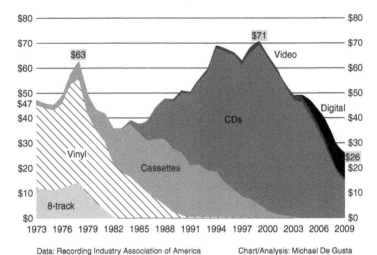

Fig. 0.1. US record music revenue, by format, 1973–2009 (2011 US$ per capita).

Source: De Gusta, 2011.

on music through the sale of CDs rose steadily until the late 1990s (De Gusta, 2011; Figure 0.1).

That the CD facilitated the production of counterfeited copies of copyrighted material was not in doubt, but such were the profits being made through the sales of CDs that such piracy could be reduced to the category of minor irritation, and which even in its most rampant form was mainly present in markets beyond North America and Western Europe and so less important to the financial health of the major record companies.[1] Moreover, as Knopper points out, record companies gradually warmed to the merits of CD, as the promise of high-quality sound made it possible to sell already recorded music— back catalogue—at a higher cost, but also because the conversion 'costs' of moving from one format (vinyl and/or cassette) to another (CD) was used to justify the redrafting of artists' contracts so that

---

[1] In addition, large-scale CD manufacturing plants producing illegal copies required considerable fixed capital and variable investment, which tended to be available only to the most organized of illegal practices. This meant that it was relatively easy to enrol the criminal and judicial system to help prevent music piracy, particularly where it impinged upon core markets in North America and Europe.

more money was retained by record companies as compensation (2009: 32).

I am not aware that any technology company sought to win over the record industry to the merits of MP3 in the 1990s in the way attempted for the CD because, unlike the CD, MP3 was not designed for the record industry. A software solution to the development of digital television, it worked its way into the music industry initially through informal channels, which meant that the industry failed to organize a response that might it see it benefit from the new format (see Chapters 2 and 3). By the time such arguments came to be pitched, MP3 had developed a life and ecosystem all of its own and the forms of digital lock-down that the music industry had insisted upon with the introduction of the compact disc proved difficult if not impossible to realize. There are signs that the industry is now finally stabilizing around the new social and technological arrangements associated with MP3 and other purely digital formats. However, this process of adjustment has been slow and painful, and has radically transformed the way in which the music industry reproduces itself. It is this process that this book documents.

The book has been put together over a long period of time, and I owe a debt of gratitude to the many people who have helped along the way. I am grateful to all those in the music industry who agreed to share their knowledge and expertise through interviews, conversation, and other kinds of exchanges. I am particularly grateful to Julie Bateman, Malcolm Atkin, and Peter Filleul of the Association of Professional Recording Studios (APRS) for their help and assistance: without them many doors would have remained closed, and through their efforts I was privileged to address a gathering of APRS members at the University of Nottingham's London Office in 2006 to help put some conceptual flesh on the bones of the crisis that they were experiencing first hand every day. I first began to consider music from a geographical perspective in the early 1990s thanks to the encouragement first of Stuart Corbridge and Gerry Kearns, and then, more importantly, by David Matless and George Revill. Dave became a colleague when I moved to School of Geography at the University of Nottingham at the end of the 1990s, and I have been fortunate to work in an environment of scholars that has both encouraged and challenged my accounts of change in the musical economy. I would like to thank Jon Beaverstock, Andy Cook, Louise Crewe, Steve Daniels, Georgina Endfield, Shaun French, Dan Grimley, Sarah Hall,

Mike Heffernan, Amanda Huskinson, Steve Legg, Sarah Metcalfe, Kevin Milburn, Carol Morris, Michael Samers, Adam Swain, Alex Vasudevan, and Charles Watkins for their comments and/or collegiality along the way. I am particularly grateful to Louise and Charles for being Acting Head of School for six months from February 2013 as I recovered from an accident caused by being hit by a car when cycling. I am also grateful to the School's Research Committee for some seed corn funding at a key moment in my research. Beyond Nottingham I would like to thank Roger Lee, Kris Olds, Jamie Peck, Jane Pollard, Adam Tickell, and Nigel Thrift for their support and encouragement over many years. Louise Crewe, Shaun French, Nigel Thrift, and Pete Webb helped to develop some of the ideas in this book through our collaborative research undertaken as part of an Economic and Social Research Council grant which examined the rise of e-commerce. They are also the co-authors of Chapter 4 in its original form and I am grateful that they have generously granted permission for a revised version to be reproduced here. The diagrams have mostly been drawn by Elaine Watts with the support of Chris Lewis. Emma Booth at Oxford University Press was a very patient yet very encouraging presence throughout.

But most of all I would like to thank Linda, Sophie, and Tom for their support and tolerance during the long gestation period of this book. Their keen and persistent willingness to prevent me taking academic life too seriously is deeply appreciated, although it may not appear so at the time. I'm particularly grateful for their love and care in helping me to recover from my accident. The period of recuperation that followed enabled me to revisit and complete this project, although it was achieved in circumstances that I would have preferred to have avoided.

I also gratefully acknowledge the permission to publish the following copyright material. Chapter 2 is a revised version of my 'Time-Space (and Digital) Compression: Software Formats and the Geographical Reorganisation of the Music Industry', first published in *Environment and Planning A*, 33(1): 49–77, 2001, and is published here with the permission of Pion Ltd, London; Chapter 3 is a revised version of my 'Scary Monsters: Software Formats, Peer-to-Peer Networks and the Spectre of the Gift', first published in *Environment and Planning D: Society and Space*, 21(5): 533–58, 2003, and is published here with the permission of Pion Ltd, London; Chapter 4 is a revised version of Andrew Leyshon, Peter Webb, Shaun French, Nigel

Thrift, and Louise Crewe, 'On the Reproduction of the Music Industry After the Internet' first published in *Media, Culture and Society*, 27(2): 177–209, 2005, and is published here with the permission of SAGE Ltd, London; Chapter 5 is a revised version of my 'The Software Slump? Digital Music, the Democratisation of Technology, and the Decline of the Recording Studio Sector within the Musical Economy', first published in *Environment and Planning A*, 41: 1309–31, 2009, and is published here with the permission of Pion Ltd, London.

Contents

List of Figures

List of Tables

List of Abbreviations

A&R   artists and repertoire (recording company department in charge of finding, signing, and developing new talent)
APRS   Association of Professional Recording Studios
IFPI   International Federation of Phonographic Industries
IP   internet protocol
IPO   initial public offering
IPR   intellectual property rights
IRC   internet relay chat
ISP   internet service provider
P2P   peer-to-peer
RIAA   Record Industry Association of America
SDMI   Secure Digital Music Initiative

1

Crisis? What Crisis?

On 28 April 2013 Apple's iTunes online music store celebrated its tenth anniversary. By any measure, Apple was surely justified in celebrating this achievement given how, within a relatively short period, iTunes had managed to implant itself firmly at the centre of the musical economy, and its history is one of rapid growth and expansion (see Table 1.1).

In its first week of operation, despite business at that time being restricted to Apple computer users based in the United States, over one million songs were downloaded. This increased to 10 million within six months, and by the first anniversary in 2004 the total had risen to 50 million and to 100 million by the end of the year. The service soon began an extensive process of internationalization, with operations being opened in twelve European countries and Canada, while the system migrated beyond the Apple ecosystem to work on computers run by Microsoft. By 2009 the iTunes catalogue had indexed more than 10 million songs. Roll forward to 2013 and by the tenth anniversary the number of downloads had risen to 40 billion. iTunes was by then operating in over 100 countries and Apple was generating profits of $4bn per quarter. iTunes had become the largest music retailer in the United States, and the popularity of the service had gone a long way to help Apple sell hundreds of millions of iPods and iPhones through which the songs on its catalogue could be played while on the move.

iTunes is the most successful of a large number of legal download services that now circle the world. These licensed sellers of recorded material support the system of intellectual property rights that underpins the music industry as it has been traditionally organized and facilitates the flow of money from consumers through the music industry to artists in return for the digital music files that have now become the default mode of listening for many music listeners. By 2013

Table 1.1. iTunes downloads (cumulative)

Year	Number
2003	10m
2004	100m
2005	300m
2006	1bn
2007	2bn
2008	5bn
2010	10bn
2011	15bn
2013	40bn

Source: ITunes Store.

the International Federation of Phonographic Industries (IFPI) even argued that digital music consumption 'had become mainstream', reporting the results of a consumer survey that revealed that 62 per cent of internet music users between the ages of 16 and 24—the main buyers of music goods and services—had 'engaged in some legitimate digital music activity in the past six months' (IFPI, 2013: 6). As these services have been rolled out in new markets, so the number of downloads from such services increased: legal download services delivered 2.3 billion downloads of single tracks and 207 million downloads of digital albums in 2012 (4.3 billion tracks in all), a year on year increase of 12 per cent (IFPI, 2013). This growth had even brought about a minor revival in the global music industry, and the year to 2012 witnessed the largest growth in recorded music sales since 1998, with the IFPI reporting with optimism the ways in which the music industry was becoming more integrated into the digital economy and, in particular, with social media.

Given this upturn in fortunes in the musical economy, and the ways in which a key music industry institution such as the IFPI was embracing engagement with the internet, it is tempting to suggest that some kind of Rubicon had finally been crossed and that the music industry was set fair for a stable and predictable era of growth based on digital music sales. Perhaps, but even if this were true, this stability would represent change in itself, because since the late 1990s the industry has been anything but stable, having been subject to an extraordinary upheaval. This was caused by a transformation in the bases of competition in the industry brought about by the rise of MP3 software formats and internet file sharing. As this book explains, the advent of MP3 was the tipping point that put the industry into a dangerous tailspin from which many practitioners feared it might never recover. While such an outcome was never really likely, the music industry has been subject to unprecedented challenges. That 2012 saw the largest growth of sales since the onset of this crisis was a significant sign of optimism for the industry, and suggested that it may have levelled out from its tailspin, albeit by flying at a much lower altitude than that to which it was previously accustomed. And the 'recovery' of industry needs to be put into context: the annual growth in sales of recorded music to 2013 was just 0.3 per cent, so for this to be the largest increase since 1998 shows just how badly the sales have been affected by events in the early twenty-first century. Moreover, although digital music sales have increased at a steady rate, overall sales remain dominated by music in physical formats such as CD (which still made up 58 per cent of the total in 2012: IFPI, 2013), the demand for which continued to decline, thereby ensuring that overall growth remained anaemic. The gradual decline in the sale of music in physical formats had led to a thinning out of the number of record shops in major markets (Jones, 2009; Zetner, 2008), which accelerated after the onset of the financial crisis, following the collapse of several major record retailers. Moreover, as the IFPI report makes clear, and to stretch the aeronautical metaphor perhaps to breaking point, the industry may be still flying but the cautionary seat-belt signs remain on, due to the clear and present danger of further turbulence. The music industry remains haunted by the spectre of file sharing on peer-to-peer social networks, where recorded music is exchanged in defiance of intellectual property law. Indeed, the IFPI claim that a third of all internet users regularly access unlicensed sites for music for which no fee is offered or received. This corroborated other industry research, such as that by consultancy Musicmetric, which reported that file sharers in the US and the UK using the BitTorrent peer-to-peer network illegally downloaded 1.1 billion tracks in the first six months of 2012 alone (Musicmetric, 2012). In other words, the number of tracks downloaded illegally within just two countries over six months was equivalent to 25 per cent of all global legal downloads over an entire year. Given that illegal peer-to-peer sites have been operating internationally for at least a decade, simply scaling up the US and UK figures across other major territories for an entire year leads to the not unreasonable conclusion that the number of illegal downloads far outweighs those downloads made from legal services.

One of the main reasons why the financial performance of the music industry has not managed to match growth levels last seen in the late 1990s is that unlicensed peer-to-peer computer networks, which made digital file sharing easy, also began to emerge at this time. The chapters in this book chart the transformation of various constituent parts of the musical economy as software formats such as MP3 emerged from their previous redoubts within relatively small computer-literate and hacker communities. They quickly migrated to wider and less technically proficient publics, through institutional and technological innovations brought into existence via the dot.com bubble associated with the New Economy (Daniels et al., 2007). The end of the twentieth century is an important reference point for this book for another reason too: not only did it remain the high water mark for growth in the music industry over a decade and a half later, but it was also the date at which the research reported in this book began, after I was first introduced to the concept of MP3 and its use in combination with the distributive power of the internet.

By 1997 I had already published work on the geography of music (Leyshon et al., 1995), and was waiting for the publication of an edited book on *The Place of Music* (Leyshon et al., 1998). Although this work was generally well received, and had helped to carve out a new line of enquiry within human geography, I was never entirely satisfied with what I was doing, mainly because I had not found a research problem that played to my strengths and interests as an economic geographer. For this reason, I remain particularly grateful to an undergraduate at the University of Bristol who was in the Department of Geography as part of the Erasmus exchange programme. Knowing I had already published work on the geography of music, he came into my office one day to present me with a CD which contained upon it what, at the time, seemed to be an impossible number of tracks, well over a hundred. As it played in the background on my PC, he began to tell me of the new phenomenon that was sweeping hacker communities on the internet, and in which he participated, that made it possible to download all kinds of music for free (although given the angular sounds coming from my computer speakers, he seemed only to be interested in a hard-core variant of German 'techno' dance music). I don't claim to possess particular gifts of insight and prediction, but I was certain that this was both an inherently geographical phenomenon, as it enabled music to move through time-space in new ways, and, because of this, was going to have important implications for the organization of the music industry; this means of capturing and replaying music was achieved in networks that lay outside the established institutional and regulatory structure of the music industry.[1]

I was fortunate to have the rise of MP3s and internet file sharing brought to my attention when it still remained below the horizon of most economic commentators, let alone social science researchers. This made it possible for me to begin to document the impact of digital technology on the musical economy from relatively early on and as it has evolved. In so doing, the work in this book is strongly informed and influenced by what Nigel Thrift (2005) has described as a 'close attention to the present', and I have at times deployed a descriptive, narrative style in order to do so, as a means of documenting the twists and turns of what he also describes as 'capitalism's ceaseless experimentation' (Thrift, 2001: 379). As Thrift has argued, one of capitalism's most notable features, and the source of its durability and persistence in the face of multiple and repeated crises that at the time might appear to be terminal, is its capacity for innovation and adaptability. The history of the music industry since the late 1990s is a particularly good example of such innovation and adaptability. It is constantly mutating, albeit within constrained parameters that set the terms and conditions on how industries and firms are able to reproduce themselves. Moreover, this is a highly political process, with winners and losers, and for many the stakes are very high. The work that follows seeks to investigate what I describe as musical networks. The approach is theoretically heterodox, and is influenced by a range of cognate fields, including social theory, geographical political economy, cultural studies, and actor-network theory. The chapters in turn address particular parts of musical networks, although the focus is mainly on networks of creativity, reproduction, and distribution. The key resource for the research is over fifty hours of material drawn from interviews undertaken with managers and employees in the music industry over several years in both the US and the UK. Apart from a minority of instances where permission

---

[1] Although I was clearly not the only person to be coming to similar conclusions at the time. Tony Wadsworth has written of the time during his tenure as Managing Director of the Parlophone record label when an employee handed him a CD-R with the entire back catalogue of The Beatles, who were originally signed to that label in the 1960s, which he describes as 'the Holy Grail of pop music assets' (Wadsworth, 2011: 2).

was not forthcoming, all interviews were recorded and subsequently transcribed for analysis.

The remainder of the book is organized as follows. Chapter 2 examines the geographical and organizational consequences of the emergence of a new 'technological assemblage' within the music industry in the late 1990s, organized around MP3s digital files and internet distribution systems. The chapter explores the relationship between technological innovation, economic competition, and the contestability of markets for digital goods and services. The chapter sets out two opposing arguments that circulated within the music industry at the end of the 1990s: one that denigrated the emergence of software formats such as MP3, and another that celebrated it. The chapter critically analyses electronic markets and their impact upon economic organization, and examines the impacts of digital content and electronic markets within the music industry through the concept of the musical network. Four networks with distinctive organizational and spatial characteristics are identified within the musical economy: networks of creativity, of reproduction, of distribution, and of consumption. All four networks were reshaped as a result of the impact of software formats and internet distribution systems, and in so doing threatened the short-term profitability of established firms within the industry, although there were already signs that forces within and cognate to the industry were seeking to restabilize around a new technological and regulatory regime designed to protect copyrights in music in software formats.

Chapter 3 focuses in more detail on the emergence of sociotechnical networks made possible by combining of software and peer-to-peer computer networks. These socio-technical networks destabilized the regime of governance that supported 'copyright capitalism' by creating a series of gift economies where the products of those industries are given away. This development had significance for a wide range of creative industries dependent upon copyright protection for their reproduction, including motion pictures, publishing, and software engineering. However, it was within the music industry that the challenge to the mode of reproduction of copyright capitalism was most acute and immediately apparent. The origins of these gift economies were founded in the academic roots of the internet. A musical gift economy centred upon MP3 emerged during the early 1990s, but was only constituted as a problem for the music industry after the commercial invasion of the internet during the late 1990s.

Dot.com start-ups transformed the specialized knowledge that was once the preserve of hackers and hobbyists into generic knowledge through the development of 'user-friendly' file-exchange systems, providing mass access to previously underground musical gift economies. The music industry mobilized the powers of law enforcement to reassert their control over the circulation of recorded music, and successfully tamed many of the firms that initially sought to extend this gift economy for commercial gain. However, in the early 2000s there emerged a set of networks that were both ideologically and substantively opposed to the interests of copyright capitalism, and that were more resistant to attempts to reassert the control of the large corporations. The existence of these peer-to-peer networks undermined the ability of large media companies to extract value from copyright in the way they have in the past, and used space and mobility to evade legal control.

By the early twenty-first century the music industry began to suffer from falling sales, negative growth, and financial losses. Explanations internal to the music industry quickly and decisively identified the cause of the crisis as the rise of internet file sharing, or 'piracy' in the industry's terminology. However, the emergence of software formats, such as MP3, and internet distribution systems is more accurately categorized as a 'tipping point' that brought into focus a set of deeper structural problems for the industry related to changing forms of popular music consumption. Chapter 4 examines responses to the crisis in the form of three distinctive business models that represented different strategies in the face of the crisis of the musical economy, an arena within which a range of experiments were undertaken in an effort to develop new ways of generating income. Nevertheless, there was reluctance within the industry to embrace the more radical organizational changes that might have allowed it to fully accommodate the impact of software formats and internet distribution systems. A key reason for this reluctance was the stake that the leaders of the major record companies had in the preservation of the existing social order of the musical economy.

As Chapters 2 to 4 illustrate, the music industry was radically transformed by software. The development of MP3 and the rise of internet file sharing had significant impacts upon intellectual property rights and distribution within the industry, with serious consequences for record companies. Chapter 5 explores another part of the musical economy, the recording studio sector, which was also transformed through code. The chapter reveals how the introduction of software into the recording process encouraged a vertical disintegration of production in musical agglomerations from the late 1970s onwards and, in so doing, helped leading recording centres to strengthen their hold on the market for recording budgets. However, the impact of software since the mid-1990s has been less benign for such centres. The rise of more affordable digital recording rigs and easier programming protocols represented a democratization of technology, making available a process that was once only accessible through the facilities and skills provided by a recording studio. Software and code ushered in a regime of distributed musical creativity, which had significant impacts on the organization of the musical economy. As a result, the recording studio sector entered a severe crisis which has produced a spate of studio closures, redundancies, and underemployment within musical agglomerations, leading to a significant depletion in the 'institutional thickness' of key recording centres.

Chapter 6 focuses on the financialization the musical economy. With the music industry in crisis since the dawn of the twenty-first century, record companies struggled to find new business models and viable income streams in the wake of file sharing on peer-to-peer networks and the arrival of new market entrants based on legal digital download systems that between them have lowered margins for incumbents. This environment was ripe for exploitation by the private equity sector, the repertoire of which includes the restructuring of struggling companies in failing industries. The chapter focuses on the implications of the purchase by private equity firm Terra Firma of EMI, the UK's last remaining large record company, in 2007. Terra Firma sought to turn around EMI by calling its culture of creativity to account, and forcing its employees to focus on the bottom line. Terra Firma's social experiment in the musical economy failed, but this was mainly due to a shift in the socio-technological bases of the musical economy and the depth and duration of the financial crisis which was its background and context.

The book concludes with an Afterword, which draws on the preceding analysis to consider the implications of the emergence of new economic forms and organizations for the contemporary musical economy.

2

Time-Space (and Digital)
Compression: Software Formats, Musical
Networks, and the Reorganization of the
Music Industry

2.1. INTRODUCTION

> Music is prophecy. Its styles and economic organisation are
> ahead of the rest of society because it explores, much faster than
> material reality can, the entire range of possibilities in a given
> code. It makes audible the new world that will gradually become
> visible, that will impose itself and regulate the order of things;
> it is not only the image of things, but the transcending of the
> everyday, the herald of the future. (Attali, 1984: 11)

This chapter introduces the problem that the emergence of MP3
created for the musical economy through an exploration of the relationship between technological innovation, economic competition,
and the contestability of markets for goods and services. In doing so
it addresses three issues of general relevance: first, the transformative impact that economic competition can have (Storper and Salais,
1997); second, the economic role of information and knowledge
(Daniels et al., 2000) and the organizational implications of electronically mediated information and computer software (Bauman, 2000;
Luke, 1998; Pratt, 2000; Robins and Webster, 1999); third, and finally,
the role of geographies of regulation and governance, and the shifting complexities of regulatory space (Hudson, 2000) within a world
of digital content and surveillance (Curry, 1996; Lessig, 1999, 2001,
2005, 2008; Leyshon and Thrift, 1999; Ryan, 1998). Specifically, the
chapter examines the impact of a new *technological assemblage*, made

up of software formats such as MP3 and internet distribution systems, upon the geographical and institutional organization of the music industry.

The argument in this chapter is developed as follows. Section 2.2 provides an introduction to the idea of software formats and examines reactions to their emergence within the music industry in the 1990s. Section 2.3 considers the economic effects of combining software products with the distributional capabilities of the internet through an analysis of 'electronic markets' and, in particular, the ways in which such markets can transform the competitive bases of industries through processes of disintermediation and reintermediation. Section 2.4 develops a theoretical approach to the music industry that helps identify the impacts made by software formats such as MP3. It develops the concept of the musical network, and identifies four distinctive musical networks within the music industry: creativity, reproduction, distribution, and consumption. Section 2.5 examines the impacts of software upon the four musical networks, and identifies those most likely to be transformed.

2.2. SOFTWARE FORMATS AND THE MUSIC INDUSTRY

The relationship between the music industry and technology has long been a close and intimate one. The industry emerged around the end of the nineteenth and the beginning of the twentieth century in the wake of innovations in sound reproduction and, especially, electrification (Frith, 1988). Thereafter, the industry evolved in lockstep with, although not determined by, a range of technological advances, from the development of vinyl as a reproductive medium, to the introduction of magnetic audiotape, up to the digitalization of music and the creation of formats such as compact disc, digital audiotape, and minidisk. These technological transformations have usually been economically beneficial to the industry in its broadest sense, although as we saw in the Preface, the industry has not always recognized this. Consumer electronics companies created new markets for reproduction equipment, while new formats enabled record companies to mine their back catalogues, selling old recordings in new forms, of which CD was the best example (Lovering, 1998; Knopper, 2009).

By the mid-1990s, this virtuous circle of technological development began to enter a new phase as the industry prepared to connect to what was described as 'the information superhighway' to distribute digital music direct to consumers along fibre cables.

Initially, the industry welcomed this vision of a world of digital distribution (e.g. see Sadler, 1997: 1931). However, by the end of the 1990s, a mood of cautious optimism had evaporated, to be replaced by one of fear and loathing. A world of cabled and wireless connectivity began to be perceived not as a boon but as a serious threat, not only to future profitability but, in the opinions of some industry commentators at least, to the long-term survival of established record companies. The reason for this was an unforeseen and hitherto unremarkable technological development originating in the considerably less glamorous world of international standards.

This development was a seemingly innocuous software program called MPEG-1 Audio Layer 3 or, as it is better known, MP3. The program was developed as an international standard for the coded representation and combination of moving pictures and audio to facilitate the development of an interactive television industry (*The Economist*, 1999). It was developed by the Motion Pictures Expert Group of the International Organization for Standardization, or ISO. Established in 1947 and based in Geneva, the ISO is a confederation of national industrial standards organizations, with a self-declared purpose 'to promote the development of standardization and related activities in the world with a view to facilitating the international exchange of goods and services, and…developing co-operation in the spheres of intellectual, scientific, technological and economic activity' (ISO, 1999). The ISO has largely existed in the relative obscurity of meetings and agreements on technical standards. It has been responsible for matters such as the agreed size and thickness of credit and bank cards, so that they can be used in automated teller machines around the world, and the tensile strength of bolts used in the aviation industry, to facilitate international air safety. Thus, the ISO is a kind of backstage fixer for organizations such as the General Agreement on Tariffs and Trade (GATT) and, more recently, the World Trade Organization (WTO), creating international technological conventions and ironing out technical differences between national economies. In this respect the ISO has probably done as much as, if not more than, the more illustrious GATT and WTO to bring globalization into being, by ensuring that it works on a practical day-to-day basis.

However, because of an unintended application of MP3, the ISO and, in particular, the Motion Pictures Expert Group, are no longer as obscure as they once were. MP3 is a compression program which reduces the size of digital audio files, making them quicker to make and easier to distribute. Compression programs analyse the profiles of digital packages to remove repetitions and redundancies in digital information (Negroponte, 1995). MP3 achieves compression through a process known as 'psychoacoustic masking' (Moody, 1999) where software analyses and filters sounds according to their degree of audibility to the human ear.[1] This filtering process means that MP3 files are much smaller than conventional digital music files, so that whereas a CD typically requires 11 megabytes (MB) of memory for every minute of sound contained, an MP3 file requires only 1 MB of memory for per minute of sound (Hedtke, 1999). Therefore, whereas a standard three-minute CD track required around 30 MB and took around 90 minutes to download onto a computer using the copper wire connectivity that undergirded the internet of the 1990s, an MP3 file of similar length required only 3 MB and took only 10 minutes. And, as telephony moved from copper wire to glass fibre and wireless from the late 1990s onwards, so downloading times per track shrank from minutes to seconds.

The size of the files had important consequences for their mobility; they were small enough to be sent down narrow band telephone lines from computer to computer via the internet, and then in large numbers, simultaneously, via broadband. Thus, it became possible to transfer digital music as pure code without the intermediation of a material disc, be it a compact disc, a minidisk, or even digital audiotape. Moreover, because the software originated within the ISO, MP3 files were produced in an open standard that was accessible to anyone with a reasonably up-to-date personal computer with a sound card. By the late 1990s, several companies began to offer MP3 player software packages, many of which were free or, for more technically advanced versions, available for a relatively modest one-off payment of about US$25 to US$30.

---

[1] The sound spectrum of an audio file is divided into narrow frequency bands, which are then sampled many times per second. Those sounds that would be masked by louder noises on nearby frequencies are discriminated against and information about them is ignored. In other words, the sounds that will be the most perceptible are produced most faithfully, whereas less perceptible sounds are reproduced less carefully, if at all.

MP3, then, could be seen as the emergence of a new kind of music format but one that, unlike existing digital formats, could be played back over a general and open standard hardware configuration (the personal computer), and so did not require listeners to purchase dedicated reproduction equipment, save for a relatively inexpensive software program. However, while the introduction of new formats for the playback of recorded music had, after a while at least, been enthusiastically supported by the music industry, this was not the case with MP3. For the most part, software formats elicited a conservative, critical response, a discourse founded in the existing social and technological hierarchies of the industry. This, as we have seen, is not unusual within the industry. However, among some groups software formats were welcomed precisely because they were seen as a means by which the music industry's established hierarchies and power relations might be dismantled. Although opposed to one another, these two positions at least agreed upon one thing: that the rise of software formats such as MP3 would bring about the end of the music industry as it was configured. I will now consider each of these positions in turn.

2.2.1. Against Software Formats

Most commentators and observers within the music industry depicted the rise of MP3 and other software formats in largely negative terms because they were considered a threat to sales and to prevailing relations of ownership and intellectual property rights. Organizations such as the Record Industry Association of America (RIAA) saw MP3 as directly responsible for the decline in the share of US music sales generated by the 15–24 age group, which fell sharply in the late 1990s (Moody, 1999). Because software formats enabled this age group to access music more cheaply and conveniently, the argument went, they were no longer spending so much money on CDs and other conventional formats within local record stores and shopping malls. More worryingly, the development of MP3 was also considered by some to be responsible for the erosion of the very economic viability of the industry because it facilitated the breach of intellectual property rights through illegal copying. As numerous studies indicated, the ability to exploit copyright has been central to the profits of the music industry almost since its very inception (e.g. Bettig, 1996; Frith, 1987a; Negus, 1992; Ryan, 1998; Sadler, 1997). It was the ease by which recorded material could be uploaded and downloaded to and from personal computers through the medium of MP3 that most animated the music industry, and accusing fingers were pointed at the rash of internet sites dedicated to the illegal distribution of copyrighted material. For example, in 1998 it was estimated that about 26,000 internet sites used music illegally (Boshoff, 1998), and some commentators claimed that by the late 1990s MP3 was the most searched for category on the internet and that over 500,000 different MP3 files could be accessed through it (Dempsey, 1999; Moody, 1999). At the same time the International Federation of Phonographic Industries estimated that there were three million downloads of MP3 files each day, and that most of these downloads were of illegal copies of copyrighted material. As a result, income from the exploitation of intellectual property rights was being 'forgone', with dire consequences for the ability of the industry to reproduce itself. As one Sony Music representative put it:

> My company invests millions of pounds each year in new writing talent and new composers. To recover that money we need to be paid. If we don't get paid because it goes on the internet and everyone gets it free, then we can't continue to make that investment in new talent. (Quoted in Boshoff, 1998)

For the music industry MP3 represented the re-emergence of the spectre of what is described as 'piracy' (David, 2010), which haunts all copyright industries, but was now manifested in a new more virulent and dangerous form. The industry has vigorously organized against breaches of copyright in the past, most notably in the campaign against 'home taping', whereby audiences made their own tapes of recorded music, either for their own enjoyment or for distribution to others (Heylin, 2003). However, although identified as an illicit activity which led to a technical loss of income, such practices were mainly undertaken by an active group of music users who also bought records and CDs as well as engaging in home taping. Moreover, any distribution of illegally taped material tended to be very local, amongst groups of friends and colleagues and, because of the relatively low reproductive quality and perishability of tape, may have induced additional purchases of the music in a more durable format. However, the rise of MP3 and other software formats was seen as a far more sinister development, because it allowed digital recordings to be copied more faithfully and, because of the distributive capabilities of the internet, to be disseminated through a music community of worldwide dimensions.[2] It is in this sense, then, that compressed computer files contained the capacity to compress time and space.

And it was not just the 'corporate suits' who bristled at the indignity of consumers obtaining their music on the cheap, and on a potentially global scale: this conservative discourse was also supported by many artists pursuing a career within the traditional system. For example, Ashley Slater, a member of the band Freakpower, could not have been clearer in his support of the power relations of the music industry:

> If my copyright isn't protected I go out [of business]—and I'm just one of tens of thousands of musicians who rely on that. Every time that happens a little twinkly light goes out in the Cool Britannia sky. (Quoted in Boshoff, 1998)

In 1998, Alan McGee, a fully signed-up member of Cool Britannia if ever there was one, being then both the founder and chairman of the Creation record label and a member of the government's Creative Industries Taskforce, made similarly pessimistic predictions about the long-term future of the music industry. He argued that in Britain at least the music industry would 'be dead within 10 years' as bands cut out the middleman and downloaded their music directly on the internet; it was, in his view, 'an industry in absolute crisis' (quoted in Boshoff, 1998). By the end of 1999 McGee's prognosis for the industry had become even more pessimistic, as he announced his intention to leave the industry, resigning from his record company so that he could devote more time to cultivating multimedia ventures and being an 'internet entrepreneur'. The music industry, he argued, was already a lost cause:

> The major record companies are absolutely running scared. I said there would be a consolidation and there has been. In the last year-and-a-half probably 20–30% of people have lost their jobs, about 20–30% of bands have lost their contracts; there's a huge bloodletting and there will continue to be. (Quoted in Waldman, 1999: 4)

---

[2] This insight into the geographical dimensions of different technological regimes of copyright infringement was obtained during an interview with a senior executive of the RIAA, Washington, DC. Retrospectively, home taping was now considered by the RIAA to have had some benefits to the industry, in that it often provided the raw material for sampling and the creation of 'new' music, as well as helping to provide a means through which knowledge about music was circulated to audiences.

2.2.2. For Software Formats

However, while extreme responses such as these were common within
the industry as MP3 and software formats emerged, they need to be
put in context, not least since levels of employment and artists' rosters
in record companies have always been volatile and unpredictable as
musical fashions change. Moreover, such comments were counterbal-
anced by a more enthusiastic engagement with the emergence of MP3
and other software formats by actors outside and on the fringes of
the music industry. Such actors produced and constituted what may
be described as a 'progressive' discourse surrounding the emergence
of software formats. It was progressive because, while it agreed with
conservative critics that this technology would bring about a radical
reorientation of the music industry, it saw this as a desirable outcome.
In other words, whereas conservative discourses were connected to
the traditional material and ideological expressions of hierarchy, ownership, and the exploitation of property rights of the music industry,
progressive discourses welcomed the possibility of the destruction of
hierarchy and the creation of a more open and accessible industry. In
so doing, these progressive discourses tapped directly into the well
of romanticism and mysticism where the creativity of musicians and
artists is seen to be in perennial opposition to the naked commercialism of the music industry itself (Negus, 1995).

A good example of this progressive discourse in practice could
be seen embodied within New York-based rap artists Public Enemy.
Following disputes with their record label about the timing of the
release of an album in 1998, the band posted unreleased tracks on
their official website and permitted them to be downloaded for free, at
least until legal action by Polygram, who owned the copyright to the
recordings, forced their removal. In subsequent interviews the band's
leader, Chuck D, justified the band's embrace of MP3 and the internet
in the same kind of vivid language Public Enemy employed in their
musical commentaries on race and inequality within urban America:

> Major record labels are like dinosaurs. They move slow. Our album
> *Bring the Noise 2000* was slated for a March 98 release, but Polygram
> slept on it. So we released it in MP3 on our [website]. Why not? Our
> fans wanted the music. And we believe in the technology. We didn't
> sell the tracks, so to us it was the same as just making more promo-
> tional copies...the lawyers came running and told my manager to take
> it down. They don't like MP3 because it can obliterate the middleman.

But the industry won't be able to pimp MP3, so they're going to have to figure out how to co-opt it...It's the chicken coming home to roost, the levelling of the playing field, the little man getting his chance...Soon you'll see a marketplace with 500,000 independent labels—the majors can co-opt all they want, but it's not going to stop the average person from getting into the game. Today a major label makes a CD for as little as 80 cents, then sells it whole sale for $10.50 so retailers can charge $14—that's highway robbery. They were able to pimp that technology. Well, MP3 is a technology they can't pimp. (Quoted in Freud, 1999)

The democratizing possibilities of MP3 were echoed by a host of other actors taking advantage of the commercial possibilities of bypassing the existing structures of the music industry. For example, in 2000, Tony Wilson, the former owner of the pioneering independent Factory record label, announced plans to establish an internet-based record label founded on MP3, which would undercut not only mainstream record labels but also existing internet MP3 distribution sites:

Wilson is convinced that by being a trailblazer in the new technology, independents can again beat the majors at selling music, but Wilson believes he can do it more cheaply than any of them. A Factory offshoot at music.com will remove 70% of the costs of selling music. According to Wilson, online retail music will triple sales of music and benefit the public and artists alike. He says the public are tired of trawling around record shops to find albums 'like The Verve's, who have three good tracks and they're the singles anyway', and plans to sell individual songs, without B-sides.[3] He claims he will undercut other [internet] operations by as much as 30p a tune, meaning 'these shits charging 99p and then saying to the artists, "You can have so much per cent" can go screw themselves'. (Simpson, 2000: 12)[4]

Meanwhile, a representative of a high-technology company manufacturing MP3 players depicted the changes that the technology would bring about as being akin to a creative and commercial nirvana. In the future, he argued, there will be

---

[3] The mention of B-sides in this context is either meant to be ironic or else is made by someone who did not fully understand MP3 technology. The B-side is of course a product of analogue, vinyl recording technology.

[4] Wilson's former record label, Factory, was notable for its sympathetic contractual relations with its artists, who typically enjoyed a 50% share of royalties. This generous approach to royalties gave the label a precarious financial footing that some commentators suggest contributed to the company's bankruptcy in the early 1990s (Simpson, 2000).

Instant access to music produced anywhere in the world, more special-
ised labels, lower marketing costs on the Web leading to more variety
and more artists, blurring between amateur and professional artists,
new ways to buy or rent tracks. (Quoted in Moody, 1999: 34)

Clearly, the debate surrounding the introduction of software formats generated a good deal of heat within the music industry. But,
with hindsight, what light can be cast upon the implications that
software formats and internet-based delivery systems had for the organization of the music industry? In order to do this, the rest of the
chapter develops the theoretical concept of the musical network to
assist in analysing the organization of the music industry through
time and over space. It draws upon a heterodox range of literatures
to sketch out the organizational and geographical dimensions of four
distinctive musical networks and to determine the impacts of software formats and internet distribution systems upon them. However,
to be able to understand the reorganization of the music industry
within a broader context, it is necessary first to turn to a more general
literature on electronic markets and the role they play within processes of economic transformation, through the disintermediation
and reintermediation of economic practices within established production, or value, chains.

2.3. FROM MARKETPLACE TO MARKET SPACE? PUTTING E-COMMERCE IN ITS PLACE

The rise of e-commerce at the turn of the twenty-first century—
defined as 'trade that…takes place over the internet through a consumer visiting a seller's website and making a transaction there' (*The
Economist*, 2000: 6)—and the stock market bubble that accompanied
it may be interpreted as symptomatic of a wider economic crisis, of a
breakneck obsession with reducing the turnover time of capital, and
of an inherent tendency within capitalism towards speculative investments of 'fictitious value'. This analysis contains within it more than
the odd grain of truth. However, this interpretation does not really
explain why capital markets became so excited about e-commerce,
and proved so willing to channel large volumes of money into companies that were, by their own admission, many years away from
making any profits (Daniels et al., 2007). To argue that the willingness

to invest was the result of a collective delusion was appealing for those who subscribed to a broadly left sentiment on such matters. But even if true, rather more in the way of explanation would still be required. What exactly were the promises of e-commerce that encouraged so many investors to part with their money in the hope of future returns, beyond the perennial qualities of faith, hope, and greed endemic to all capital markets?

One of the principal reasons for the focus on e-commerce was the way in which it promised to bring about a major process of discontinuous change (Christensen, 1997; Clarke and Clegg, 1998) in the nature of economic organization. Quite simply, advocates of e-commerce argued that it would rewrite the rules of organization, providing significant first-mover advantages to firms in the vanguard of its development. Many of these claims were founded upon a hybrid business-economics literature which can be traced back as far as the late 1980s, but which only really began to flower 10 years later. This literature, in the main, approached the economic role of the internet through the application of concepts such as transaction costs, paying particular attention to the role of information within processes of market exchange. A key concern was to explore the capacity of a new technological assemblage of hardware and software to disintermediate and reintermediate production networks and value chains within established industries (e.g. Evans and Wurster, 1997, 1999; Hagel and Armstrong, 1997; Hagel and Singer, 1999; Rowe, 1998; Sivadas et al., 1998; Strader and Shaw, 1997).

Before proceeding, it is necessary to post a health warning in relation to much of this material, for at least three reasons. First, much of the literature on the rise of e-commerce contained a tendency towards futurology, which mixed established economic concepts with speculations about the future shape of economy and society. Second, and relatedly, much of the work was consultancy driven, and appeared in books and articles written by employees of leading management consultancy firms and hurriedly published in imprints such as Harvard Business School Press with an eye to hybrid business-academic audiences. Third, many of these accounts were shot through with neoliberal normativity and are economically reductionist, so that they directly and indirectly valorized e-commerce through its ability to expedite serial acts of individual consumption. However, to be aware of the limitations of this literature is not to necessarily denigrate its theoretical and empirical significance. Indeed, in many respects, this distinctive embryonic literature undoubtedly had formative impacts upon its subject, because of the constitutive ways in which economic theory 'performs, shapes and formats the economy' (Callon, 1998: 2), and the voracious appetite businesses have for new organizational paradigms (Clarke and Clegg, 1998; Micklethwait and Wooldridge, 1997; O'Shea and Madigan, 1997). The e-commerce literature may also be seen as an example of what Miller describes as virtualism, whereby 'the economy is increasingly forced to change itself in order to match the descriptions of abstracted models that are produced by academic economists' (2000: 201).

A particularly useful description of an abstract model of that kind is the 'electronic market hypothesis' (EMH), first developed by Malone and his colleagues in the late 1980s (Malone et al., 1987), and subsequently updated by Daniels and Klimis (1999). The EMH predicted that the rise of electronically mediated forms of information would bring about a decline in the costs of economic coordination. The rise of the internet and the emergence of the phenomenon of e-commerce, it was argued, made electronic markets an everyday reality. The growth of software devices such as search engines and intelligent agents (Corradi et al., 1999; Hagel and Armstrong, 1997; Hagel and Singer, 1999; Wise, 1997, 1998) made it possible for buyers to search electronic markets at speed and at low cost for supplier and product information that is both rich in content and geographically extensive (Evans and Wurster, 1999). By lowering the costs of economic coordination in this way electronic markets would bring about the disintermediation of production chains and a decline in the importance of hierarchies, in favour of market coordination made possible by agent software that enable consumers to make more effective searches of product markets (Daniels and Klimis, 1999).

In addition, such markets would facilitate a new form of integration between buyer and seller, ensuring faster transactions between counterparties, but also allowing both parties to exchange and store information about transactions (Daniels and Klimis, 1999), albeit that this information tends to be more important to sellers as they seek to build up information about consumers (see du Gay, 1996).

Electronic markets also have the potential to reconfigure fundamentally the competitive bases and the contestability of markets. Thus, not only do electronic markets have the potential to break down established market hierarchies through disintermediation, but established firms may well be disadvantaged as markets are reintermediated through electronic channels. Established firms tend to have significant sunk costs within physical infrastructures, and it is for this reason that electronic markets offer significant competitive opportunities for new or marginal competitors within existing industries:

> The paralysis of [dominant market] incumbent[s] is the greatest competitive advantage enjoyed by new competitors...the paralysis of the leading incumbent is also the greatest competitive advantage for the marginal incumbent, who has lost the old game and has every motive to change the rules. (Evans and Wurster, 1999: 65)

In other words, this perspective argued that a range of product and service markets were up for grabs because, although established firms start with significant competitive advantages, they are unable to react quickly enough, creating spaces for smaller, more nimble, firms to move in.

The next two sections of the chapter seek to determine the extent to which e-commerce brought about a reconfiguration of the music industry and, in particular, changed its contestability. These processes of reconfiguration are considered in section 2.5. But first, it is necessary to come to a theoretical understanding of the organization of the music industry prior to the advent of electronic markets, so that the impact of e-commerce upon it may be properly assessed.

2.4. APPROACHING THE ECONOMY OF MUSIC

Analyses of the economy of music may be found within a number of academic disciplines, including economics, organization studies, geography, sociology, and cultural studies. Across these disparate literatures there emerges a general consensus that the musical economy consists of a series of sequential processes. Although these accounts differ in their identification and naming of such processes and in the relative importance they ascribe to each within the musical economy as a whole, there is a general consensus that the different processes are connected to one another through complex networks of social relations that link actors, organizations, and technologies.

This section of the chapter approaches the musical economy by combining a process-oriented approach with one that explicitly addresses the spatiality of such processes. Such an approach makes it possible to more accurately identify impacts of software formats like MP3 and internet distribution systems upon distinctive parts of the industry and to determine their geographical consequences. This is particularly important because of the potential that this new techno-logical assemblage has to 'shrink' space through an enhanced capacity to transmit music over space through computer networks. However, before we can speculate on the degree to which the geographical or-ganization of the industry might be overturned in the ways predicted by commentators both within and outside the industry, it is necessary first to identify the traditional configuration of the music industry. In order to do so in a way that combines sensitivity to musical processes and to their spatiality, I deploy the concept of the musical network.

2.4.1. The Musical Network

The concept of the musical network was originally developed by Jacques Attali (1984) in his provocative and, in many ways, prescient historical materialist reconsideration of the role of music. According to Attali, the economy of music operates through networks based upon the composition, representation, and repetition of musical forms.[5] He argues that musical networks are both emblematic and constitutive of distinctive types of social and economic relations within human soci-ety. Thus, at the dawn of capitalism, a musical network of representa-tion brought about a transformation in the musical conventions and practices that surrounded the performance of music, which began to move away from the purview of patronage and towards the market, so that musical production become monetized and the 'concert hall performance replaced the popular festival and the private concern at court' (1984: 46–7).

Then, at the beginning of the twentieth century, a new musical net-work emerged, in the wake of technological developments in the field of sound capture and reproduction (Kittler, 1999). This network of

---

[5] Attali also identified what he describes as a sacrificial network, but which is not relevant to the analysis presented here. Within this network music is produced for largely ceremonial purposes within non-capitalist, traditional societies, and it acts as a system of distribution 'for all of the orders, myths, and religious, social or economic relations of symbolic societies' (1984: 31). Within such societies, music was a 'Tool of the political' (1984: 48), and music was made possible through the patronage of the aristocracy.

repetition emerged initially to capture and reproduce the sound of music produced within networks of representation, although it eventually gained an energy and dynamism of its own, and provided the basis for a 'new organisational network for the economy of music' (Attali, 1984: 32). Music increasingly became a corporate enterprise (see Farrell, 1998), and became incorporated within large-scale production processes.

Finally, Attali conjures up a utopian vision of the future for his final network, that is, a network of composition. The parallels between Attali's description of this network and Marx's dream of an idyllic communist existence are clearly discernible in Attali's prophecy that, in the future, 'music could be lived as composition, in other words, in which it would be performed for the musician's own enjoyment, as self-communication, with no other goal than his own pleasure, as something fundamentally outside all communication, as self-transcendence, a solitary, egotistical, non-commercial act' (1984: 32). It is a network that effectively inverts the musical economy, wherein music is made for its own sake, rather than for purposes of representation, repetition, or, critically, as part of the reproduction of the capitalist economy as a whole.[6]

Rather than use the concept of the musical network in Attali's broad-brush manner, to argue that the music is symbolic of broader social relations within particular stages of economic history, I will use the concept in a far narrower and more restricted sense. Subject to some modification, Attali's approach to the economy of music is of value to the analysis being pursued in this book in that it is suggestive of the existence of a set of overlapping and complementary networks that, between them, configure the musical economy. That is, the musical economy is simultaneously made up of networks of composition, of representation (or performance), and of repetition (or recording). Moreover, partly because of the fruitful engagement between geography and network approaches, Attali's approach is suggestive of a route through which the processes and practices of musical economy can be analysed through time and over space within geographical networks.[7]

---

[6] The development of music composition computer programs such as Apple's Garage Band is an illustration of how such networks of composition can be realized and performed.
[7] It is recognized that there are a number of limitations to the use of the network metaphor. One problem, identified by Latour (1999), is that, thanks to the kinds of

However, before attempting to chart such a route, it is first necessary to attend to some of the limitations of Attali's analysis, and to suggest counteracting modifications. There are at least three problems with Attali's approach as originally conceived. First, heavily freighted with the trappings of Marxist political economy, it adopts a 'stages' approach to social change, whereby each successive musical network is held to symbolize a distinctive shift in broader social relations through time. Thus, although Attali admits that it is possible that the 'four modes of [musical] production [might] interpenetrate in time and space', he argues that there exists an 'economic logic of succession: *In music, as in the rest of the economy, the logic of the succession of musical codes parallels the logic of the creation of value*' (1984: 41; original emphasis). But, by privileging the temporal exclusivity of networks, Attali gives the impression that they are far more coherent and unified than they really are. For example, consider the space of the recording studio since at least the 1960s. It is difficult to imagine where the networks of composition, of representation (performance), and of replication (recording) would begin and end. The recording studio is not just a site of replication, but it is also a site of performance, and it has become a compositional tool in its own right (Cunningham, 1998; Tamm, 1995; Thérberge, 1997). At important points of intersection then, such as the recording studio, musical networks overlap in space as well as in time. Therefore, it is necessary to subsume composition, performance, and recording within a broader network of creativity.

Second, Attali's political economy perspective means that he elides the role of consumption within the musical economy, which he submerges within the network of repetition. However, the proliferation of work on consumption in the years since Attali's work was first published[8] means that much greater attention needs to be paid to the ways in which a network of consumption is not only an essential element within the musical economy, but is also an increasingly powerful one (see e.g. Miller, 1995).

processes described in this chapter, the term has entered common vernacular to such an extent that it can no longer convey a sense of surprise or puzzlement in a social science context. If not exactly a dead metaphor, it is certainly not as robust and healthy as it once was. However, the metaphor is used here in a restrictive and specific way to combine a focus on both process and spatiality within the musical economy. The network metaphor still works effectively to convey a sense of incomplete connectivity over space.

 [8] The book was originally published in French in 1977.

Third, Attali's analysis of the music industry has been superseded not only by the passage of time but also by a proliferation of work on cultural industries which has provided more careful and nuanced accounts of the flow of cultural products through commodity chains (Leslie and Reimer, 1999; Lury, 1993; Pratt, 1997, 2000). For example, Sadler (1997), drawing on the work of Aksoy, suggests that the music industry is an information business which is made up of four distinctive processes. These are: (1) production—innovation—creation; (2) packaging—publishing—reproduction; (3) distribution—transmission—diffusion; and (4) facilitation—integration—servicing. Whereas stages (1) and (2) bear a strong resemblance to the networks of creativity and networks of reproduction, stage (3) draws attention to the importance of a network of distribution within the industry, which acts as a bridge between the networks of creativity and reproduction on the one hand and the network of consumption on the other. It ensures that musical output is delivered to consumer markets.

Therefore, a conceptual overhaul of Attali's original schema results in the identification of four distinctive musical networks which possess distinctive but overlapping functions, temporalities, and geographies. To recap, these networks are as follows: first, a network of *creativity*, formed from the fusion of networks of composition and representation, wherein music is created through multiple acts of performance; second, a network of *reproduction*, which is a narrower definition of the original network of repetition, and which includes the manufacture of multiple copies of audio recordings; third, a network of *distribution*, as described earlier; and, fourth, a network of *consumption*, incorporating retail organizations of various kinds.

One of the advantages of this approach is that it offers the possibility of analysing the various functions necessary for the reproduction of the musical economy, while addressing its complex and often messy organizational structure, as well as providing a useful conceptual framework for the task of locating these functions within geographical space. This framework is particularly useful in analysing the impacts of software formats such as MP3 within the musical economy given the claims made about their potential to dematerialize the musical economy and, thereby, effectively efface space within it.

I now examine each of these networks in turn, to provide a brief sketch of the overall geographical organization of the music industry and as a precursor for a subsequent analysis of the impacts of software formats like MP3 upon it.

2.4.2. Working through Musical Networks

What might these musical networks look like? A useful way forward is to begin with Scott's (1999a) schematic overview of the organization of the music industry. Scott locates artists and record companies at the heart of the record industry complex, with the contractual relationship between these two groups of actors acting as a fulcrum around which the rest of the industry turns. Each individual record company, or label, performs a dual function, that is, firms act as 'A&R (artist and repertoire) recruitment organisations and as the publishers of finished recordings' (Scott, 1999a: 1968).

> Around this core lies a constellation of distinctive economic and culture-producing functions ranging from song writing and the provision of musical instruments on the one side, to manufacturing and promotion-distribution on the other. At various intermediate stages come such other essential components of the production process as legal services, music publishing, recording studios, producers, sound engineers, and various accessory services. To these may be added a number of specialized operations...such as record mastering, video production, graphic design, sleeve printing, packaging, and so on.

Scott also provides a diagrammatical representation of the anatomy of the industry, a modified version of which is presented in Figure 2.1. What is particularly valuable about this depiction is that it assists in allocating the different functions of the industry to the four musical networks identified.

In what follows, the four musical networks are examined in more detail, to determine the geographical organizational significance of each within the musical economy as a whole. This serves as a prolegomenon for the succeeding section of the chapter in which the impact of software formats upon each of the four musical networks is examined.

Networks of creativity

In order to ascertain the ways in which networks of creativity are configured, it is useful to refer to two related concepts which have sought to explain the generation of new music within the musical economy. These concepts, the creative field and the musical scene, suggest that networks of creativity take the form of dense spatially agglomerated interactions between a relatively large number of actors, institutions, and technologies. The concept of the creative field has been coined by Scott to argue that musical creativity is a spatially agglomerated process.

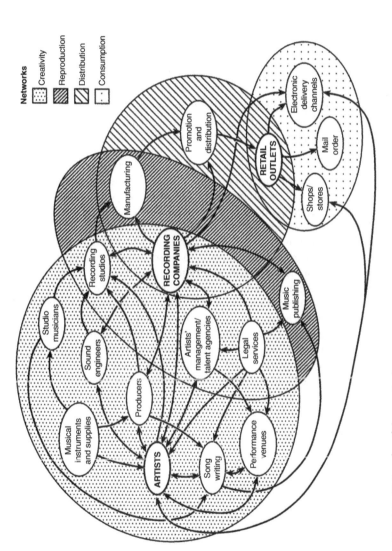

Networks

- ☷ Creativity
- ▨ Reproduction
- ▧ Distribution
- ⠿ Consumption

Fig. 2.1. Networks of the musical economy.

Based on an analysis of the US recorded music industry, Scott argues that, like other culture industries, the music industry tends to be 'rooted in communities of workers anchored to particular places' which, once established, become 'magnets for talented individuals from other places who migrate to these centres in search of professional fulfilment' (1999b: 809). In addition, such centres contain concentrations of specialized institutions that engage in dense and regular inter-firm transactions. Scott argues that in the United States centres such as New York and Los Angeles, and to a lesser extent Nashville, are particularly important creative fields for popular music, and are sites of significant traded and untraded interdependencies within the musical economy:

> agglomerations of any sort represent not just spatial accumulations of physical capital, but also evolving pools of human skills and aptitudes. These pools or communities of workers are also the preserve of accumulated traditions and conventionalized sensibilities (including cultural norms as embodied, for example, in particular musical genres), and they function as potent frameworks of cultural reproduction and arenas of socialization.... To these factors we may add the urban environment generally as a cultural setting, and specifically in the case of the music industry, the clubs, theaters, and other live performance venues within which players and audiences come face to face and in which new musical idioms and tastes are often worked out. In New York and Los Angeles, such venues actually represent critical functional and spatial adjuncts to the industry at large. Additionally, the human capital endowments of individual communities are typically sustained by educational and training institutions that focus on local, agglomeration-specific needs, as well by inward migration of new talent from other areas. (Scott, 1999a: 1974–5)

In alluding to the importance of the spatiality of the cultural milieu within which music is produced, Scott pursues an argument which runs parallel to cultural analyses of musical creativity which suggest that new and distinctive popular music forms emerge from musical scenes, or distinctive spaces of musical activity. According to Shank (1994: 122), a musical scene may be defined as 'an over productive signifying community [wherein] far more semiotic information is produced than can be rationally parsed', but which nevertheless struggles to convey this information through the bodily performances of artists and audiences, within and through institutions, technologies, and spaces. Thus, an important prerequisite for the development of a

local scene includes the presence of 'a situated swirling mass of transformations, signs and sweating bodies, continually reconstructing the
meaning of a communion of individuals in a primary group' (Shank,
1994: 128). It is through such bodily acts that new music emerges. It
does so, too, through a mixing of musical styles and genres in place.
Straw has drawn attention to the creative potential of musical scenes,
arguing that they are cultural spaces 'in which a range of musical
practices coexist, interacting with one another with a variety of processes of differentiation, and according to widely varying trajectories
of change and cross-fertilization' (1991: 373).

Musical scenes are able to reproduce themselves most successfully
when they produce a set of stabilizing institutions, such as performance venues, specialized record shops, rehearsal and recording studios, specialized music press, and record labels. These institutions
facilitate the circulation of, and interactions between, artists, specialized labour, dedicated institutions, and, significantly, audiences,
which facilitate the combination of skills and technologies to create
new musical forms.

Networks of musical creativity, therefore, may be defined as centres of musical knowledge, both in the sense of being a repository
of the requisite technical competencies to be able to compose, perform, and record music, but also of knowledges of what different
compositional, performative, and recording styles signify within a
wider cultural and subculture context. They are, as such, not only
centres of production, but also of interpretation (see Thrift, 1994).
Networks of musical creativity influence the ways in which musical forms circulate and are recombined through acts of creativity.
Thus, it is important to draw attention at this point to the blurred
and fuzzy nature of the four musical networks identified in this
chapter, and to the ways in which information and activities may
take place simultaneously in more than one network. For example,
Hennion (1989: 402) has argued that the process of record production involves 'progressive attempts to extend what has first been
localised in the studio'. This extension is achieved not in the manner
of a process of diffusion, but rather as part of a series of negotiations
with an audience, which is not merely 'an abstraction that comes
along or (or not) at the end of the route to sanction the work of
production: it is [more accurately] a circle of actual auditors that is
gradually widened' (Hennion, 1989: 416) as recorded music moves
through the four networks.

For Scott, it is the spatially agglomerated yet organizationally disintegrated nature of musical creativity that ties this form of musical network to urban agglomerations:

> in contrast to innovative clusters in industries such as semiconductors or biotechnology, innovation in the music industry does not so much involve continual 'improvements' in final products as it is represented by constantly shifting registers of cognitive content and the formation of new consumer tastes or fashions,...new sensibilities, insights, and procedures are likely to be engendered as these moments of contact occur, above all where contrasting or incommensurable perspectives are brought into conjunction with one another and then negotiated out to some unexpected conclusion. By extension, the large agglomeration can also be seen as a sort of repository offering endless combinatorial possibilities for such encounters, so that the number of different 'experiments' that can occur in products is effectively unlimited. The latter point is doubly decisive given that novelty is the lifeblood of the recorded music industry. (1999a: 1975)

And it is the spatially inextractable nature of these interactions that, Scott argues, will ensure that, despite the potential for music to be distributed via the internet, 'major production clusters are still likely to remain as dominant centres at creative and production activity' (1999a: 1975). I will examine the veracity of this statement in regard to the rise of MP3 and other software formats in section 2.5 and through the book.

Networks of creativity are linked to networks of reproduction through record companies, which are powerful in the former and dominant in the latter. The traditional *raison d'être* of record companies is to make profits by exploiting their ownership of property rights in sound recordings. They are thus active in networks of creativity in order to unearth and develop new artists and repertoire, and to produce sound recordings of them for commercial sale. Thus, the creative departments of record companies tend to be concentrated in large urban agglomerations, to be close to cultural developments in the musical economy, but also to expedite the transaction-intensive process of contractual dealings with artists and their managers and lawyers over issues such as advances, royalties, and the required recorded output over the length of the contract.

Record companies are instrumental in providing the wherewithal to enable artists to use the specialized labour and institutions that configure networks of creativity. That is, they provide the initial contracts and money needed to hire the specialist workers such as record producers, sound engineers, and session musicians, and the dedicated institutions such as rehearsal and recording studios which are required to produce recorded output. One of the key tasks of a record company is to 'discover' artists or bands that will be successful in a rapidly changing market. However, the difficulties of successfully doing so is reflected in the fact that the majority of recordings are commercially unsuccessful and fail to recoup the initial investment made in them. Indeed, traditionally between 80 and 85 per cent of recorded music output fails to cover costs (Caves, 2000), so that the viability of a record company relies on a small minority of recordings to cover the cost of the rest (Ryan, 1998).

Therefore, an important ingredient for success in the industry is that record companies should have 'deep pockets' and be sufficiently well capitalized to be able to afford investment in highly risky projects (Bettig, 1996). For example, in the early 1990s it was estimated that the recording budget for an album in the United Kingdom ranged from £200,000 for minor artists to almost £2 million for major artists (MMC, 1994). Although three-quarters of this outlay was in the form of advances to artists and producers which were potentially recoupable from the royalties, each album release required a record company to put significant sums of money at risk. For example, 96 different singles and 185 different albums were released each week in the United Kingdom in 1992 (MMC, 1994). The majority of these releases did not sell enough copies to recoup the investment in their production. But those recordings that do can sell in such large numbers to more than make up for the losses incurred by the majority of releases, particularly because the marginal costs of reproduction are low. It is this characteristic of the industry that has encouraged a long-term tendency towards capital concentration. By the 1990s the music industry worldwide was dominated by just five corporations: BMG, Sony, Polygram, Warner, and EMI. Between them, these companies were responsible for over 80 per cent of global recorded music sales. The volatility and unpredictability of the market for recorded music means that it is difficult for smaller record labels to survive for any length of time. Such companies are dependent upon a relatively small roster of artists that have to be consistently successful if the label is to survive over the long term. The survival of companies that depend upon the exploitation of copyrights has been shown to be closely related to the size and range of their portfolios of exploitable products (Ryan, 1998). This has encouraged many smaller record labels to forge links with larger companies (Negus, 1992). The smaller company is expected to provide its larger partner with preferential access to artists that it discovered through its own A&R department, and in return gains a greater degree of financial stability and access to the large record company's greater efficiency and effectiveness within networks of reproduction and distribution.

Networks of reproduction

When music enters networks of reproduction it enters a new world of production, one that was traditionally far more stable than networks of creativity. When music was dominated by playback formats such as vinyl records and CDs, this was based upon mass production, where the emphasis is upon economies of scale. Accordingly, the geography of these networks was very different from that of networks of creativity. All record companies owned manufacturing affiliates, which were located within 'global regions', so that the entire European market for recorded music, for example, could be sourced from just a handful of large production facilities (Figure 2.2). The benefits of large-scale production were not realized merely in terms of savings on overheads; large capacity was also seen to be beneficial in managing volatile orders, which could ebb and flow from week to week in extreme cases. In addition to these large corporate operations, there was also a set of smaller independent manufacturers, which were used mainly by independent record labels and by the large record companies for short production runs, especially for items such as singles, the sales of which were very volatile (MMC, 1994). These plants tended to be located on the margins of large urban agglomerations (for example, in the United Kingdom they tended to be located in the outer suburbs of Greater London or the rest of the South-East: Figure 2.3).

Therefore, in comparison with networks of creativity, networks of reproduction are spatially diffuse, conforming to the logic of an industrial world which requires standardized inputs and produces generic outputs (Storper and Salais, 1997).

Networks of distribution

It is within networks of distribution that record companies seek to exploit the property rights they hold over sound recordings. Thus,

Fig. 2.2. Networks of reproduction: manufacturing sites for the UK and European market, EMI and Polygram, 1994.

Source: compiled from data in MMC, 1994.

networks of distribution ensure that copyrighted product is delivered to final markets. Traditionally, this has taken place through processes of physical distribution, whereby distribution companies take delivery of manufactured output from production plants and distribute this onwards to retail outlets or mail order companies. This too is a highly concentrated network, so that the distribution of music in the United Kingdom was controlled by just nine major distribution companies in the early 1990s. Moreover, five of these companies, all owned by the major record companies, controlled over 85 per cent of

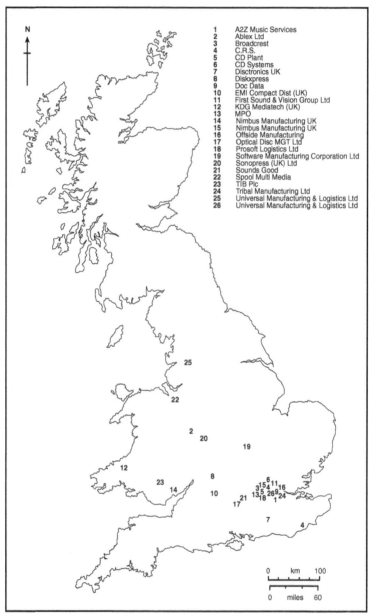

1   A2Z Music Services
2   Ablex Ltd
3   Broadcrest
4   C.R.S.
5   CD Plant
6   CD Systems
7   Disctronics UK
8   Diskxpress
9   Doc Data
10 EMI Compact Dist (UK)
11 First Sound & Vision Group Ltd
12 KDG Mediatech (UK)
13 MPO
14 Nimbus Manufacturing UK
15 Nimbus Manufacturing UK
16 Offside Manufacturing
17 Optical Disc MGT Ltd
18 Prosoft Logistics Ltd
19 Software Manufacturing Corporation Ltd
20 Sonopress (UK) Ltd
21 Sounds Good
22 Spool Multi Media
23 TIB Plc
24 Tribal Manufacturing Ltd
25 Universal Manufacturing & Logistics Ltd
26 Universal Manufacturing & Logistics Ltd

Fig. 2.3. CD manufacturing plants in the United Kingdom.

Source: Showcase, 2000.

the distribution market. The major distribution companies sought to capitalize on their domination of the market by undermining existing intermediaries, such as record wholesalers, by dealing directly with retailers. By the early 1990s, the share of product passing through wholesalers before entering the retail section had fallen to as low as 40 per cent (MMC, 1994).

Over time networks of distribution expanded to include a range of parallel media-based channels through which additional revenues from the exploitation of copyrighted material might be realized. The 1980s and 1990s saw music companies become parts of larger media agglomerations, forging links with cable and satellite television companies to ensure channels for the dissemination of musical products to audiences, 'both as a source of profit in its own right and as a means of encouraging customers to buy the work of certain artists' (Sadler, 1997: 1928).[9] Therefore, like networks of reproduction, networks of distribution tend to be capital intensive, which encouraged capital concentration and organizational integration (Sadler, 1997).

Networks of consumption

Networks of consumption incorporate those locations in which musical products created within other networks are purchased. They are made up of organizations, delivery systems of various kinds, and consumers themselves. Traditionally, in the United Kingdom at least, this network was made up of a constellation of relatively small independent specialist shops and the recorded music departments of general retailers and department stores. Until the early 2000s, independent record stores remained important sites of consumption, particularly among active and enthusiastic consumers of music, and many independent stores survived by occupying a niche in the market by holding extensive stocks of particular musical genres. Moreover, historically such stores played an important part in networks of creativity, as they acted as meeting points for encounter and informative exchange between actors with an active interest in music, either as audiences or as performers, or both. However, in the early twenty-first century independent record shops began to close as sales of CDs declined (Jones, 2009).

---

[9] This argument is developed further in Ch. 4.

By then large chains such as Virgin, HMV, and Tower Records dominated the industry, largely through the buying power they exerted back up the production chain. As a result, there was a marked shift of power from distribution to retailers. During the 1980s and 1990s distributors came under pressure to operate on a just-in-time basis as large retailers reduced the volume of capital tied up in inventory, with orders being placed and dispatched on a day-to-day basis (MMC, 1994).[10] Retailers were able to exert such influence through the value chain of the industry not only because of the scale of their bulk orders, but also through what du Gay and Negus (1994) describe as the ability of the large chains to 'construct' the consumer of recorded music. That is, through a combination of 'hard' and 'soft' managerial technologies, firms became much more knowledgeable about consumers. This, in turn, enabled music retailers to regulate and manage consumer behaviour more effectively. In so doing, firms were able to influence consumption, by directing consumers to some products rather than others and promoting certain artists at the expense of others. Sometimes this was done inadvertently, as in the case of more general retailers who stocked only the Top 40 selling records and, therefore, by definition, limited consumption in their stores to what was already popular.[11]

Networks of consumption also constituted a highly lucrative part of the musical economy: music retailers traditionally enjoyed margins of 25 per cent of the sale price on record and CD sales (Wallis et al., 1999: 14). As du Gay and Negus observe, the power over consumption vested in the large retailers even prompted the chairman of the UK industry's trade association, the British Phonographic Industry, to advocate that record companies should 'take action against the inexcusable power of retailers who control what we sell to the public' (quoted in du Gay and Negus, 1994: 395). As we shall see in the next section, this statement has a particular resonance in the light of the development of software formats and internet distribution systems within the music industry.

---

[10] e.g the Monopolies and Mergers Commission reported that one major record company indicated that between 1988 and 1992 the number of units it shipped declined by 24% while at the same time the number of orders processed increased by 42%, and the number of records per order decreased by 47% (MMC, 1994: 118).

[11] I am grateful to Andy Pratt for the 'Top 40' observation and, in a personal communication, he also drew attention to the role of the music press and media in circulating information about consumption (through reviews and the like).

I have sought to map out here the configuration of a set of distinctive, but strongly overlapping and interrelated, musical networks: of creativity, reproduction, distribution, and consumption. Each of these was seen to have distinctive geographical and organizational logics. In the next section attention is shifted towards the impacts of the rise of MP3 on the networks of the musical economy.

2.5. ELECTRONIC MARKETS AND THE DISINTERMEDIATION AND REINTERMEDIATION OF MUSICAL NETWORKS

The purpose of this section is to incorporate the argument developed in the previous two sections to determine the impacts of software formats and internet distribution systems on the networks of the musical economy. It should be noted that even now the impacts are still working their way through the system, and these are in large part the subject of the rest of the book. Nevertheless, it is possible to discern a number of very significant developments that have implications for the institutional and geographical organization of the music industry.

2.5.1. Networks of Creativity

Activities in these networks have relatively high levels of asset specificity in the complex combination of skills and technologies manifest within them. Arguably, such networks also have high levels of product complexity, given the difficulty of describing music other than on its own terms (Daniels and Klimis, 1999). For these reasons networks of creativity appear to be reasonably resistant to electronic disintermediation. The significance of embodied skills, performances, and subcultural knowledges effectively tie these networks to established centres of the musical economy through practices such as A&R as well as record production, engineering, and management that are enacted within core institutions such as performance venues, rehearsal spaces, and recording studios. To this extent, Scott (1999a) is surely correct to argue that centres of creativity are unlikely to disappear in the wake of the capacity to distribute music as pure digital content.

However, this is not to argue that there are not dangers to incumbent actors and institutions within networks of creativity from the rise of software formats and related digital technology. The extent to which these networks are tied to urban agglomerations is already being undermined by parallel developments in composition and recording software that can turn personal computers into mini recording studios. This, as well as the falling costs of home studio equipment, has made it far easier to record music and, with the aid of software formats, to upload this music quickly to internet sites. The increasing prevalence of this activity is likely to have at least two important implications. First, as in other areas of the economy, electronic markets in music have had deflationary outcomes (*The Economist*, 2000), putting pressure on the hourly fees charged by recording studios and by specialized labour within networks of creativity. This has caused a crisis in the recording studio sector (see Chapters 5 and 6). Second, as Wallis et al. (1999) argue, these changes at least made it possible for artists to set up their own internet-based record labels and publishing companies to exploit their intellectual property rights (IPRs) in sound recordings:

> Artists who become famous are often locked into long-term contracts with intermediaries. When such contracts come up for renewal, superstars are in an extremely strong position to recover and retain their IPRs. Such artists are commodified products in themselves they [increasingly have] access to alternative means of finance, and they may use new distribution technologies to control globalisation and delivery process. This is the great fear of the multinational companies. (Wallis et al., 1999: 9)

Wallis et al. argue that this strategy could be followed only by artists with well-established fan bases and sufficient capital to be able to mount marketing campaigns to draw audiences to their websites. However, although it is far more difficult for less established bands to pursue such a strategy, it is not impossible, as Brindley (2000a, 2000b) illustrated in the case of bands that found commercial success by distributing their music through their own websites. Moreover, the dominant position of traditional record companies within networks of creativity has been destabilized by the growth of internet companies established as 'incubators' for new and unsigned acts and as 'portals' to guide and attract audiences interested in particular types of music.

2.5.2. Networks of Reproduction and Distribution

These networks are considered together here because they share a number of similarities in being the most stable networks of the record industry. The products within them have low levels of asset specificity and low levels of product complexity. Therefore, these networks were always the most likely to be subject to processes of disintermediation and reintermediation through electronic markets. It is within these capital-intensive and concentrated networks that we find much of the music industry's ambivalence towards software formats and digital distribution. The traditional configuration of these networks was, in itself, a fairly effective barrier to entry to the industry (Alexander, 1994). But the advent of software formats like MP3 changed the bases of competition and made it possible for these barriers to be circumvented, along with the industry being 'locked in' to an outdated paradigm of manufacturing and distribution. There was an understandable reluctance within the industry to embrace open software formats and electronic methods of distribution which would undercut investment in established production and distribution paradigms. In this sense, software formats and internet distribution systems may be seen within the music industry as a 'disruptive technology' (Christensen, 1997), that is, one that 'overturns a traditional business model, which makes it harder for an established firm, with its own cultural interior, to embrace' (*The Economist*, 2000: 16). The reluctance of incumbent music industry firms to embrace software formats gave new entrants a two to three year competitive advantage in electronic distribution (see, in addition, Chapter 4). Major record companies belatedly began to explore the potential of this new production and distribution paradigm from the late 1990s, mainly by strategic investments, of which the tie-up between Time Warner and internet service provider American Online (AOL) in 2000 was perhaps the most notable example. This merger signalled the beginning of a wholesale reconfiguration of networks of reproduction and distribution to incorporate digital content and distribution directly. Indeed, in the medium to long term, processes of disintermediation and reintermediation offered the industry even greater profits from the exploitation of intellectual property rights because of the savings that could be made as traditional networks of reproduction and distribution

were scaled back.[12] Moreover, there were some grounds for arguing that internet distribution channels would help to support traditional networks as much as undermine them, through the potential
for generating online orders while a shift towards software formats
would save the costs of production and distribution associated with
material formats such as CD, vinyl, and cassette, and helping to access the 'long tail' (Anderson, 2006) of demand for relatively obscure recordings that was previously too geographically distributed
to reach effectively.

However, these opportunities would be fully realized only if the industry could ensure that the illegal copying of digital content could be
controlled. And it is here that we confront the real dilemma that faced
the music industry in all this: the dominant software format for music
was MP3, an open and insecure medium from which innumerable
copies may be made, and which is difficult to regulate (see Andersen
et al., 2000).

The industry's favoured solution to this problem was to seek to develop secure digital formats containing 'watermarks' to make it impossible to make multiple copies of sound recordings. To speed this
development, the RIAA sponsored the development of the Secure
Digital Music Initiative (SDMI). Established in 1999 the SDMI
recruited around 200 members, made up of companies and organizations involved in recording, consumer electronics, and information
technology. However, the RIAA's aim of protecting copyrights in an
open digital environment through a collaborative and cooperative
process was undermined by the fact that the SDMI was an uneasy
alliance, including traditional industry incumbents such as the
large record companies, as well as the smaller MP3 start-up companies that were instrumental in forcing the industry to search for
a secure digital platform in the first place. To ensure that an ac-
commodation between consortium members could be reached, the
SDMI did not seek to produce one software format, but rather what
it described as 'a voluntary, open framework for playing, storing

---

[12] The progress of the merger between Time Warner and AOL was held up during
the summer of 2000 due to the fears expressed by the European Union about competition and monopoly within the entertainment industry. Ironically, one of the solutions
offered to get the EU to sanction the deal was for the new company to withdraw from
manufacturing and distribution, passing these activities on to third parties. The analysis presented in the chapter indicates why such forced divestments were in line with
future strategy.

and distributing music in a protected form' (<http://www.sdmi. org>). The compromise option of seeking a regulatory framework, rather than the development of a specific format, was justified as follows:

> SDMI's work is based on the core principles that copyright should be respected, but those who wish to use unprotected formats should be able to do so. SDMI is not producing a single format, technology, or design. The specification developed by SDMI will answer consumer demand for convenient accessibility to quality digital music, enable copyright protection for artists' work, and therefore enable technology and music companies to build successful business.

This rather loose and non-prescriptive formula seemed designed only to unleash a digital music version of the 'format wars' that have beset consumer electronics industry in the past. Indeed, there quickly emerged a diversity of software formats associated with leading firms such as Sony, Microsoft, IMB, and AT&T, to add to generic formats such as MP3. But the open nature of MP3, and the first-mover advantage this technology held in comparison with proprietary software formats, meant that its leading position was difficult to displace. Moreover, MP3 software was actively supported by a body of users in the same way as computer operating systems such as Linux, which was also an open format (DiBona and Ockman, 1999; Raymond, 1999) (this is discussed in more detail in Chapter 3). The prospects of the SDMI producing a broadly agreeable regulatory framework soon became less propitious, given that just one year into the initiative the RIAA launched a legal action against one of the consortium members, MP3.com, for alleged violation of copyright law following the introduction of a new software product. This action was indicative of an ideological divide within the SDMI about the borders of copyright, with the established firms wanting tight and rigid borders, whereas the newer companies wanted looser, more flexible limits.[13] These differences proved to be insurmountable, and the SDMI initiative was abandoned in 2001.

---

[13] The action revolved around a service called Beam-it, which enabled users to upload MP3 copies of CD tracks to the MP3.com site, which could then be accessed remotely through any PC. Although MP3.com indicated that this should be used only for purchased CDs, there was no way to ensure that the CDs were owned by the user (for more on MP3.com, see Ch. 3).

2.5.3. Networks of Consumption

The impact of software formats upon networks of consumption is significant because, within these networks at least, traditional record companies actually had much to gain and relatively little to lose. Here it was the large music retailers that feared a shift to digital content and internet distribution. Just as record companies were slow to respond to the possibilities of software formats within networks of reproduction and distribution because of problems of lock-in, so retailers were tethered to networks of consumption as traditionally configured. Thus, by the late 1990s incumbent retailers were already being bypassed by a first wave of disintermediation, a process that consisted of internet-based retailers selling CDs from their websites at discounted prices and delivered by mail. Traditional music retailers also faced displacement through second and third waves of disintermediation and reintermediation. On the one hand, retailers were in danger of being overtaken in their abilities to understand and influence consumer behaviour by the development of electronic-based techniques of 'forensic marketing' and the 'narrow-casting' of products to highly distinctive market niches. Such practices were made possible by the mass of detailed consumer information generated by digital transactions, which enabled firms to develop new ways of 'making up' and constructing consumers (Kozinets, 1998; Sivadas et al., 1998; see Pratt, 2000, for a discussion of 'on the fly' advertising using such technologies), in a way that prefigured the later emergence of 'big data'.[14] On the other hand, retailers were also threatened by the plans of the large record companies to establish digital distribution channels that would supply music in digital content direct to consumers. This was the clear vision of the future embraced in the early 1990s when the potential of the internet began to be recognized, but which clouded somewhat in the wake of the panic surrounding MP3. Belatedly, the record companies began to pilot such schemes, which were parallel

---

[14] e.g. software company RealNetworks was revealed in 1999 to have been compiling detailed information from the computers of all those who downloaded its RealJukebox program which permitted the recording and playback of MP3 files. This information included the number of music tracks stored on users' hard drives and their formats, the preferences attached to tracks, the type of portable music player connected to the computer, and, critically, a Global Unique Identifier that identified each user by name, e-mail address, and postcode (McIntosh, 1999).

and complementary initiatives to the SDMI. A secure digitally distributed future was seen in some quarters of the music industry as a highly effective measure to neutralize the power of the retailers, given the pressure they have exerted over the rest of the industry over the last fifteen to twenty years or so.

This vision of the future, if successfully realized, would indeed have seriously undermined the viability of music retailers as they were traditionally organized, as the retailers themselves soon recognized. For example, in the wake of the announcement of the planned merger between AOL and Time Warner, a senior executive of Virgin Megastore, a leading music-retailing chain, suggested that a shift to digital distribution would undermine margins sufficiently that firms such as his might be forced to withdraw their investments and move out of the industry altogether (Ward, 2000).[15] This executive was half-right: the combination of software formats and the internet would account for Virgin's retail music business, which closed in 2007, followed by a management buyout that itself failed in 2009. But it was not because the record companies had successfully taken control of retail distribution. Rather, as we saw earlier, it was because a technology company, Apple, pioneered paid-for downloading and positioned itself in a powerful position at the centre of networks of distribution.

2.6. CONCLUSIONS

This chapter has considered the implications of software formats such as MP3 upon the geographical organization of the music industry. The concept of the musical network was used to help understand the configuration of the musical economy and of the impacts of processes of disintermediation and reintermediation. The evolution of this new technological assemblage within the musical economy has had significant organizational and geographic impacts upon all four of its constituent networks.

---

[15] Given that margins in record retailing were estimated to be in the region of 25% of the cover price, sales of CDs would have to fall significantly to warrant such a decision, when the statement was made it was thought that there was more than a little hyperbole within such a threat. However, this prediction was for the most part accurate.

Nevertheless, it is important to stress that, as software formats and internet distribution became central to the organization of the musical economy, the processes by which musical networks stabilized around these technologies moved at different speeds, for at least three reasons. First, although the share of music sales mediated through the internet is growing rapidly, it is still at a relatively low level, particularly compared to the volume of sales in the 1980s and 1990s when CD was the dominant format. Second, the market is partly limited by hardware requirements, as it is mediated by networked personal computers or mobile devices, the costs of which are not insignificant. Moreover, although MP3 titles are compressed, if stored in any number they can still command significant amounts of memory which can begin significantly to slow the speed at which computers and devices work for other purposes.[16] Third, there is a tendency for the debate surrounding software formats and internet distribution systems to skip into a mode of thought that accepts that its introduction will be to the exclusion of existing modes of organization within the music industry. Yet, it is possible to see that the new technological assemblage may, in some respects, complement rather than undermine the current configuration of networks in the musical economy. For example, many of the internet sites offering free downloads of MP3 files from obscure artists are doing so not out of altruism but as samples or tasters in the hope that consumers will buy copies of the artist's music, or consume the artist's material in other ways, such as through live performance or artist-related merchandise. Moreover, even as the record companies worked through their problems with digitally distributed music and began to embrace it, they found resistance on the part of at least some consumers reluctant to abandon the wider aesthetic process of music consumption which involves building up a physical collection of recordings. For such consumers, the compilation of file names on a computer directory was not seen as an acceptable substitute to the collection of material things.[17]

---

[16] Although costs have fallen in real terms and alternative means of access have expanded, especially with the development of mobile telephone technologies that permit the transfer of sizeable or unlimited data packages, the development of internet access through other domestic appliances (such as, ironically, given the origins of MP3, interactive television) and devices such as digital tablets, and the ability to store files 'at-a-distance' through cloud computing.

[17] Although I should point out that this has not been a problem for this particular, active consumer of recorded music, who has quite happily set aside his collection of

Indeed, contrary to the celebratory and romantic ways in which formats such as MP3 have been welcomed by actors on the fringe of the industry, it remains the case that record companies that make profits from the exploitation of the intellectual property rights contained in sound recording have, for the most part, not failed (but see Chapter 6 on EMI). Although the proliferation of companies dedicated to exploiting the potential of software formats and internet distribution systems increased levels of competition, the familiar process of capital centralization and concentration in the music industry served to regulate competition.

For similar reasons, then, we have yet to witness the growth of some kind of alternative musical economy, which early advocates of MP3, such as Chuck D for example, suggested was just over the horizon. Thus, even though Public Enemy deserve credit for pioneering the idea of selling an album in digital form for a discounted price ahead of the release of the CD version, they were still selling the downloads for profit. The political ethos surrounding the growth of software formats is, appropriately, akin to that attributed by Wise (1997) to the community of organic intellectuals that has developed around *Wired* magazine, which he describes as 'one of the central sites [for] the politicization and culturalization of information and communication corporations (1997: 151). Thus, the discourse that advocates MP3 and other digital futures as an alternative to the current configuration of the music industry may well be anti-organizational and anti-hierarchical, but it is certainly not anti-market, conforming as it does to a kind of 'capitalist libertarianism'. It was, therefore, ironically appropriate that the press release that accompanied the release of Public Enemy s *There's A Poison Goin' On* in MP3 format included a quote by Chuck D who argued that the availability of music in downloadable format not only provided 'consumers with options they've never had before' but it was also 'the modern day equivalent of Dylan going electric'.[18] Although Bob Dylan's abandonment of an acoustic folk vernacular in 1965 for the use of electronic instruments in the 'contemporary style' is certainly considered by popular music historians to be a significant development in the evolution of the genre, it

---

vinyl, tape, and CD recordings built up over forty years for music in software format and which, incidentally, is playing on the speaker system of my PC as I type this.

[18] See <http://www.atomicpop.com/aboutatomicpop/Pepr2.html>.

was also interpreted by large sections of his audience as an unforgivable 'sellout' to the forces of 'commercialism'. As the industry began to stabilize around software formats and internet distribution, the statement was possibly more prophetic than its author realized. These ideas are developed in more detail in the next chapter.

3

Scary Monsters? Software Formats, Peer-to-Peer Networks, and the Spectre of the Gift

> All old...established industries have been destroyed or are daily being destroyed...And as in material, so also in intellectual production. The intellectual creations of individual nations become common property. (Marx and Engels, 1977 [1848]: 39)

> Napster and Gnutella work poorly as actual threats to the business of the music industry, [but] they have considerable promise as *scary* stories to tell legislators, particularly if one were lobbying for government assistance in preserving the current shape of the market. (Boyle, 2000; emphasis added)

> They created a *monster*...(US District Judge Marilyn Hall Patel, on the Napster peer-to-peer file-sharing system, quoted in Borland, 2000a; emphasis added)

3.1. INTRODUCTION

A spectre is haunting capitalism, the spectre of the gift.[1] An emergent socio-technical network, understood here as a network of human actors, information and communication technologies, and institutions, is challenging those domains of the capitalist economy that rely upon the exploitation of intellectual property rights for their reproduction. These domains, which I describe as copyright capitalism, have become ever more extensive, a product both of increases in the knowledge and information content of the economy and of the subsequent rise in the measures taken to defend ideas, images,

---

[1] The phrase is borrowed from Marx and Engels (1977: 34), 'A spectre is haunting Europe, the spectre of communism', via Barbrook (1999: 1), 'A spectre is haunting the Net: the spectre of communism'.

and creativity through laws and regulations pertaining to copyrights and patents (Boyle, 1996; Lessig, 2005; Rifkin, 2000; Thurow, 1997). Although concern about the emergence of this challenge to intellectual property rights is widespread and generally felt, it is most intense within the culture industries, broadly defined. These industries tend to be dominated by large corporations that translate acts of creativity into commodities which, for the most part, are sold in mass markets on a per-unit pricing basis. However, since the late 1990s, business models have emerged from the corpus of the 'new economy' (Cassidy, 2002; Daniels et al., 2007; Frank, 2000; Lewis, 1999) that reduced the per-unit marginal cost of cultural commodities such as music, movies, and texts virtually to zero, while the fixed initial costs required to produce these commodities remained high.

In this chapter I focus upon the 'scary monsters' which were summoned into existence through socio-technical networks that destabilized the regime of governance supporting copyright capitalism, and which enabled its leading corporations to become globally significant institutions. These changes had significance for industries such as motion pictures, publishing, and software engineering, among others. However, it was in the music industry that the challenge to the mode of reproduction of copyright capitalism was initially most acute as new musical networks, made up of digital music, software formats, and internet distribution systems, profoundly destabilized this most highly concentrated and centralized of industries (Alderman, 2001).[2] This is also where the spectral outlines and manifestations of what Barbrook (1998) described as a 'hi-tech gift economy' could be discerned most clearly. This gift economy—or more accurately, gift economies—has had important implications for economic governance more generally, for it indicates how new competitive and regulatory norms were introduced through the hardware and software that forms electronic spaces such as the internet and the World Wide Web (Sassen, 2000; Thrift and French, 2002), and is arguably the vanguard of a mode of exchange with significant implications for conventional business models across a range of capitalist industries.

The argument in the chapter proceeds as follows. In section 3.2 I provide some background and context, recapping briefly on the crisis within the musical economy. In section 3.3 I look at the development

---

[2] For analysis of similar processes of destabilization within the motion-picture industry, see the work of Andrew Currah (2003, 2006, 2007).

of hi-tech gift economies. In section 3.4 I consider the emergence of a gift economy in recorded music in the mid-1990s. Founded upon the specialized skills of computer 'hackers' and hobbyists, its narrow base meant that this early manifestation of the hi-tech gift economy was seen more as an irritant than as a direct threat to the revenues of the music industry. In section 3.5 I look at the ways in which this irritation was transformed into a major strategic concern during the late 1990s as, driven on by the phenomenon of the new economy, new dot.com start-ups began to devise new business models for the music industry. The models transformed specialized knowledge, once the preserve of hackers and hobbyists, into generic knowledge through the development of 'user-friendly' file-exchange systems, thereby providing mass access to a once 'underground' musical gift economy.

3.2. THE MUSICAL ECONOMY IN CRISIS

Over its relatively brief history the music industry has been constantly shaped and reshaped by what Christensen (1997) has described as 'disruptive' technologies: that is, artefacts that, through their social application, produce episodes of socio-technical change which have profound implications for organizational structures by changing the bases of competition within and between industries. The music industry has been beset by numerous crises triggered by the introduction of technologies originally developed for use beyond the musical economy but which migrated there some time after their original applications. The current crisis in the music industry has been brought about by the emergence of software formats.

Software formats, such as MP3, are examples of powerful disruptive (socio-)technologies, and their impacts upon the music industry were largely unforeseen and unintended. As outlined in Chapter 1, MP3 is a software 'compression' program that reduces digital files to around 10 per cent of their original size, with very little loss of quality. The program was originally developed to reduce the size of digital motion picture files and audio files as part of the efforts by the International Organization for Standardization to establish protocols and conventions for the emerging interactive television industry. However, by the mid-1990s MP3 programs were being used to compress digital music files extracted from media such as compact discs, reducing them to a size that made it possible for the files to be sent as e-mail attachments or, more commonly, to be posted on websites and available for downloading onto personal computers. These files were usually copies of copyrighted material, but were made available as part of complex processes of gift exchange (see sections 3.3 and 3.4).

It is around the issue of copyright that the crisis in the musical economy revolves. The exploitation and protection of copyright has long been central to the music industry as a means of defending investments made within the musical economy. Copyright is a social convention developed to encourage cultural creativity. Emanating from debates on authorship and literary property in seventeenth-century and eighteenth-century England (Rose, 1993), copyright is a compromise that balances the interests of producers with the distribution of knowledge within a broader public commons. According to Vaidhyanathan (2001: 177), 'copyright law is a system—an institute of practices and habits—that regulates information by creating artificial shortages for limited times and limited purposes'. By making unauthorized copying of material illegal for a fixed period, copyright enables cultural producers to exploit an economic rent from their creations. When the copyright on a work expires, the material passes into the public domain, enabling cheaper copies to be made available.[3]

As far back as the nineteenth century, music publishers were already fully conversant with the language of copyright, which was used to protect investments within the production of sheet music. Performing rights societies were established from the mid-nineteenth century onwards to collect royalties for composers and publishers every time their music was performed in front of an audience. To similarly protect investments in sound recording, after its development in the early twentieth century, the music industry pushed for the revision of copyright law to include the payment of 'mechanical' royalties for 'each cylinder, record or piano roll manufactured, in addition to revenues already derived for live performances' (Garofalo, 1999: 322). Such mechanical rights endured and were adapted as formats and technologies changed, and were supplemented by royalties earned from performances both live and pre-recorded in other

---

[3] These periods have tended to increase over time. Take the example of US copyright law (Vaidhyanathan, 2001). Until 1831 copyright lasted for just fourteen years, for twenty-eight years until 1909, and for fifty-six years until 1978. Between 1978 and 1998 copyright was extended to the lifetime of the author plus fifty years.

developing media such as radio and television. Indeed, over time as record companies evolved into larger entertainment corporations, partly as a result of mergers with organizations within the publishing, broadcasting, motion picture, and electronic-manufacturing industries (Sadler, 1997), the *raison d'être* of such companies began to change. Increasingly, they

> began to think of themselves more as exploiters of rights than producers of records. Their new mission was to develop as many 'revenue streams' as possible. Music-television and cross-media marketing—particularly movie tie-in—were crucial to this development. (Garofalo, 1999: 343)

A concern with copyright was extended to encompass the broader idea of intellectual property rights and their exploitation (Vaidhyanathan, 2001), which became ever more central to the production of profits by such firms. This encouraged a concerted and ultimately successful movement to encircle the intellectual commons further (Boyle, 1996; Lessig, 1999, 2001) and to enact regulation that ensured the maximum extraction of value from copyrighted material:

> corporate capital has expanded its hold over intellectual property rights in at least three critical areas: extending the term of copyright, narrowing the arena for fair use, and creating brand-new intellectual property rights. In the 1990s both the European Community and the United States extended the term of copyright to a point that effectively eliminates the public domain for music written in the twentieth century. In a sweeping revision designed to bring the United States in line with changes in the European Community dating back to 1993, the Sonny Bono Copyright Term Extension Act of 1998 extended U.S. copyrights owned by corporations to ninety-five years and individually held copyrights to the life of the author plus seventy years. While the move was spearheaded by Disney because, under the existing law, Mickey Mouse was about to enter the public domain, such legislation obviously serves the interests of transnational capital, which is becoming better organized on an administrative level. (Garofalo, 1999: 348)

The importance that record companies attach to the protection of copyright is based upon valid enough concerns. The music industry is characterized by chronic uncertainty and by high levels of information asymmetries, so that it is generally accepted that only a small percentage of recordings recoup the investments made in them, which take the form of advances to artists and other production and marketing costs. However, the low marginal costs of production mean that the recordings that are successful usually recoup sufficient returns to cover the costs of those that do not. But such are the problems of uncertainty that run through a fickle and fashion-conscious market, record companies are never able to predict which of their recordings will be successful. As a result, record labels adopt a portfolio approach to their rosters of artists, which are increasingly turned over, as acts that fail to generate profitable recordings for any length of time will fail to get their contracts renewed. Moreover, this low ratio of success to failure also explains the industry's perennial concerns about copyright infringement because the ability of customers to obtain illegal copies of material is considered to directly reduce sales, thereby lowering income and reducing the amount of money that record companies are prepared to invest in artists, particularly those that do not earn any money.[4]

In light of the relationship between the music industry and copyright, software formats and internet distribution systems were claimed by the record companies to be a particularly potent threat to their continued existence. It is important to put these claims into context. At one level, software formats raised exactly the same issues as did the adoption of earlier reproduction technologies such as audiotape and videotape. In both cases, the entertainment industry argued that the ability of consumers to make tapes of music or motion pictures would destroy markets for these products. However, both industries were able to overcome the perceived problems of 'home taping' through successfully securing a tariff for the sale of blank cassettes and by selling their products through new distribution channels (such as rental and sell-through in the case of VHS videos) (Ryan, 1998), and redrafting contracts on terms less favourable to artists. Moreover, the music and motion picture industries were able to differentiate successfully their products from taped copies through the development of products with high reproduction quality (such as CDs in the 1980s, DVDs in the 1990s, and the upgrading of the cinematic experience

---

[4] However, the argument that the acquisition of illegal copies of music acts as a substitute for purchases is contentious. Indeed, there is some evidence to suggest that illegal copies circulate most rapidly among active music listeners who also buy more legal copies of music than average. For example, according to one estimate, whereas the average consumer bought four CDs per year, those who downloaded music bought between twenty and thirty CDs (Talacko, 2001).

across both decades). However, the music industry argued that the 'digital dilemma' is different from that of taping, for at least four reasons. First, as a digital format, MP3 offers a near-perfect copy of the original recording,[5] which does not deteriorate over time as is the case with other recording media, such as audiotape. Moreover, software formats overcome what Pratt (2001) has described as the 'physical drag effect', which in the past meant that copies were either of inferior quality or expensive to produce. Second, and to compound this problem, MP3 is an insecure format, which means that copies, once made, can be copied indefinitely and on a potentially worldwide basis because of the reach of the internet. To give some illustration of this, Figure 3.1 shows just how far these files can travel. It reveals the geographical distribution of users logged into one online music provider, Audiogalaxy, at one moment in the early 2000s. An MP3 file made available by a user could potentially have been downloaded by 15,560 users in at least sixty-four different countries. Third, although the companies that provide MP3 player software have to pay mechanical royalties to the music industry in a fashion that is almost as old as sound recording itself, most of the MP3 files in circulation were illegal copies of copyrighted material for which no royalties were paid or received. Fourth, and finally, MP3 files were being exchanged in an environment that was not merely indifferent to copyright law and intellectual property but, in many respects, overtly hostile towards it. This was particularly problematic as the music industry sought to adopt the internet for commercial use (Lessig, 1999). The industry was required to enter an environment that was created for an alternative purpose, and which posed a challenge to the enforcement of copyright law. It is to the development of this economic space within the infrastructure of the internet that I now turn.

---

[5] However, the sound quality of MP3 was far lower than that of CDs, and although MP3 players can be connected to hi-fi systems, most MP3s were, initially at least, played on the sound-reproduction equipment of PCs or through the cheap headphones of MP3 players. These technical deficiencies acted as a deterrent for some music consumers who placed considerable importance on the 'high fidelity' reproduction of music.

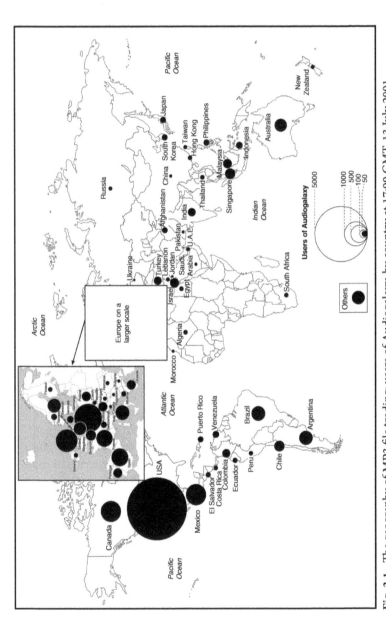

Fig. 3.1. The geography of MP3 file trading: users of Audiogalaxy, by country at 17:00 GMT, 13 July 2001.

Source: Audiogalaxy website, http://www.audiogalaxy.com/.

3.3. THE SPECTRE OF THE GIFT

By the late 1990s, the process of making the internet an infrastructure for the generation of profit via commodity exchange was well under way. The case for a 'new economy' founded upon the internet was advanced by a complex mixture of advocates, made up, according to Feng et al. (2001), of internet 'visionaries', management consultants, mainstream economists, and 'gonzo journalists'. The appeal of this new economy was founded upon the possibilities of harnessing electronic networks, which promised to extend the geographical reach of companies at the same time as they reduced costs (French and Leyshon, 2004; Daniels et al., 2007). Encouraged by the riches that e-commerce might deliver—and by the startling stock prices of the rash of dot.com start-ups (Cassidy, 2002)—being 'net-centric' became the latest business fad (Feng et al., 2001; Williams, 2001). However, although exchange was one of the founding principles of the internet, and had driven its development from its earliest years, efforts to import models of monetary and commodity exchange from the mainstream economy ran into difficulties in some areas because the kinds of exchange upon which the internet was founded were for the most part non-pecuniary in nature. Indeed, not only was the internet initially a difficult place for companies to do business but, according to Barbrook (1998), it actually posed a significant challenge to the mainstream economy because elements of it constitute what he describes as a 'hi-tech gift economy'.

The origins of the internet were as a system for the US military and it developed subsequently within the academic community. Therefore, although the internet was used as a means of exchange, it was used largely as a means of exchanging information within a peer-to-peer culture that was motivated more by the accumulation of cultural capital than by economic capital. The basis of advancement within the academic community is generally the building of reputation and esteem through the development of a body of work that is, to all intents and purposes, given away. In other words, academic outputs are gifts, given away in the anticipation that they will generate cultural capital for the giver. If accumulated in sufficient quantities, this cultural capital can be converted into economic capital through career progression, as academics are given promotions and receive job offers. However, the point is that much prestigious academic output is simply given away:[6]

---

[6] Although not all of it is. The obvious exception is the publication of books, which can earn authors royalty income. However, books are bought by libraries, and are

Reformatted

Funded by the state or by donations, scientists don't have to turn their intellectual work directly into marketable commodities. Instead, research results are publicised by 'giving a paper' and by 'contributing an article' to professional journals...academics acquire intellectual respect from each other through citations in articles and other forms of public acknowledgement. Scientists therefore can only obtain personal recognition for their individual efforts by openly collaborating with each other through the academic gift economy. Although research is becoming increasingly commercialised, the giving away of findings remains the most efficient method of solving common problems within a particular scientific discipline. (Barbrook, 1998: 3)

In other words, the act of giving away is proliferative in this instance, for both the receivers and the givers of such gifts, as repeated and multiple acts of academic gift giving ensure that there are greater resources to draw upon than if knowledge was restricted or made available only for a fee that reflected the costs of its production. Structured as such, the academic model is predisposed towards a highly distributed system of knowledge diffusion that should produce, in turn—given the existence of appropriate institutions and media, such as libraries with up-to-date journals and books, for example—a distributed system of knowledge production.[7] The architecture of the internet is predicated upon the same model of proliferation, based as it is upon what Tim Berners-Lee—widely credited as bringing the World Wide Web into being—describes as 'a decentralised technical architecture and a decentralised social architecture' (Berners-Lee and Fischetti, 2000: 220). The strong academic influence over the building of the

available there free to borrowers. It is also important to note that publishers make money from the giving away of research articles as universities are required to pay subscription fees to gain access to the papers that their employees sign away. It was in response to this evident asymmetry that the Open Access model for academic publishing emerged.

[7] However, as work on the sociology of scientific knowledge and its geography teaches us, knowledge is 'stickier' in some places than in others, which reflects the fact that scientific knowledge is not only a relational achievement between academics, but also a relational achievement between academics and non-human actors such as laboratories, equipment, and suitable grant-funding bodies (Latour, 1987; Latour and Woolgar, 1986). Therefore, the academic gift economy produces an uneven geography of academic knowledge production that, at a global scale at least, maps onto the geography of wealth and income. This is because this gift economy requires that funds are available to ensure that a library does have up-to-date stocks of the latest journals and books, that academics work in sufficiently well-resourced environments which facilitate their research, etc.

internet has meant that it too has been structured towards the free exchange of information based upon the norms of the academic gift economy:

> the founders of the Net never bothered to protect intellectual property within computer-mediated communications. On the contrary, they were developing these new technologies to advance their careers inside the academic gift economy. Far from wanting to enforce copyright, the pioneers of the Net tried to eliminate all barriers to the distribution of scientific research. Technically, every act within cyberspace involves copying material from one computer to another. Once the first copy of a piece of information is placed on the Net, the cost of making each extra copy is almost zero. The architecture of the system presupposes that multiple copies of documents can be easily [transferred] around the network. (Barbrook, 1998: 3)

Thus, of all the branches of corporate capitalism threatened by the internet it is that which relies upon the exploitation of intellectual property rights that has the most to lose by the generalization of a gift economy through the mediation of the internet, because it supports the giving away of all kinds of creative, intellectual products.

However, although Barbrook's thesis is interesting and provocative, it is weakened by the fact that it deals only superficially with the concept of the gift itself and makes little attempt to distinguish gift exchange from commodity exchange. Fortunately, definitions of gift exchange, and the qualities that distinguish it from commodity exchange, can be derived from a large body of anthropological writings on the subject (e.g. Carrier, 1991; Gregory, 1982; Parry and Bloch, 1989; Schrift, 1997a). The first point to make is that gift exchange and commodity exchange should not be seen as necessarily oppositional or mutually exclusive. Nor is it the case that gift giving is a purely altruistic and innocent activity whereas the exchange of commodities is purely instrumental and calculative (Parry, 1989: 65). As has been pointed out, in numerous studies from Mauss onwards, expectations of reciprocity and 'return' mean that gift giving can be coercive and socially damaging (e.g. see Mauss, 1990 [1950]; Parry 1989; Schrift, 1997b). The obligation that gifts bestow upon the receiver means that no gifts are ever really free (Bourdieu, 1997; Douglas, 1990). Moreover, systems of gift exchange and commodity exchange have coexisted alongside and entangled with one another over a long period of time (Bloch and Parry, 1989; Carrier, 1994; Curry, 1999;

Miller, 2002), and gifts have long been used to induce commodity exchange (in the form of the free sample, the offer, and so on).

Nevertheless, there are broad differences between the nature of gift
exchange and commodity exchange, and at least three of these are
significant to the argument being developed here. The first distinction
revolves around the alienability of the objects being exchanged, and
the nature of the relationship between the transactors. In Gregory's
classic definition, gift exchange involves the exchange of inalienable
objects between interdependent transactors (1982). Gifts are considered inalienable because their ownership is symbolic of the relationship between the transactors, so to transfer them subsequently to
someone else would represent an undermining of that relationship.
Gifts carry traces of the gift giver, to whom the recipient is bound
in some way until the gift is reciprocated. Commodity exchange,
meanwhile, is defined as the exchange of alienable objects between
independent transactors (Gregory, 1982; see also Bloch and Parry,
1989; Schrift, 1997b). The second distinction revolves around the
issue of time. Thus, for Bourdieu (1997), commodity exchange takes
place within an economy based upon the instantaneous exchange of
objects of equivalent value—that is, the exchange of commodities for
their equivalent value, usually in monetary form—whereas within gift
economies there is usually a time delay before exchanges are equal-
ized. The third and final distinction is that gift exchange is motivated
less by the accumulation of economic capital than by the accumulation of cultural, or symbolic, capital. As Bourdieu argues,

> The gift economy, in contrast to the economy where equivalent values
> are exchanged, is based on a denial of the economic (in the narrow
> sense), a refusal of the logic of the maximization of economic profit,
> i.e. of the spirit of calculation and the exclusive pursuit of material (as
> opposed to symbolic) interest, a refusal which is inscribed in the object-
> ivity of institutions and in dispositions. It is organized with a view to the
> accumulation of symbolic capital. (1997: 237)

It is this latter quality alone—the accumulation of cultural capital—
that Barbrook uses as the defining feature of the hi-tech gift economy.
This exercise in conceptual clarification makes it easier to identify the
ways in which the musical gift economies to be described conform
to conventional understandings of gift economies, and the extent to
which they might differ from internet-based commodity exchange.
Therefore, in the next section of the chapter I consider the emergence

of internet-based gift economies founded upon the exchange of MP3 files.

3.4. THE MP3 GIFT ECONOMY

From the 1990s onwards, the internet facilitated the development of a series of gift economies occupied by hobbyists and enthusiasts of various kinds. The exchange of digital commodities, in the form of picture and sound files, has been described by Slater (2000) as a 'postscarcity' economy. These exchanges developed around internet relay chat (IRC) networks, which made it possible for users to transfer digital files of all kinds between one another. Although not entirely costless—as Slater points out, there are transaction and opportunity costs involved, including the cost of equipment, telephone and broadband bills, plus the time it takes to build and transfer such material—the material was free at the point of supply:

> The material exchanged [via IRC] is indeed 'free' in the sense that there is no monetary value or payment involved: just dip into the sea and take what you want. There is also no effective property right: web sites pay lip service to copyright, but IRC circulates everything indiscriminately without reference to any ownership or authorial origins. It is a Sherwood Forest in its notion of the moral economy. [It]…employs a version of freedom located in an anti-commercial anarchism of the 'property is theft' variety. (2000: 128)

Users created the material for these exchanges by uploading files to their sites on the network, therefore making the material available for others to download. It is in this sense that these files constitute gifts, although it could be argued that a more accurate way of describing them would be as 'takes' rather than gifts. They are unusual gifts in another sense, too. They may be seen as proliferative gifts because downloading files from one computer to another creates a copy—so that the 'giver' does not experience a loss of the object, as happens in traditional acts of gift giving. These are gift economies that operate beyond scarcity.

Moreover, as Slater observes, another unusual characteristic of these 'take from the rich' worlds is that, despite their relaxed approach to the use of copyrighted material, their inhabitants are 'completely obsessed with property rights, with rules of exchange and with exchange ratios' (2000: 130). Although nominally free from the regulatory gaze of governments or the commercial agencies whose copyright they are infringing, users nevertheless are expected to conform to a normative expectation of behaviour when conducting such exchanges.

This much is clear from Cooper and Harrison's study (2001) of MP3 trading via IRC during the mid-1990s. Using the normative language of the music industry to demonize those who break copyright laws, they identify what they describe as an audio-piracy subculture.[8] They reveal a community that is organized around the search for (sub)cultural capital, as participants earn 'respect' by providing diverse and up-to-date MP3 audio files. The community is exclusionary and status-driven, which is in part a product of the high level of computer knowledge required of users if they wish to be able to participate in IRC MP3 exchanges:

> The audio pirate often uses several computerized tools simultaneously, sometimes with multiple and distinct windows open at any one time to different destinations in each. A typical 'upper class' audio pirate might have open two FTP clients, an IRC client talking in four channels, a web browser and an FTP server. By rapidly multiplexing which of these interactions to focus upon, the pirate will never run out of things to do, and can spin about for an unbounded amount of time, moving files from place to place, building social status and all the while continuously conversing with others. (Cooper and Harrison, 2001: 77)

Cultural capital was also earned by the roles that participants played within this community. According to Cooper and Harrison, there were at least three categories of participant, which commanded different levels of respect within the community. The least-respected participant within IRC communities was the *leech*. Leeches took files but gave nothing back. As Slater has pointed out, despite the fact that obtaining a file does not deplete its source, 'leeches are the lowest of

---

[8] Richard Stallman has drawn attention to the way in which copyright capital has used language to inflate the seriousness of acts of copyright infringement through the use of terms such as 'copyright theft' and 'piracy', where in the case of piracy the act of 'sharing with your neighbour is the moral equivalent of attacking a ship. If you don't believe in that, refuse to use the word "pirate." There are plenty of neutral terms, such as "unauthorised copying," that you can use, that will express no opinion about it. Or, as I do, you could describe it as "sharing with your neighbour," and express positive opinion about it. But if you feel obliged to be neutral, be neutral, don't use the other side's propaganda word' (2001).

the low on IRC, and leeching is probably the greatest insult to IRC as such' (2000: 130). The refusal of leeches to recognize the unwritten rule of gift economies, that the receipt of a gift incurs an obligation to return it (Bourdieu, 1997), meant that many site operators imposed trading ratios, whereby files could be downloaded only in strict proportion to the number of files uploaded to the site. This feature may be seen to weaken the status of such sites as gift economies. The anxiety experienced, by those who uploaded files to their sites, about the unreciprocated taking of their gifts, suggests that at times exchange resembled the transfer of alienable objects between independent traders. However, Cooper and Harrison argue that the interdependence of transactors was reinforced through the requirement of many site operators that potential transactors presented personal recommendations from other site owners before they were given access to files. Moreover, although many site owners did not insist upon an instantaneous exchange of equivalents, merely of exchange in proportion, the fact that these kinds of exchanges were made almost simultaneously makes them more closely resemble commodity exchange than gift exchange.

This form of behaviour was routinely practised by the next category of user, the *trader*. Traders obtained files by exchanging them in reciprocal deals with other traders. The social community of MP3 exchange via IRC was completed by the *citizen*, who commanded the greatest amount of cultural capital, and whose activities most closely resembled that of an archetypal participant within gift exchange. Citizens played a foundational role within these communities by making sufficient material available through uploading, which could then be subsequently traded or leeched by others. In other words, citizens provided the 'liquidity' that made the reproduction of these gift economies possible.

As the number of people exchanging files via IRC grew steadily over the 1990s, so copyright capitalists began to get concerned about the circulation of copyrighted material that was being made available without cost to consumers (Alderman, 2001), particularly as some of those using IRC to download MP3 files adopted a studied indifference to copyright law, as Cooper and Harrison (2001: 87) revealed in their online interview with MP3 trader 'dox':

> Copyright law doesn't interest me. It doesn't pertain to my existence in any way because it could never affect me. I buy the software I use for

business, and steal the software I use for pleasure. I buy CDs that I want
to listen to, but I download MP3 files of music that I don't think is worth
buying or that I can't find for a reasonable price. It's not like I can get
caught, so why not?

But the overall impact of these communities upon the total level of
copyright infringement was relatively limited because, by the close of
the 1990s, they remained relatively small. According to Cooper and
Harrison, even on the largest IRC network there were only 135 channels devoted to MP3 file exchange (out of a total of over 17,000 channels), and at any one time there was an average of twenty users on
each channel (2001: 74–5). The reason for their limited size, particularly in relation to the online models to be discussed in the next part
of the chapter, is that they had significant barriers to entry in the level
of technological knowledge required to operate successfully within
them. Therefore, although this early form of the MP3 gift economy
generated concern within the music industry, and was a herald of the
file-sharing models that would consume much of its legal energies in
the future, in retrospect the MP3 gift economy of the mid-1990s to
late 1990s can be interpreted as little more than a more efficient and
'space-shrinking' form of the small-scale copyright piracy suffered by
the music industry since the advent of home-taping technology (see
Chapter 2). Constituted as a hi-tech gift economy, MP3 file exchange
actually presented a relatively minor threat to music as a commodity.
However, things began to change when, as part of the dot.com boom,
an attempt was made to convert these gift economies into income
streams. It is to this process of transformation and translation that
I now turn.

3.5. CAPITAL WILL EAT ITSELF: IMPROVISING NEW BUSINESS MODELS

From the late 1990s, capitalism began to colonize the gift economies
of the internet. Fuelled by the torrents of money made available by
venture capitalists (Cassidy, 2002; Daniels et al., 2007; Frank, 2000;
Kenny and Florida, 2000; Thrift, 2001), a host of new start-ups began
to explore the possibilities of harnessing the trade in MP3 to commercial ends. Making money from digital music had been part of
the long-term strategy of the large music corporations since the early

1990s when these firms first recognized the possibility of delivering music directly to consumers through what was then being described as the 'information superhighway' (Alderman, 2001). However, music industry concerns about copyright protection meant that more money and effort was invested in developing technologies that would make digital music 'secure' than in developing ways of delivering music online. Given that the record companies were strongly wedded to a price-per-unit business model, such reticence was understandable. As far as the music companies were concerned, until it was possible to develop a digital-music format that would prevent consumers making multiple unauthorized copies it would not be possible to develop a viable business model for the online delivery of music.

As the large corporations hesitated, the new economy start-ups began to pioneer experimental music business models. As Feng et al. (2001) have argued, the 'business model' became the predominant means of securing sufficient money from venture capitalists in order to attempt to realize the promises of e-commerce. The *raison d'être* of such models was knowledge transformation; they made generic the highly specialized and technical knowledge previously the preserve of the hackers and hobbyists that dominated the MP3 gift economies. These models made it possible for those with lower levels of computer networking abilities to gain access to the MP3 economy. As with many new economy businesses these were largely improvised, but three main variants emerged which marked these firms out from the conventional music-industry business model. These were: streaming and web casting, cyber lockers, and digital downloads. Of these, streaming and web casting posed the least significant challenge to the music industry as it was then configured, for it operated as a form of 'internet radio', which played a continuous stream of music of various genres. The order of music could not be controlled by the listener, nor could individual pieces of music be downloaded, and the owner of the site derived revenue from selling advertising space on the site, and in return paid royalties to the copyright owners for use of the material. The remaining two business models were more interesting as not only did they represent new ways of making money from music that threatened the revenues of incumbent music industry firms, but they also significantly extended the MP3 gift economy from a constituency of several thousand to one of tens of millions.

These models will be explored through three brief case studies, which represent different variants of these models. Two of the models were choked off by legal action, and were incorporated into the sphere of copyright capitalism. However, in the third case, incorporation proved more difficult, and the networks of exchange produced were both practically and ideologically more difficult to tame.

3.5.1. The 'Cyber Locker': MP3.com

MP3.com was established in San Diego in 1997 by Michael Robertson, a twenty-something graduate of the University of San Diego, who had already been president and chief executive of two other software companies before founding the company that eventually became MP3. com. The firm was initially created as an aggregator site that grouped together the formerly independent websites of new and unsigned bands and artists that offered MP3 downloads of their own music. From this it evolved into something approaching a record company with an online capacity. Although not signing artists to contracts as such, it nevertheless arranged to press CDs for them, which could be ordered from the MP3.com website (Alderman, 2001).

One or two tracks from each album would be available as MP3 files that could be freely downloaded from the site, as samples or tasters to prompt consumers to buy the album online. This low-cost and streamlined way of doing things no doubt also helped contribute to an additional novel feature of the firm, and that was the very generous (by industry standards) royalty rate of 50 per cent offered to artists. However, the fact that the company made little effort to market these acts meant that sales remained low (Alderman, 2001).

Swept along by the boom in internet stocks, the company was incorporated in 1998 and underwent an initial public offering (IPO) in July 1999. The stock was priced at $28 per share but, on issue, rose to over $60, so that during 1999 the firm was valued at over $740 million.[9] This was achieved despite the fact that the long-term business model for the company at the time remained opaque.[10] However, despite the vote of confidence placed in the firm by the capital market,

---

[9] This market valuation was calculated from the MP3.com website <http://www. MP3.com/investor/index.html#management> and from NASDAQ data <http:// quotes.nasdaq.com>.

[10] e.g. according to Alderman (2001: 79), when Robertson was asked what business MP3.com was in prior to the IPO his reply was 'the IPO business'. This, it should be said, was not unusual for many of the dot.com firms of the time (see Cassidy, 2002).

the relative obscurity of the artists with whom the company had re-cording deals limited the number of users making repeat visits to the site. As Robertson himself admitted in a 1999 article in the internet magazine, *The Industry Standard*, 'One of the complaints with MP3. com, and it's a warranted complaint, is that people say, "You're doing all these great things with music, but it's not the music we like." We need to have all the music' (quoted in Rosen, 2000).

In 2000 the firm introduced a new service designed to overcome these problems, based upon a free software package which the com-pany gave away at its website. The service was called 'My.MP3.com', and it signalled the firm's attempt to increase the number of visitors to its site, which would increase the likelihood of people listening to its artists and buying its music, but would also enable the firm to charge more in advertising revenue for space on the site. The service intro-duced the concept of the 'cyber locker': a virtual storage space where people could deposit their music, which could then be accessed from a computer anywhere in the world. The system was based upon the company's 'Beam-it' technology, another piece of software which, it was claimed, would be able to read the digital information contained on a music CD and transmit it to MP3.com's central server. All that the MP3.com users would then have to do is to access the site, log in, and then listen to their music collection, without having to have the CDs physically on them.

It was this move which raised the hackles of the RIAA, which be-came an increasingly important actor in the governance of the music industry during this crisis as it sought to come to terms with the emergence of software formats and internet distribution systems. The main role that the RIAA took was to mobilize legal action against copyright infringement, which, given the number of cases they brought, was widespread. In 2000 the RIAA sent more than 7,400 copyright-infringement notices to commercial sites offering down-loads, and a further 2,500 notices to sites that linked to sites which were deemed to be infringing copyright (Borland, 2001). However, the RIAA's actions against MP3.com, and later against Napster, were pivotal to a strategy of protecting the profitability of copyright capital within the musical economy.

The RIAA complained that MP3.com's new service was encourag-ing copyright infringement. Although MP3.com asked users of the Beam-it service to give a declaration that the CD about to be pro-cessed was owned by them, there was no way to ensure that this was the case. Making copies of purchased recorded material is considered as fair use, but it is prohibited to make copies of material that is not owned. As the legal action moved forward, and information about the system was disclosed, the RIAA's lawyers discovered what they saw to be a considerably more serious infringement of copyright law. Despite its suggestive title, the Beam-it software program did not actually transmit the sound files to the MP3.com server, but only transmitted the track listings. This information enabled MP3.com to copy the relevant tracks from its database of 45,000 copyrighted CDs, which it had bought to facilitate the service, to the user's space on the server.

All the major music corporations combined to sue MP3.com when the service was launched, claiming extensive copyright violations. The industry's position was made clear in an open letter from the head of the RIAA to Robertson ahead of the case in 2000:

> your company's violation of the copyright law is brazen on its face. Simply put, it is not legal to compile a vast database of our members' sound recordings with no permission and no license. And whatever the individual's right to use their own music, you cannot exploit that for your company's commercial gain. MP3.com's actions not only violate the rights of our member companies but also are an affront to artists, music publishers and writers, producers and other retailers. We regard MP3.com's business choices to be in serious disregard of the law with serious consequences to the company and its shareholders. (Quoted in Rosen, 2000)

The company mobilized the concept of fair use, but the fact that it was MP3.com that made the copies, and not the owners of the CDs, placed it in a weak position, and prompted the firm to settle out of court for a figure of $170 million (Hu, 2000). After such a capitulation, the firm had one of two choices. First, it could have gone back to its original, if not entirely successful or coherent, business model. Or, second, it could throw in its lot with the large music corporations. It chose the latter option. Having effectively broken the firm in its original form, the five major record companies agreed licensing deals on the back of the My.MP3.com service, whereby registered users would be able to store up to twenty-five CDs on the service for free—despite the fact that prior to the case such storage was deemed to infringe copyright—and between twenty-five and 500 CDs for an annual fee of $50 (Luening, 2000). This process of incorporation was taken further in 2001 when the company agreed to be acquired by Vivendi—owners of Universal—for $372 million so that MP3.com could provide a technological platform for a new online music delivery service being developed as a joint venture by Vivendi and Sony (Learmonth, 2001a). However, at about the same time as the interests of copyright capital were successfully quelling this particular challenge to their interests, a new venture-capital-funded variant of the MP3 gift economy was emerging in the shape of Napster.

3.5.2. The Centralized Peer-to-Peer Network: Napster

Napster was established in Redwood, California, in 1999 to explore the commercial possibilities of a software program written by Shaun Fanning during his undergraduate course in computer science at Northeastern University. Fanning dropped out of university to found the firm, and his company quickly began to extend the MP3 gift economy from a few thousand people to a community of tens of millions. As an undergraduate, Fanning had been an avid user of IRC and of the informal gift economies that grew up around it, and developed the Napster software to make it easier for him and his fellow students to exchange MP3 files over the internet (Alderman, 2001).

Napster was a file-sharing program that utilized the distributed capacity and power of personal computers attached to the internet. It was the best-known example of a category of computer applications described as peer-to-peer, because such networks take 'advantage of resources—storage, cycles, content, human presence—available at the edges of the Internet', and that exist in 'an environment of unstable connectivity and unpredictable IP addresses' (Shirky, 2001: 22). These contingent technological assemblages, made up of human and non-human agents, are formed through the temporary connections forged between the machines running the peer-to-peer program at the same time. Peer-to-peer networks are made up of

> tiny endpoints on the Internet, [that] sometimes without knowing each other exchange information and form communities. There are no more clients and servers or at least, the servers retract themselves discreetly. Instead, the significant communication takes place between co-operating peers. (Oram, 2001: p. ix)

Thus, peer-to-peer networks are radically decentralized systems that use the internet to take advantage of the potential of underutilized computing power and capacity distributed across space and time. In particular, they bring together the individual power of personal computers with internet connectivity to form a much more powerful collective (Levy, 1997) which, in Shirky's suggestive phrase, harnesses the 'dark matter of the Internet' (2001: 24).

Napster was not the first example of a peer-to-peer program—the earliest was the SETI@home program, which was set up in 1998[11]—but it has been by far the most successful. By downloading the free Napster software, users were able to exchange MP3 files held on the hard disks of their PCs; this was coordinated through a central server that provided a search facility enabling users to find songs by particular artists, with particular titles. One of the keys to the success of Napster was its ease of use, which meant that even those with relatively limited levels of computer literacy could gain entry to the formerly arcane and exclusive world of MP3 file exchange. However, unlike the world of IRC, there were no normative rules about the amount of files one could take in relation to the number uploaded. To be sure, users no doubt fell into the categories of leech and citizen identified by Cooper and Harrison in their analysis of IRC-based filed exchange. There were no traders as the nature of the system made it impossible for a user to negotiate terms of exchange with other users: the files were either available to be downloaded, or they were not. There was no space in this system for users to negotiate about the relative use value of different files. But even leeches acted as citizens of a sort because, although they may not have actively made new material available for uploading, everything they downloaded was available for other users to access thereby increasing the 'liquidity' of the system and the likelihood of finding files in searches. Thus, by logging on to the system, users were offering up as gifts all the MP3 files they had previously downloaded from Napster and any others that they made accessible from other parts of their hard disk.

Napster accumulated users at an extraordinary rate. In just eighteen months, without any advertising, it had attracted 38 million users; in two years, this number had risen to almost 60 million. With over 500,000 people logged into the system at any one time in the year 2000 (Alderman, 2001), the system demonstrated the efficiency and capacity

---

[11] SETI@home set about enrolling the computing power of PCs to assist the Search for Extra-Terrestrial Intelligence, a project to detect intelligent life beyond the Earth, which began in the late 1950s. The program has been downloaded by over 2 million people. By using the collective power of so many PCs, SETI@home was able to outperform the world's then largest supercomputer, located in the US Department of Energy. This machine worked at a peak rate of 12.3 trillions of floating-point operations per second (TFLPOS); SETI@home operated at a rate of 20 TFLPOSs (Anderson, 2001).

of a distributed system as it became the richest and most active musical archive in the world. Nevertheless, it was hard to discern what the logic of the Napster business model actually was. One conclusion was that, much like MP3.com, the long-term purpose of Napster was to ride the wave of interest in the new economy and secure an IPO, thereby leveraging money from the financial markets into the hands of its owners and venture capitalists. The software was free, as were the downloads of music files, while the site did not carry advertising. However, the company did vigorously assert its copyright over the Napster name and logo, which in a short period of time gained global recognition, with a view perhaps to exploitation through clothing and other branded products. As Alderman (2001: 134) observed, 'when it came to protecting its intellectual property, Napster was… clearly bullish.'

It was perhaps appropriate, then, that Napster soon came under legal attack from the representatives of copyright capital. The RIAA took action against Napster for 'contributory and vicarious copyright infringement and related state law, alleging that the system enables and encourages piracy, either by downloading pirated songs or by sharing illegal files' (Carey and Wall, 2001: 45). In addition, the RIAA was joined in its action by the record companies it represented and even by a number of individual artists.[12]

---

[12] It was joined most notably by Metallica and Dr Dre. Metallica's position was pointedly satirized in an episode of *South Park*. Stan, Kyle, and Kenny are arrested by the FBI for filesharing and then given an illustration of the consequences of their actions through the 'hardship' endured by musicians who consequently had to 'forego' royalty income. Metallica's drummer, Lars Ulrich, a strident opponent of Napster, is depicted as crying by the edge of his swimming pool. The boys are informed by the agent that Ulrich 'was hoping to have a gold-plated shark tank bar installed right next to the pool, but thanks to people downloading his music for free, he must now wait a few months before he can afford it' (Comedy Central, 2003: 'Christian Hard Rock', *South Park*, season 7, episode 9). This effectively captured the feelings of many downloaders who, brought up on a diet of the programmes such as MTV's *Cribs*, which depicted the home lives of variously talented musicians in more or less opulent luxury, thought that in the circumstances illegal downloading was fair game. The irony of Dr Dre's action is signified by the fact that, having begun his career with Los Angeles 'gangsta rap' band NWA (Niggaz With Attitude)—which included as part of their repertoire the song, 'Fuck da police'—he should subsequently call up the powers of law enforcement so readily to protect his copyright (see Alderman, 2001, for a discussion). Not all artists were so hostile, and many welcomed the ability of Napster to distribute their music to new audiences. Indeed, the LA-based Rage Against the Machine issued an apology to their fans on their website after their management company forced Napster to remove users who were downloading the band's songs from its system, and the band then sought unsuccessfully to get the users reinstated (Borland, 2000b).

Napster lost the action, and was ordered to remove all copyrighted material from its system, and required to pay copyright owners $26m in settlement of unauthorized uses of music, plus an additional $10m advance against future licensing royalties. The appeal of the system soon declined and the numbers of users visiting the site decreased precipitously (Reuters, 2001). However, the future of the firm appeared to have been secured even before the case had been settled through the intervention of Bertelsmann Media Group (BMG). Having undertaken market research that indicated that 80 per cent of Napster users would be prepared to pay a $15 monthly fee to use the system, the firm entered into an alliance with Napster to convert the system into a fee-based subscription service (Reuters, 2000). In return, BMG would then make its entire catalogue available to Napster users. The objective of this deal was to adapt the distributive capacity of Napster to ends that would also protect the income of copyright capitalism.

However, reconciling these two divergent aims was problematic. For one thing, as has just been indicated, the number of Napster users fell rapidly as copyright material was removed. Moreover, the system closed down altogether in the middle of 2001 to be reconfigured ahead of its conversion to a subscription service, so the service not only had to convert users to subscribers but also had to recruit them again. This was more difficult than BMG suspected for there soon emerged a number of media within which MP3 gift economies were able to proliferate and which, as we shall see, were more difficult for copyright capitalism to subdue or co-opt.[13]

3.5.3. Distributed Peer-to-Peer Networks: Gnutella and Freenet

The legal victories of the RIAA and its clients over the likes of MP3. com and Napster were made possible, in part, by the geography of their computer networks. Both firms operated central computer servers, located at their headquarters, which coordinated the networks of users that drew on their services. To use the terminology

---

[13] For BMG, the point became moot in Sept. 2002, when a bankruptcy court prevented the firm acquiring Napster's assets. As a result, Napster was closed and liquidated. Thereafter the brand was bought and sold repeatedly as various companies sought to convert it into a viable subscription service.

of actor-network theory, the servers were obligatory passage points that users had to pass through to gain access to the services provided by the companies. Therefore, by exerting power over the company to shut down or modify the actions of its server, the state, acting on behalf of the RIAA and the large music corporations, was able to exert control over the entire network centred on MP3.com and Napster. However, at the same time there also emerged a set of computer networks that did not rely upon the intervention of a central server. These systems may be described as decentralized networks, or true peer-to-peer networks.

The Napster system was actually a hybrid peer-to-peer system; although users downloaded files directly from each other's hard disks, the directory of files at the heart of the system was centralized, and the system required the central servers to broker search queries in relation to the distributed inventory of files (Minar et al., 2001). True peer-to-peer networks abandon server–client hierarchical relations to create flatter, decentralized systems. Indeed, the operation of these networks carries more than an echo of Deleuze and Guattari's concept of the 'rhizome', which they deploy as a biological metaphor to oppose the 'principle of foundation and origin which is embodied in the figure of the tree' (Marks, 1998: 45). Thus,

> The model of the tree is hierarchical and centralised, whereas the rhizome is proliferating and serial, functioning by means of the principles of connection and heterogeneity. In simple terms, any line can be connected to any other line. (Marks, 1998: 45)

Decentralized peer-to-peer networks are truly 'acentred', and operate as software that exists within the multiple nodes of the internet to which it has been downloaded. Once set in motion, these systems are in a constant state of flux and 'emergence'. The development of such systems has direct relevance to the proliferation of MP3 gift economies for they are both substantively and philosophically opposed to conventional ideas of copyright protection. I will deal briefly with two of the most important of such systems, Gnutella and Freenet.

Gnutella

Given the significant challenge that Gnutella posed to copyright capitalism, it is perhaps surprising to note that it was written by software engineers within a subsidiary of AOL, Nullsoft, at the very same time—spring 2000—that AOL was lining up a merger with Time Warner to create the world's largest rights-driven organization (AOL Time Warner). However, the project was quickly shelved by AOL, being declared an 'unauthorised freelance project' by the engineers that devised it, as its potential to undermine digital copyright protection was immediately recognized (Kan, 2001: 96).

The inspiration for the project is revealed in its name. The appellation GNU betrayed Gnutella's links to GNU and the free-software movement, which by the late 1990s had evolved into a distributed, global community of programmers and software engineers mobilized around the concept of open source (DiBona et al., 1999; Himanen, 2001; Moody, 2001; Raymond, 1999; Wayner, 2000). Open source is based upon software programs where the source code—that part of computer programs that is readable by humans—is kept 'open' and so modifiable by subsequent users, and has produced a continuous and decentralized process of development and improvement of programs. It was this community that salvaged Gnutella, reproducing it through a process of reverse engineering and then publicizing it on a GNU website.[14] From there, the program spread rhizomatically, as users downloaded the software, enabling hosts to interact with one another and permitting users to search for digital files. These included MP3 files but, unlike Napster, also included other media such as picture files.

Thus, Gnutella did the same kind of work as Napster, but supported all kinds of digital media, not just MP3. Moreover, as far as its users were concerned, Gnutella had an advantage that Napster did not. Its advocates claimed that it was beyond the regulatory reach of the RIAA and its agents. Gnutella effaced place: it existed only as a relational entity between points of the internet, between those PCs that were running the program at any particular time.

> To join the network, you simply download one of [the] software packages from the Web. This turns your computer into a 'servent' [sic]— both a client and server. Once you've done that you're ready to find some other servents—their locations are publicised on websites and chat rooms—and make contact with them. The connections are made over the Internet, and all the computers are identified by their Internet

---

[14] Although Richard Stallman, the creator of GNU, has cast doubts on whether Gnutella is really part of the free software or open source movement, as it is not clear whether its source code is modifiable by users (see Vaidhyanathan, 2001: 225).

Protocol (IP) addresses, the basic numeric addresses that identify computers on the Internet. But Gnutella is not the World Wide Web. Your computer communicates directly with the servent it knows about, and those servents pass messages back and forth to yet more servents, which do so in an ever expanding net. (Fox, 2001: 32)

In this sense, Gnutella had no 'location', which in turn had implications for the control of copyright infringement:

> In a decentralized world, it's tough to point fingers. No one entity is responsible for the operation of the Gnutella network. Any number of warrants, writs, and summons can be executed, and Gnutella will still be around to help you find recipes for strawberry rhubarb pie and...MP3s...Gnutella doesn't have a mailing address, and, in fact, there isn't anyone to whom to address the summons. (Kan, 2001: 99 and 119)

However, the system was not as invulnerable as it advocates claimed. It was well recognized that the number of users actively uploading files to such systems—the 'citizens' of such communities—was relatively small, with about 50 per cent of all files being provided by about 1 per cent of users (Carey and Wall, 2001; Fox, 2001). The RIAA targeted this 1 per cent of the Gnutella community by seeking out their IP addresses, identifying their internet service provider (ISP) and writing 'a threatening letter or writ [to]...have the user kicked off or force the ISP to reveal a name that can be pursued through the courts' (Fox, 2001: 32). However, such actions were unsuccessful in shutting Gnutella down, and it became the base protocol for a succession of branded P2P networks, including Limewire and KaZaA.

Freenet

Developed by University of Edinburgh undergraduate Ian Clarke, Freenet was expressly designed in opposition to copyright capital and to promote the total freedom of information. He was also opposed to copyright capitalism, which he argued was inhibiting free expression (Clarke et al., 2002). Freenet was a more sophisticated system than Gnutella, being a self-organizing, learning network. Whereas Gnutella sent out thousands of requests in response to a search command, Freenet sent out just one message, which moved across the network from computer to computer. When the material was found, the source was stored on 'nodes' within the network, so that the system became more intelligent and more efficient at moving information in the future (Learmonth, 2001b). But it also worked akin to underground or guerrilla cells, in that each node in this network only knew about a limited number of other nodes, and there was no way of individual nodes tracing the route that files took after a search request. This has important consequences for the ability of regulatory authorities to trace acts of copyright infringement:

> If the powers that be request a file from a node, they'll get a copy. If they seize that node they'll definitely find a copy. But it would be impossible for them to prove that the file was there before they requested it, so the exercise amounts to entrapment....And because documents are stored in encrypted form, the node's owners can argue truthfully that they had no idea any particular document is held there. What's more, as the act of requesting a document generates new copies, censorship is self-defeating. (Fox, 2001: 32)

Both Gnutella and Freenet were maintained by volunteers operating across several continents, in the open source mode. This movement produced a successful computer operating system—GNU Linux—which is a viable alternative to the Microsoft and iOS operating systems which dominate the market. Indeed, the success of the open source movement caused Microsoft to rail against the project, implying that it is destructive of intellectual property, and therefore 'un-American' (Naughton, 2001).

Although the open source movement was a highly political project, it is in fact neither strictly of the left nor of the right, but is a curious admixture of both. The open source movement conforms to what Barbrook has described as the 'Californian ideology', an alliance of New Left and New Right ideas that 'simultaneously reflects the disciplines of market economics and the freedoms of hippie artisanship' (Barbrook and Cameron, 1996). Thus, this movement was not opposed to capitalism per se, but merely big, corporate capitalism, which was seen to be too powerful and influential within civil society. These ideas were expanded on at length by Eric Raymond, a leading figure in the open source movement, who promoted the idea of the gift economy as a way of introducing a different kind of market, not as a way of replacing the market altogether. A black belt in karate and a believer in the Wicca religion, he advocated an economy made up of a self-correcting system of selfish agents:

> Raymond believes that 'the techniques and attitudes that I've learned from Zen and neo-paganism are very much part of what makes me

publicly effective'. They are also completely consistent with the other beliefs that are central to his life: free software, no gun control—or 'an armed and self-reliant citizenry', as Raymond prefers to put it— and libertarianism, which he explains as 'the original individualist-, small-government, free-trade, rely-on-the-market-not-on-coercion ideology'. More specifically, he describes himself as belonging to a group called 'market anarchists' who 'would like to abolish government altogether'. (Moody, 2001: 153)

Therefore, this vision of the hi-tech gift economy was certainly not a progressive utopian alternative to capitalism, but was seen by some of its influential participants as a precursor to a more distributed, more efficient market economy, with a strong libertarian edge. As Fox has observed, although Freenet provided the means to support gift economies in the face of regulatory authorities that would attempt to close them down, and also provides a vehicle for voicing criticism without fear of punishment or retribution, it can also act as an uncontrollable medium for the circulation of child pornography or for instructions to make weapons of mass destruction (2001). Thus, technologies such as Freenet were morally ambivalent; they appealed both to a progressive sensibility that welcomed its capacity to undermine the ability of large corporations to maintain monopolies over certain kinds of knowledge, and to a libertarian impulse that would enable the circulation of material considered profane and offensive within the existing norms of society.

3.6. DISCUSSION

This chapter has examined the extent to which internet-based gift economies developed in the face of the opposition from 'copyright capitalism', paying particular attention to the musical economy, and to the emergence therein of MP3 trading networks from their earliest incarnation via IRC networks to their development through new economy start-ups and peer-to-peer networks. I have sought to determine the veracity of Barbrook's argument that the growth of the internet from the 1990s onwards brought into being a series of hi-tech gift economies. Barbrook's original thesis did little to actually distinguish between gift exchange and commodity exchange, a deficiency that this chapter sought to rectify. To recap, gift exchange and commodity exchange may be distinguished by: the relative alienability of the objects being exchanged and the interdependence of the transactors; the timing of the exchange of equivalences; and whether exchanges are motivated mainly by the accumulation of economic or cultural capital. Having explored the evolution of systems of MP3 exchange from IRC exchange onwards, we are now in a position to determine the extent to which these systems may accurately be described as gift economies.

It would appear that none of the systems described qualifies as a gift economy on the first criterion alone: that is, the exchange of inalienable objects between interdependent transactors. Even in the case of IRC-based exchange, where access to files often had to be negotiated within interdependent online communities, once the files had been secured their new owners had no compunction in making them available to other users. Their willingness to do so is perhaps understandable given the special qualities of digital files as objects, in that the process of giving them away involves giving away a copy, so that the giver's stock of objects is not denuded. But it would appear that, because these communities are relatively impersonal and anonymous, these objects circulate more like quasi-commodities than like gifts.

These systems of exchange resemble gift economies more strongly in relation to the second criterion, which is the temporality of the exchange of equivalents. Although, as both Slater and Cooper and Harrison report, some IRC site owners enforced trading ratios, which necessitated some simultaneous exchange of objects, these exchanges were usually not directly equivalent and for the most part files were made available to be taken without any thought of immediate reciprocity. This delayed reciprocity was institutionalized within peer-to-peer networks.

A third criterion of gift exchange is that it is driven by the accumulation of cultural capital. This quality would seem to apply to IRC exchange and the distributed peer-to-peer systems of Gnutella and Freenet, but certainly does not apply to either MP3.com or Napster. IRC exchange, Gnutella, and Freenet exist as loose, self-organizing networks held together by the actions of hobbyists and hackers, whereas MP3.com and Napster were firms with ownership structures, brought into being through venture capital and so are firmly linked to the accumulation of economic capital.

Therefore, of the examples we have considered in this chapter, it is IRC-based systems of exchange and distributed peer-to-peer networks that most strongly resemble gift economies, as they are traditionally understood. However, even these were unusual gift economies to the extent that the objects were alienable and exchanged among independent transactors. Moreover, they operated according to a dynamic that was the inverse of most other gift economies, for within hi-tech gift economies objects were not actively 'given' by one actor to another; rather, these hi-tech gift economies should be seen as institutional arrangements that enabled actors with needs or desires to 'take' from those with resources, albeit at no cost to the latter because of the nature of digital reproduction.

Thus, Barbrook's claims for the emergence of hi-tech gift economies deserve qualified support. While the systems of exchange identified may perhaps be more accurately described as 'weak' or 'inverse' gift economies, there is little doubt that they are of wider significance because they constituted considerable challenges to modes of governance and regulation across the range of industries that make up copyright capitalism. This is not least because of the libertarian challenge to copyright that is embedded within P2P networks which were actively supported by advocates of the gift economy in the global community of hackers and programmers in the open source movement. The ability of such 'virtual' networks to efface space by existing on top of the internet poses a significant challenge to corporations and regulators who would wish to close such gift economies down. It was initially difficult for traditional legislators to tackle such viral and rhizoid entities, which are not 'in place' and which cover their tracks, despite all the efforts made by commercial interests to impose individual digital identities upon the internet (Lessig, 1999; Sassen, 2000).

This did not stop the RIAA and other authorities seeking to take action against such networks, especially after they provided the platform and model for corporate P2P networks like Grokster, Kazaa, and Morpheus, for example. However, while the networks were decentralized, the companies behind them were not and legal action finally caught up with them despite their efforts to move offshore (David, 2010). However, the decentred nature of such networks means that they always have the tendency to be elusive and are constantly evolving. For example, the BitTorrnet protocol for file sharing through P2P systems was developed in 2001 and within ten years was responsible for a large share of all internet traffic and became the framework for a new generation of networks opposed to copyright capitalism, including Pirate Bay (David, 2010).

The advance of these networks across the internet holds out the prospect of an even greater extension of gift economies. In so doing, it raises some intriguing questions about the ability of creative industries that were reliant upon the marginal costs of large-scale production to reproduce. At this juncture, it is useful to return to the argument made at the start of the chapter that the shape of the music industry—like every industry—is socio-technologically contingent, and has mutated at various moments in its history. It was at one such moment at the beginning of the twenty-first century. Thus, music listeners were faced with the prospect of a postscarcity economy, where all music of all kinds was immediately available at a marginal cost.

But this raised large and significant questions. How would the industry reproduce itself? How would artists be paid to ensure that they could make a living within this field? It quickly became apparent one way would be through a revalorization of live performance. The abundance of recorded material inversely increased the value and novelty of co-presence, of the 'human attention' that is produced through face-to-face interaction (Rifkin, 2000), which would generate more in the way of both cultural and economic capital (Thrift and Dewsbury, 2000). Indeed, this was already a strategy employed by artists who were not really that creative anymore, and whose material is abundant in the sense that their fans have already purchased most of what is worth buying. Such acts, like the Rolling Stones for example, have for years earned more money from touring and performing than they ever do through sales of recordings, because they have sufficient 'brand recognition' to ensure that their touring income is boosted by considerable corporate sponsorship (Klein, 2000) (and see Chapter 7). Performance is also the *modus operandi* of musical economies such as that of Jamaica, where the nature of civil society means that copyright law is only ever partially and fitfully enforced. The lack of copyright protection has produced a high-speed musical economy where ideas and styles are 'borrowed' without impunity, thereby placing much greater emphasis upon live performance to differentiate one act from another (see Power and Hallencreutz, 2002; Vaidhyanathan, 2001). Thus, music might become a multimedia product, which is bundled up with other services. Appropriately, this was also a business model developed within the open source software movement, where the software is often given away but enables income to be earned through the sale of additional services or products that enhance or develop the software, which is often delivered in person.

However, the generalization of such a model still has some way to go, and perhaps its greatest problem is the enduring allure of corporate capitalism. As Chapter 7 points out, the new production regime faced by artists offers more freedom but it is also more insecure than previously. While P2P networks have the potential to extend quasi-gift economies across time and space in new ways, their use nevertheless requires a degree of computer knowledge which constitutes a barrier to entry for non-'digital natives'. The success and appeal of MP3. com, Napster, and the numerous other similar firms that followed in their wake is that they developed services that were easy to use, even for those with only a rudimentary knowledge of computers. Part of the reason for this is that their ultimate aim was the accumulation of capital, so that through the attraction of outside investment, the creation of shareholders, and management structures, they quickly assimilated the discourse of marketing that focused upon attracting mainstream users and which emphasized ease of use.

Freenet and even Gnutella were produced under a very different aesthetic. They were services that were created not for the accumulation of profit, but for the accumulation of cultural capital among fellow hackers and software engineers. This they earned for their creators in substantial volumes. But such systems also assumed a level of knowledge and a commitment to the cause of the gift economy that is beyond the average user or consumer. Indeed, there are strong asymmetries of commitment among the communities that participate in gift economies enabled by Napster, Gnutella, and Freenet, as indicated by the fact that only a very small proportion of users perform the role of 'citizens', which means that, in the absence of traders, the majority of participants perform the role of leeches. There are clear parallels here to the weaknesses in other projects to develop alternative economies, such as local exchange and trading systems, which also rely heavily upon a small core of activists who disproportionately bear the burden of reproduction on their shoulders (see Leyshon et al., 2003). Therefore, it could be that, to paraphrase Oscar Wilde, although the idea of the hi-tech gift economy is capable of gaining wide support and appeal, for the majority of people, like socialism, it just 'takes too many evenings'.

4

On the Reproduction of the Musical Economy after the Internet

4.1. INTRODUCTION

This chapter explores some of the ways in which the music industry was transformed by the emergence of a new regime of socio-technical organization outlined in the previous chapters. By the middle of the opening decade of the twenty-first century the musical economy was dominated by four large corporations—AOL-Time Warner, Sony/BMG, Universal, and EMI—that were responsible for 80 per cent of global music sales and had significant interests across the media, entertainment, and technology sectors. The music divisions of all these companies had experienced a reversal of fortune, linked to falling sales and numerous misplaced investments. This marked a significant break with what, in retrospect, will be interpreted as a 'golden era' in the history of the music industry, during which it enjoyed about fifteen years of steady growth in recorded music sales following the introduction of the compact disc (CDs) as the predominant format for the playback of recorded music (see Figure 1.1). For an industry used to year-on-year sales growth, this reversal had serious consequences, with the leading firms in the sector posting disastrous financial results. Vivendi-Universal, for example, recorded a staggering $12bn loss for the first nine months of 2002 (*The Economist*, 2003a), although part of this loss was due to activities in other areas, such as motion pictures. EMI, which was the least diversified of the major companies, and most reliant upon sales of recorded music, posted a financial loss of £54.4m in the six months to September 2001 (*The Economist*, 2003b).[1] The other companies experienced similar losses

[1] Although, for reasons outlined later in the chapter, the company subsequently managed to reverse these losses.

and, as a result, the major record companies resorted to dramatic acts and gestures. Rosters of artists and repertoire were reduced, and turned over more rapidly. In extreme cases under-performing acts were bought out of their contracts altogether, so that the companies could avoid future outlays on production and marketing for material that, in their estimation, would not be recovered. The rapid circulation of artists through record companies was accompanied by a similar high turnover of staff, within what was already a precarious industry in which to work.

In seeking to account for the poor performance of their businesses, record company executives were almost as one in their identification of the main cause of their malaise: the internet. Or, more particularly, it is the rise of digital file-sharing systems, such as the peer-to-peer (P2P) networks discussed in the last chapter that significantly increased the rate of circulation of illegal copies of copyrighted music, which was identified as the clear and present danger to the survival of the mainstream musical economy (Alderman, 2001; Jones, 2002; McCourt and Burkart, 2003; David, 2010). As long ago as 2002 there were almost 1 billion music files available to be downloaded on the internet (Sanghera, 2002), and it was estimated that even then 27 per cent of Americans and 13 per cent of Europeans regularly downloaded music through such networks (*The Economist*, 2003c). Bodies such as the RIAA and the IFPI, were particularly vocal in condemning practices that they claimed were contributing to the death of the music industry. The industry pointed to an inverse correlation between the decline in sales and the rise of software formats such as MP3 to suggest that the former is a result of the latter. The head of the IFPI claimed that the fact that only one CD sold more than 10 million copies worldwide between 2001 and 2002 was a direct result of file sharing (*The Economist*, 2003c). The industry argued that illegal copying and transferring of music over the internet was increasingly acting as a substitute for sales, which reduced the inflow of capital to the industry that would otherwise be used for the discovery and the development of new acts. In making such claims, the industry revised and updated arguments that first began to circulate from the 1970s onwards, following the growth of music cassette recording technology, when it was argued that 'home taping was killing music' (see Chapter 3).

There is no question that what the industry describes as 'piracy' has caused the music industry to forgo potential earnings in some parts of the world where, for reasons such as a weak civil society or official disregard of acts of copyright infringement for geo-economic reasons (Vaidhyanathan, 2001), the majority of sales of recorded music are in the form of counterfeit cassettes or CDs. For example, the IFPI reported that the global 'pirate' music market totalled 1.9 billion units in 2001, and that as much as 40 per cent of all CDs sold worldwide were illegal copies, with the largest markets being China (where 90 per cent of the total market was pirated material), Russia (65 per cent), and Brazil (55 per cent) (IFPI, 2002). In such economies, little or no money flows back to the record companies that funded the recording and marketing of the music in the first place, and the pirate music business was often controlled by organized crime syndicates. Some commentators even sought to make a link between what might be described as 'traditional' musical 'piracy', such as the counterfeiting of music in media such as cassettes and CDs, and what has become known as 'internet piracy'.

However, while some aspects of the internet economy may be controlled by criminal elements—with the adult entertainment industry being perhaps the best example (see Zook, 2003)—online music would appear to be an unlikely area for career criminals to colonize, if only because it makes little if any money. Unlike the adult entertainment industry, consumers have shown a great reluctance to pay for music in digital form, mainly because so much music has been made freely available on the internet. As set out in the last chapter, a quasi-gift economy of music has developed since the mid-1990s, emerging first from IRC networks and evolving into P2P networks of the kind pioneered by Napster but then developed further by systems such as Gnutella, Morpheus, and Kazaa (Beuscart, 2002) and then BitTorrent. While these activities may be illegal, in that they facilitate the breaching of Euro-American copyright laws, they have failed to develop a convincing business model that would make their operations viable commercial propositions.

Moreover, while such networks are clearly damaging to the profitability of the music industry, there is evidence to suggest that the rise of internet piracy cannot be held solely responsible for the depth and severity of the crisis of the musical economy. Rather, the emergence of software formats and internet distribution systems represent what can be described as a 'tipping point'[2] that has

---

[2] While the term 'tipping point' is suggestive of the leveraging effects of the cumulative impact of different events, it is used here with caution, and at some remove from the more impressionistic use of the idea in Gladwell's (2000) book-length treatise on the subject.

triggered a wholesale reorganization of the music industry and the experimentation with new business models. The problems facing the music industry have not suddenly been manifested overnight, or even in response to online digital file exchange, but rather have accumulated over time in response to a set of broader cultural forces that have changed the role of music within society, and relegated its immediacy and importance among many of its consumers. While these problems have dogged the industry over many years, it took an anomaly such as the emergence of musical gift economies to begin to bring about recognition of the need for institutional and organizational change.

The remainder of the chapter is organized as follows. Section 4.2 explores the relationship between music and value, and develops the argument that the music industry's problems are deeper and more long-standing than MP3 and other software formats alone. Nevertheless, the emergence of file sharing through P2P networks was an important episode in the history of the music industry, and was a catalyst that ushered in a period of significant reorganization. In section 4.3 I consider the proliferation of music-business models that emerged within the industry's expanded ecology as it responded to, and sought to incorporate, online distribution models. These models emerged as forms of accumulation and reproduction opposed to the per-unit pricing model upon which the music industry had been based for most of the twentieth century. Section 4.4 contains a discussion and summary of the empirical material.

4.2. VALUING MUSIC

One of the classic criticisms of the popular music industry is that it trivializes and debases what is otherwise a potentially radical form of affect. Criticisms of this kind are associated in particular with Theodore Adorno, who argued that popular music 'was bad, bound to be bad, without exception' (1976: 225). His criticism was fuelled by his belief that popular music, produced in line with capitalist means of production, was merely an appeal to the lowest common cultural denominator and distracted its audiences from the realities of their social subjugation. Adorno argued that the value of more 'difficult', classical music was that it demanded that its audiences pay it their full attention. Such acts of concentration were rewarded by the listener being made aware of the possibilities of a world of creativity that exists more or less for its own sake, rather than for the purposes of the reproduction of capital. The 'right' kind of music, Adorno insisted, has the radical potential of affect, which can influence the conscious and subconscious mind, and bring into being alternative social possibilities. Popular music, on the other hand, uses repetition and predictability to stultify critical faculties, and to support impoverished social and economic institutions.

At the time that Adorno was writing (in the 1940s), there were a number of developments that seemed to support his suspicions about popular music. These included the increasing use of background music in the workplace to improve efficiency and its emergence in places of consumption to induce spending (Lanza, 1995). In addition, there was the steady growth of the popular music industry as an important sector of the economy in its own right (Chappel and Garofalo, 1977; Frith, 1987b; Garofalo, 1999; Sanjek, 1988). Arguments supporting Adorno's thesis continue to resurface from time to time, mainly to bolster conservative and elitist critiques of musical culture that are anxious to claim classical musical production and consumption as a superior and more demanding form of expression (e.g. see Johnson, 2002). However, under the weight of a sustained critique since the 1960s, Adorno's arguments have largely been dismissed as those of a well-meaning but mistaken elitist. For one thing, the making of classical music is not undertaken in a vacuum of social relations free of power and inequality. In its earliest forms it was dependent upon aristocratic patronage, while from the eighteenth century onwards it too was increasingly dependent upon the market, manifested in the growth of the concert hall within large urban centres (see e.g. Attali, 1984; and Chapter 2). Meanwhile, as a range of studies within cultural studies has shown, popular music is not necessarily passively received but can be given meaning and significance which, in the same way that texts escape their authors, breaks free of the intentions of its producers and is given agency within a wide range of subcultural movements (see Gelder and Thornton, 1996). Therefore, consumers are not necessarily the dupes of the capitalist record industry as many high cultural critiques of popular music would suggest, but can often subvert these commodities to support lifestyles that cut against the grain of conventional society.[3]

While such subcultural uses of popular music continue, their significance is diminishing as music has increasingly begun to sink into the background of contemporary society. Thus, in a manner that both supports and undermines Adorno's position, music has become an increasingly important part of the infrastructure of capitalist society, and is now an essential crutch to all manner of acts of consumption (DeNora and Belcher, 2000). But, significantly, this development has actually served to *weaken* the music industry; popular music is decreasingly valued for itself, but is, instead, increasingly valued more for the ways in which it is consumed in relation to other things. This tendency is one of the key reasons why the emergence of internet file sharing through P2P networks is such a decisive tipping point for the industry, and is manifested in at least three ways.

The first manifestation may be seen in developments within the popular music industry. One of the most important genres of the last thirty years or so has been dance music and the associated growth of club culture (Malbon, 1999; Thornton, 1995). This genre cut across normal music industry expectations in a number of ways. Dance music proved resistant to the industry's attempts to exploit it in accordance with normal practices because the producers of such music were relatively faceless. It has often been produced through a highly distributed network of recording artists, many of them utilizing relatively cheap computer hardware and software (Hesmondhalgh, 1998). For this reason it was not so much the artists but the DJs that play the music, and the clubs within which the music was played, or the locations in which the clubs are based, that were elevated to the status of stars. The celebrity of both was earned mainly through performance within place, so that while the industry sought to capitalize upon the reputation of DJs and clubs through branded CDs, the real cultural (and economic) capital attached to the music was earned through actually 'being there'. Thus, the predominant mode of dance music consumption was as a collective experience within a public space (the club). This inverted the normal practice within the music industry

---

[3] Although this tendency towards subversion has itself been commodified, so that a strand of romanticized 'opposition' has been used over many years to nurture new musical genres within the music industry (see e.g. Negus, 1995).

where live music was used as a promotional and marketing tool to support the main source of income, the sale of recorded music, and which was an early indicator of the direction in which the music industry would soon turn. Moreover, equally as important as the sound of the music within the consumption of dance music was the physical and immersive experience of music played at volume within the confined space of the club.

This is linked to the second manifestation, which is the ways in which the consumption of music became increasingly linked to other kinds of media, where music was valued less for its own qualities than for its association with other phenomena. Thus, the use of music within advertising or within a motion picture or television soundtrack can trigger a significant increase in sales, often outstripping the sales of artists being promoted through conventional marketing channels.[4] Ironically, the perceived advantages of cross-selling music on the back of other cultural artefacts—such as motion pictures, for example—was one of the main drivers behind the construction of the large media conglomerates, of which many of the leading record companies became constituent parts (Negus, 1992; Sadler, 1997). However, the financial benefits of media 'synergy' proved elusive, partly because, according to *The Economist*, 'Amid dizzying talk of convergence, so much attention (and cash) has been devoted to securing and developing new forms of distribution that the critical importance of content has often been neglected' (2003a).[5] Moreover,

---

[4] e.g. the UK band Dirty Vegas won a 2003 Grammy award for a track used in a TV advertising campaign for Mitsubishi Motors in the US. The track sold more than a million copies in the US, but only 100,000 copies in the UK, where they remained a relatively obscure act (see <http://news.bbc.co.uk/1/hi/entertainment/music/2793511.stm>).

[5] The way in which synergy was *supposed* to work has been outlined by Breen (1995: 500): 'The [example] comes from Sony and is drawn from the corporation's plans to use Arnold Schwarzenegger in a combination of "star power and salesmanship"…. "Arnie" combined these two roles in Sony Corporation's *Last Action Hero*, a US$60 million film. Coming from the Colombia Studios, owned by Sony, the Corporation anticipated that the "tie-ins" provided across the media would promote Sony products. The film promoted the use of Sony Hardware—by what is known as product placement—so a Sony Walkman mini CD player is used by the film's star. "Arnie" places a call on a Sony cellular phone. The bands Alice in Chains, AC/DC and rapper Cypress Hill, all signed on Colombia records and Epic, appear in the film. It is difficult to separate music from the film and technology marketing fetish of the corporation. Music becomes an avenue down which the marketing logic of the corporation moves, constructing contemporary life around the processes of entertainment promotion.'

although there are many examples of musical 'assets' having being used successfully in synergies with other cultural products, there was considerable pressure within media conglomerates to use them in relation to the conglomerate's other internal media assets, as if to justify the existence of the conglomerate, rather than to use them in combination with other cultural products that might be more appropriate but which lie outside the company in question.

The third and final manifestation of the longer-run nature of problems facing the music industry is the way in which popular music no longer commands the attention of consumers in the manner that it perhaps once did. In the immediate post-war period, popular music underwent a significant period of growth as it developed seemingly in lockstep with the identification and naming of the sociological phenomenon of 'the teenager'. Linked to growing levels of affluence and disposable income, it was in the 1950s that people in their teens and early twenties became the most important market segment within the music industry. The industry would lose significant numbers of consumers as they aged and popular music became less of a central dynamic in their lives, crowded out as it was by the development of other tastes and interests. But, as these older consumers became less interested in popular music, they were simply replaced by new generations of willing music consumers.

However, there is evidence to suggest that, for a number of reasons, the ability of music to command the disposable income of those between the ages of 14 and 24 has been ebbing away rapidly. The most simple explanation for this is that other, newer, media and consumer electronics industries began to compete successfully for this market segment, so that the amount of money young people have to spend on music has been reduced accordingly. New passions, be it computer games, mobile (cell) phones, or even the internet itself, all attracted expenditure that, in many cases, was previously spent on music (*The Economist*, 2003c). The comments of the head of BMG UK and Ireland, in an interview with the *Financial Times*, neatly outlined the dilemma for the music industry when he compared his musical consumption as a youth to that of his own children:

> When I was a kid, I'd buy an album and spend hours listening to it and reading the sleeve notes and everything...But my kids get an album and they'll flick through a couple of tracks while they're on their mobile phone and playing on a computer or watching TV. They consume music differently—and when you're spending £20 a week on a mobile phone,

how much money do you have to spend on music? (Hasse Breitholtz, quoted in Sanghera, 2002: 19)

But again, it is important to stress that this phenomenon is not a product of the internet alone. Indeed, Breen argued in the mid-1990s that the music industry had been close to crisis for a long time and that this had been successfully postponed only by a series of innovations in re-production technology and the successful opening up of new markets:

> without the introduction of CDs, without classic hits radio, and without new markets in Asia and Latin America, popular music as we know it would no longer exist. The evidence is clear that popular music as a com-modity is passing through a rapid transformation, assisted by the introduc-tion of video games from Sega and Nintendo and related new technologies, which has heightened the anxiety circulating among some in the music promotion business. (Breen, 1995: 497–8; see, in addition, Sadler, 1997)

As already argued, the growth of file sharing may be seen as the tipping point that has converted this anxiety into a fully fledged crisis of reproduction. But it is a tipping point in the sense that it has legiti-mized participants within the industry to openly talk about a crisis in a way that was more difficult to do previously, if only because it is eas-ier to blame a process that may be located as external to the industry itself. File sharing also unleashed a wide range of new organizational forms as businesses sought to take advantage of the opportunities afforded by the impact of the internet to seek to develop new business models for the music industry.

As argued in earlier chapters, the industry began a period of ex-perimentation with new organizational and institutional forms to develop new modes of production, distribution, and consumption around which the music industry could be restabilized to more effect-ively reproduce itself after the shock of internet piracy. One outcome of this period of experimentation was a more diverse ecology of the musical economy. In the next section of the chapter attention turns to the proliferation of new organizational forms within the music in-dustry, developed in response to the impact made by the internet.

4.3. REPRODUCING THE MUSICAL ECONOMY

Record companies have traditionally reproduced themselves through a combination of per-unit pricing and the enforcement of copyright law. With per-unit pricing, music is viewed as a commodity where each physical unit commands a price that flows back from networks of consumption to the record companies. Copyright law supports this system by enabling those parties claiming ownership of the music and the sound recording—that is, the publishing and recording arms of the record companies—to earn royalties on each unit sold. Strong copyright legislation is important to record companies because it is a notoriously inefficient industry. However, while the fixed costs of musical production are high, the marginal costs of its reproduction are low, so that very successful recordings—which can sell in their tens of millions worldwide—can generate large volumes of money. The trade-off between fixed and marginal costs has traditionally enabled the industry to recoup the costs of the estimated 90 per cent of recordings that fail to recover the investment made in their production.

That the industry loses money on so much of its business has been explained away by the difficulties of operating within such a volatile and fickle market, which is moved by fashion and taste, and which is very difficult to predict (Scott, 1999). But the precarious imbalance between success and failure also explains why the industry is so concerned about copyright infringements and piracy, because the possibility that piracy might substitute for conventional sales makes it even more difficult for record companies to produce a profit. It is for this reason, then, that internet piracy may be seen as exactly that tipping point; piracy and copyright theft, which was previously seen to be an endemic problem within developing markets, was brought home to its core markets in North America and Europe, exacerbating the other problems facing the music industry discussed earlier. Indeed, evidence from interviews with record company executives suggested that by the mid-2000s only 3 per cent of recordings recouped their investments, and it is upon this very narrow base, in an environment of falling sales, that the rest of the industry became precariously placed.

The remainder of this chapter focuses upon three firms that represent distinctive organizational responses to the current crisis of the music industry. The three firms, whose identities are disguised to comply with assurances given to informants about confidentiality, are all based or have offices in Southern California. The case studies were chosen to illustrate some of the strategies and business models being tried out in the face of the crisis of reproduction within the industry. The companies included a large traditional, music conglomerate, an

online subsidiary of a large record company, and an independent artists and repertoire company.

Global Records Inc.

This company is one of the 'big four' media conglomerates that domi-
nates global record sales, with major offices in Los Angeles, New York,
and London. The material in this subsection is drawn mainly from an
interview undertaken in the Los Angeles office with the company's
Senior Vice-President for New Media, with responsibility for new
media policies across forty different labels that made up the record
company as a whole. The company's strategic response to the crisis
induced by the advent of software formats and internet distribution,
like that of other major record companies, combined a set of defensive and offensive manoeuvres intended to attack internet 'piracy'
while, at the same time, seeking to promote the company's strengths
and developing internal business models that would enable the company to make money from distributing music in electronic form.
Thus, in addition to giving strong support to the RIAA in its aggres-
sive legal actions against companies such as MP3.com and Napster,
for example, the company was also a leading mover in the formation
by the leading record companies of joint ventures to provide music
online, for a fee.[6]

A significant defensive strategy prosecuted by Global Records was
to support and participate in the legal actions brought against P2P
file-sharing networks. This strategy was time-consuming and expensive, but slowly yielded results for the large record companies.
Networks such as Napster and Audiogalaxy were successfully closed
down through legal action, and the industry and the RIAA continued
to vigorously pursue P2P networks through the courts on the grounds
of copyright infringement (McCourt and Burkart, 2003). However,
there soon emerged a significant number of competing P2P networks,
many with complex organizational and ownership structures, which
presented new challenges to legal action, such as, for example, the P2P

---

[6] In addition, it should be noted that these services not only require users to pay a
subscription, but are also charged per download, with restrictions being placed on the
number of times that the music can be copied and, in some instances, how many times
it can be played. Thus, in some respects, the service being offered by PressPlay and
MusicNet are an uncomfortable mix of a per-unit pricing scheme with a rental service.

network Kazaa. A defining feature of P2P networks is that they are a-centred, and difficult to 'ground' once in operation. They exist as relational entities, self-organizing software programs that operate on the internet through the computers that happen to be running them at any particular time (see Chapter 3). However, Kazaa was organized in such a way as to make the task of legal authorities even more difficult, by dividing its operations across a number of different regulatory spaces.[7] Thus, Kazaa's servers were based in Denmark, the software was programmed in Estonia, the domain name was registered in Australia, with the company that owned the network, Sharman Networks, registered in the 'no names given' Pacific tax haven of Vanuatu. Therefore, it was extremely difficult to prosecute and the company managed successfully to negotiate its way through successive legal attacks launched against it within US[8] and European courts,[9] until 2006 when the suit by the IFPI finally won a claim for $100m in damages against Sharman Networks, which forced Kazaa to change its business model to a legal download service.[10]

Given the limits and costs of this form of defensive strategy,[11] Global Records also sought to develop more offensive strategies, such as emphasizing the competitive advantages of the traditional roles of a record company, such as the promotion, marketing, and 'breaking'

---

[7] Thus, P2P networks are pursuing strategies of 'regulatory arbitrage' more commonly associated with the global financial system (see Leyshon and Thrift, 1997).

[8] By 2003 the RIAA was pursuing cases against Streamcast Networks, the designers of the Morpheus, Grokster, and Kazaa software (<http://www.mi2n.com/press.php3?press_nb = 45017>). The fact that the cases were aimed at the software designers illustrates the difficulties the RIAA faced in countering P2P networks once they are in action. Moreover, the music industry's pursuit of such entities through the courts has been interspersed with serious legal setbacks, such as a Los Angeles Federal judge's decision in April 2003 that Streamcast and Grokster were not responsible for copyright infringements committed on their networks (Borland, 2003).

[9] Kazaa was also pursued through the Netherlands courts, where the company that initially owned the network was based. It was in response to the court action that the network was sold to the 'nebulous and elusive' Sharman Networks (Tehranian, 2003: 18).

[10] However, this was unsuccessful and the service slowly died out. One of the ways in which Kazaa generated revenue for its owners was by embedding 'malware' on users' computers which provided advertising (adware) and tracking data (spybots) for other companies (<http://www.eweek.com/c/a/Security/Spyware-Trail-Leads-to-Kazaa-Big-Advertisers>).

[11] Indeed, Tehranian (2003) makes a convincing case that legal action by the music industry against P2P networks has the effect of increasing the number of users of such networks, as the media coverage of such cases brings the existence and possibilities of P2P to a wider audience.

of artists in a way that the internet cannot do. The Global Records VP gave the example of a band that had played in relative obscurity in the Bahamas for eleven years, during which time they recorded six albums that had sold a combined total of 4,000 copies. Global Records signed the band, took receipt of a new album, and built an intensive marketing campaign around it, which included placing a track from the album within a feature film. The track became a globally successful single and the album sold over one million copies. In contrast to this, the company clearly believed that the marketing potential of the internet was limited:

> There's this model called MP3.com, where anybody could self-publish and put up their own stuff, and what it really was, was geocities for music. The majority of traffic was the band preparing it on site and their friends saying, 'Oh nobody's discovering new music!', because discovering new music happens to be a very difficult and arduous thing. You need to get turned on by somebody whose face is right, [by] your peer group, or [get] your stuff elected into a genre on a radio station, in life, in culture. And that's how you get [music sold]. (Senior VP for New Media, Global Records, Interview)[12]

Large record companies justify their role within the musical economy through their ability to make popular music both possible and successful. Companies insist that music does not just emerge spontaneously, but is produced through the intervention of a set of intermediaries that act upon and channel the music from producers to consumers (see Hennion, 1989). These intermediaries include producers and engineers, artists and repertoire (A&R) specialists, marketing and media experts, and so on (see Figure 2.1). The intermediation of such roles and functions represents a significant investment that works to develop talent and make it successful. The early internet-based challenges to the music industry were unable to successfully redirect *revenue* from the established music companies.[13] Rather, models such as MP3.com, Napster, and P2P networks were parasitical in that they were free riders upon the investments of the

---

[12] For more on the MP3.com business model, see Ch. 3.
[13] P2P networks have merely reduced, rather than redirected, revenue flowing to the music companies. The major exception here, of course, is iTunes and streaming services such as Spotify. While they generate revenue for the industry they do so at reduced rates per unit than hitherto.

music industry but did nothing to actively seek to reproduce the industry through the cultivation of new music.

Nevertheless, a series of extant contradictions and complexities within the music industry became significantly more problematic in the face of the challenges posed by internet piracy. Musical 'assets' are split between different interests, including the record companies, songwriters, recording artists, and publishers. The tensions between record companies, who own the rights to the sound recording, and music publishers, who own the rights to the musical work, are often manifested within the same organization—because all entertainment companies contain both kinds of companies—and I shall outline an example of such conflict shortly. In addition, the geography of ownership rights and royalty computations is extraordinarily complex, and is the product of largely national solutions to the problem of generating and collecting income for musicians through mechanical and performance royalties.

These geographically differentiated computations made the attempt by record companies to offensively exploit the internet, through systems such as PressPlay and MusicNet, significantly more difficult, because of the way it acts against the grain of the traditional price-per-unit industry model:

> So what happens is when...on the internet, [you say], 'I'm going to download a song of a French band, covering a Beatles tune, owned by Sony Publishing, for myself in Hong Kong, and I'm paying for it with a Japanese credit card.' Okay, is there VAT? Is there sales tax? Under what royalty rates do the song publishers and the bands get [paid]? What country did the transaction take place in?...You suddenly realize that for a hundred years our contracts were album based, order based. (Senior VP for New Media, Global Records, Interview)[14]

This complex set of ownership rights and regulatory regimes, and the growing tensions between record companies and their publishing arms, meant that the industry was often slow to exploit new markets as they emerged. The VP at Global Records used the example of the use of 'ring tones'—tunes that play pieces of music to indicate an incoming call—within mobile telephony. The market for ring tones has increased rapidly over recent years, for example, by 58 per cent

---

[14] However, as the global spread of services like iTunes clearly illustrates, these problems were not exactly insurmountable.

between 2001 and 2002, generating \$71m for artists (*The Economist*, 2003d). This market was a potentially significant source of revenue for Global Records, but after it set up the first deal with a small northern European mobile phone company, the company was sued in each territory by the collection societies (on behalf of the music publishers) on the basis that the ring tone was a public performance, and therefore payment should be in the form of a performance royalty. A ruling in favour of the collection societies—because ring tones were initially synthetic versions of songs, rather than the actual sound recordings—meant that neither Global Records nor any other record company was able to earn any revenue from ring tones in their earliest manifestation (although music publishers and artists were).

A further complication emerged from the fact that most record companies are part of larger media conglomerates that have divisions that pursue strategies that threaten the reproduction of the musical economy. For example, one of Global Record's media conglomerate competitors had a recorded music division and a technology division that produced computer hardware, including CD rewriters. To the extent that file sharing and illegal CD 'burning' reduced the sale of music within traditional formats, the music division was being undermined from within, so to speak. Another competitor contained a large internet service provider; it was argued by some that it was in the interests of this division to *encourage* internet piracy, which might in turn spur more consumers to buy broadband if music was available for free on P2P networks. Therefore, once again, the suggestion was that the interests of the ISP division might be in direct competition with the wing of the company that develops artists and sells music. The major corporations have contradictory and divisive tendencies that lead to various elements within the companies pulling in very different directions.[15]

However, the large record companies also sought to turn the internet to their advantage by exploring links with new companies that were trying to exploit a niche in the online market. These were subscription-based companies, and included firms such as Listen. com, Fullaudio, OD2, DX3, and Rhapsody. Their business models varied: some permitted downloading and burning, while some were

---

[15] As David (2010) points out, Apple would hardly have been able to make such a success of their launch of iPods if it were not for the large stock of illegal copies of music in circulation that created a market for a portable player.

merely streaming or jukebox type services. All these companies were reliant upon signing licensing deals with the major companies to ensure that they had content to offer in exchange for their monthly subscription fee. Global Records signed numerous deals with such subscription companies, and adopted a wait-and-see strategy to determine which business model proved most effective in a period of chronic uncertainty. The next section of the chapter turns its attention to one such innovative business model, which was pioneering a radically different way of distributing and selling music via an online subscription service.

Online Music

The origin of this company, based in an out-of-town industrial park in San Diego, was as a dot.com start-up in 1995. Originally an online seller of CDs, it evolved into a subscription-based, online service for downloading music in MP3 format. It was purchased by one of the 'big four' companies in 2001, following which it operated as a wholly owned yet autonomous subsidiary within a division that included a set of other recent new economy purchases.[16]

Like many other new online music company start-ups that sought to provide a 'legitimate' service, Online Music was soon forced to confront the dilemma of persuading consumers to pay for music when so much was already available for free on P2P networks. The company's relative independence from its parent prior to its purchase by a private equity company was reflected in its decision to attempt to find a 'work around' to the problem of internet piracy, rather than attempt to eradicate it through the defensive legal and technological measures prosecuted by big companies such as Global Records:

> You don't beat piracy with security; you beat the piracy by providing added value, better service, making it basically easier for people to buy than it is for them to steal, giving them more advantages to buy it. And

---

[16] The timing of this purchase would seem to confirm McCourt and Burkart's (2003: 341) observation that the sharp decline in 'technology stocks' from 2000 onwards, and the consequent drying up of venture capital funds to music-orientated dot. coms that followed the Napster lawsuit in the same year, enabled the five large record companies to acquire internet distribution systems such as On-line Music for 'below market value, [which] also saved research and development costs', as these companies pioneered new technologies at the expense of venture capitalists and the capital markets (see also Feng et al., 2001).

then of course you do enforcements on people that are breaking the law and illegally distributing it. So that's been our philosophy from day one. (Vice President, Online Music, interview)

Repeating an objective expressed by other e-commerce operations, the company indicated that its *modus operandi* was 'to follow the customer', to focus first on what consumers wanted and then to attempt to provide that service. The company entered the music business thinking that it could set up an online record company. However, like other companies before it, it quickly discovered that this was 'not a good business to be in' (Vice President, Online Music, interview). One reason for this was that the people running the putative record company had backgrounds in the software industry, not the music industry, and therefore were not sufficiently knowledgeable about its complexities.

When still an independent business, the company mutated into an online distribution vehicle for a number of independent music labels. The business model that slowly emerged, through trial and error and practical experimentation, was a subscription service that allowed unlimited downloads for a monthly fee of just under US$10. The system worked as follows. For each track downloaded by the customer, Online Music made a payment of 7 cents, to be shared between the publishers of the music and the record company that held the rights to the sound recording. However, given that the subscription was $9.99 per month, a user downloading more than 143 tracks per month—on average, about twelve albums—would guarantee that there would be no revenue left from their subscription for Online Music to accrue, even before costs. However, the unlimited download model was justified as follows:

> We advertise Online Music as a discovery service. Part of the allure of music online is that there are no barriers to entry to try a new artist or a new genre of music. As soon as you place a cap on downloads you are changing the psychology and forcing customers to carefully consider what they download... As soon as you tell the customer that they get x downloads for x dollars, you are placing a value on each download. As a result the customer will feel that they are not getting their money's worth if they do not download their allotment every month. (VP, Online Music, interview)

This business model was based upon a traditional system of cross-subsidization. In this case, the company anticipated that the majority of subscribers would be relatively light users of the service. At the same time, the company sought to control and limit what were seen to be 'abuses' of the system, such as continuous and unbroken acts of downloading over twenty-four hours or more. The advantages of the subscription model over the price-per-unit model is that it provided a steady cash flow and the possibility of developing ever more detailed customer databases. However, subscription systems tend to be less profitable than price-per-unit, and it involves negotiating highly complex licensing deals with record companies (McCourt and Burkart, 2003).

Online Music's strategy seemed to be to position itself as a niche player, operating within the relatively small market served by independent record labels. On the one hand, given that at the time of the interview Online Music was owned by one of the big four record companies, this strategy might be seen as one which enabled a large company to derive income from independent competitors that were formerly outside their control, through a capital-intensive distribution system that independent labels could not hope to replicate. On the other hand, it also propagated a more diverse ecology of the musical economy, a trend which could be accelerated even further by artists taking album-by-album distribution deals with Online Music. Our informant illustrated this through an example of an artist who had considerable critical and commercial success with a band in the late 1980s and early 1990s and thereafter pursued a career sometimes as a solo artist and sometimes with new bands. His albums normally sold 75,000 copies per release, far lower than the numbers that a large record label would require to cover the costs of recording and marketing. However, since embarking on his new career, the artist took greater control over his commercial affairs and signed distribution deals with labels on an album-to-album basis.

Moreover, the fact that he owned his own recording studio, and used a traditional 'live to two-track' recording technique,[17] meant that the time taken to record material and, significantly, the costs of doing so, were seriously reduced. Therefore, sales of fewer than 100,000

---

[17] That is, the songs are recorded in one take, with the voice and instruments being recorded upon just two tracks of tape. The standard modern recording technique is to use multi-tracking techniques, which can include up to 100 separate recording tracks (Cunningham, 1998). See, in addition, Ch. 5.

copies per release generated significant earnings for this individual and his employees.[18]

Online Music thus inhabited a distinctive part of the musical economy ecology that represented a viable post-internet model for the industry and many of its artists. Negus (1992) has described the music industry as being a 'web of major and minor companies', suggesting that the outlook and philosophy of both sets of companies are similar but differentiated by scale. In particular, independent labels were seen as akin to creative research and development divisions for the major labels, discovering and sifting new talent that might be turned into successful acts and sell sufficient quantities of music to make them attractive to large record companies. The emergence of companies such as Online Music performs a similar role to that of off-line independents in the past—significantly, not in the development of artists but rather in the development of *business models*. In other words, they represent 'research and development divisions' in the quest to develop strategies compatible with a reformatted industry.

Clearly, Online Music represented a significant departure for the traditional music industry model. However, it proved too radical for the record label that owned it, which sold it on to a private equity company. While the new owners liked the subscription model, which helped to generate a regular flow of income that both helped fund the deal and provide returns of investment (see, in addition, Chapter 6), it did not like unlimited downloads which created too much uncertainty over profit and loss, so introduced a new, tiered subscription menu, with strict limits on the total number of downloads, to more closely resemble a traditional per-unit charging structure familiar to record labels.

The third and final case study points the way to an even more radical reorganization of the music industry, where the traditional role of the record companies would be significantly reduced, if not removed altogether.

MusicBroker.com

MusicBroker was an independent A&R company, which used the internet to manage an online roster of unsigned acts that it searched

---

[18] A similar argument emerged in the third case study, that of MusicBroker.

for talent in response to demands from major entertainment companies. The company's business model was based upon a perception that the A&R departments of record companies were overstretched and unable any more to successfully trawl the clubs, bars, and demo tapes for new signings. The company's Chief Operating Officer (COO) and founder described the *raison d'être* of the company as follows:

> This company's function is to act as a quality filter service for the record industry, to help unsigned bands, artists and songwriters get their music onto the desks of major record companies. (COO, MusicBroker. com, interview)

The company took advantage of the high rate of labour turnover in the music industry by employing, on a pro-rata basis, music experts to judge and evaluate music. Their team of evaluators—which included former vice-presidents of A&R at major record companies, former programme directors of radio stations, producers, successful songwriters, managers of bands, etc.—to give feedback to bands or individual artists who registered with the company for a $300 annual fee and a payment of $5 for each song submitted to the company. The feedback took the form of a report, which was passed back to the artist, which contained a 'MusicBroker rating' plus suggestions on how to improve the work. If the material was good enough, it was sent on to record or film companies that had previously expressed an interest in music of a particular type or genre. The system worked as follows:

> Record companies tell us what they're looking for... we send out information to unsigned artists, bands, songwriters, all over the globe in thirty different countries, via the internet, via snail mail, if we must, and they respond by sending us music and the response to... specific requests. We don't disclose that it's Warner Brothers looking for X, Y, Z, it'll just say vice-president of A&R of a major label looking for this or that. So the bands can't do an end run around us and inundate the people at the record companies, instead they send the music to us, with a code number on it for that specific request. It goes into a bin with all the other material that's come in for that request. We hire industry experts—who have all been really high-level people who have been involved in the selection and placement of hit music—and we pay them a really good sum of money to come in here and work by the hour to screen every single piece of music for every one of those requests. (COO, MusicBroker.com, interview)

The company was driven by two key assumptions. First, to be successful, it had to provide value-added services to the music industry without undercutting the industry's existing A&R functions. Thus, the company inverted the logic of traditional A&R activities by obtaining funding from prospective artists, rather than from retained earnings. The $300 annual registration fee, derived from subscriptions from more than thirty different countries,[19] generated sufficient cash flow to enable the company to be able to reproduce itself. Second, the changing nature of recording equipment (Thèberge, 1997; and see Chapter 5) and its increasing affordability meant that there were a significant number of musicians making high-quality recordings but who were unsigned:

> the advent of home recording equipment [makes] it plausible if not probable that hundreds of thousands of people on a global scale, maybe millions of people.... now have the ability to make very high-quality demos for next to no money, whereas before they needed to raise $20, $30, $50,000 to go to a legitimate studio. They no longer need to do that. I figured that that influx of recorded talent, [combined with] the small number of A&R people [meant] that setting up a conduit for those people with a filter on the record company end would be welcomed by both parties. (COO, MusicBroker.com, interview)

An important revenue stream was sourcing music for TV and motion picture companies, because it was cheaper for such companies to source new music than pay publishing companies and record companies for the rights to use their music for incidental and background purposes. MusicBroker begins where the A&R function of major companies ends, covering the ground conceded by traditional A&R departments in the wake of a continuing tendency towards capital centralization and concentration, as well as the day-to-day difficulties of looking after existing artists. As a result, 'Artists development long dropped off the map of A&R departments' (COO, MusicBroker.com, interview).

---

[19] Although 85% of subscribers were based in the USA. In Oct. 2002 subscribers to the MusicBroker service also came from the following countries: Australia, Belarus, Belize, Cameroon, Cayman Islands, Central African Republic, Egypt, Faroe Islands, Great Britain, Ghana, Guatemala, Italy, Lithuania, Luxembourg, Mexico, Netherlands, Somalia, Sri Lanka, Switzerland, Syria, Trinidad, UAE, and Ukraine. The list also includes 'East Africa' and the 'West Indies' (MusicBroker, personal communication, 2002).

Therefore, the company managed to carve out an institutional space for itself between the large entertainment companies on the one hand, and a highly distributed mass of unsigned artists and bands on the other, by utilizing the communicative capacity of the internet. The company was a particularly good example of the externalization of A&R functions, and one that represented a consolidation of the music industry within dominant cultural centres such as Los Angeles (see Scott, 2000). However, whereas the activities of the company were complementary and beneficial to the industry, the vision that the company had for the future of the musical economy, and of its role within it, had more serious consequences for the large entertainment conglomerates. The role that MusicBroker saw itself playing in the future was as a filter or recommendation service for new music on on-line distribution services that bypassed and supplanted the traditional networks of the music industry.

This role was predicated upon two predictions about the future of the industry, expressed forcefully during the interview. The first was that, as argued earlier, the advent of software formats like MP3 and of internet distribution systems has made the traditional music industry business model unsustainable, but also that the executives running the industry were reluctant to make their organization adapt to a new mode of operation:

> Q: So why do you think [the record companies] are having so much trouble [in adapting to MP3 and the internet]?
> A: ... they get paid way too much money, they're definitely afraid of losing their jobs. Based on those things they are afraid to make decisions, they're afraid to take chances, their Boards of Directors demand instant profits, the days of artist development are long gone ... All the record industry needs to do is go back and copy what it did twenty-five years ago and the problem is solved. But the problem is that it's going to take two or three years of dreadful profits before they're going to start reaping the rewards of that investment in time, energy, and straight thinking ... because they know their jobs generally only last for a short amount of time, so why rattle the cage or rock the boat when they're going to be out of the boat in a few years anyway and who gives a shit, they can take their money and their house in Beverly Hills and retire. (COO, MusicBroker.com, interview)

The second prediction was that the industry would move over to a subscription service but, rather than the earlier example of Online Music, this will not involve downloading. Rather, the dominant

players in the music industry of the (near) future would be internet
service providers (ISPs), such as Microsoft Network or AOL, which
will control subscription-based interactive music channels:

> people with the most income, who are people who are [early 40s],
> we grew up loving music, we made the music industry as big as it is
> today, yet we buy very little music now, because we don't have time and
> we don't like that pimply-faced little kid with the attitude behind the
> counter at Blockbuster or wherever. However, we still do love music…if
> you could pay, $10, $20, $30 a month to have a subscription service
> where you don't download anything, it's all streamed and you've got
> your 'hard drive in the sky', with your own list, [your own] 'country list',
> [your own] 'pop list', [your own] 'R&B list', all the *Billboard* hot 100 this
> month for country, R&B, pop, you know, your list to taste or somebody
> else's list is modified to taste with your stuff or anybody's list in any form
> at all, random if you want it. And that is manageable by your computer
> or by your TV set, and follows you to your cell phone…It's your station,
> [one] that follows you anywhere. You never need to download anything
> because why do you need to possess something on a hard drive and
> then transfer [it] to a device, or put it on a disc and take it to your car,
> if you can get it instantaneously anywhere you are, any time? (COO,
> MusicBroker.com, interview)[20]

MusicBroker planned to position itself between artists and ISP subscription services by offering an imprimatur of quality. Artists would
progress through the MusicBroker filter service and obtain a rating
from the company. On the basis of this rating, the artists would be able
to sign contracts with ISPs, earning money from what MusicBroker
describes as a 'per-chanical' royalty payment; that is, a royalty that is
a hybrid of a performance and a mechanical royalty.[21] The case for
such an arrangement was based on combining the scale of ISP networks with a system of micropayments to artists each time the music
is played by subscribers to web-based music channels. This is outlined
in the following, necessarily extended, interview extract:

> let's say that you have a subscription service with 30 million people on a
> global scale, that's doable—you get 35 million people on AOL—so take
> that 30 million people on a well-developed, big-time network, globally,

---

[20] In outline form this was a fairly accurate description of the streaming services,
such as Spotify, that would emerge after 2008.
[21] Performance royalties are paid to music publishers for musical performances,
while mechanical royalties are paid to the owners of the sound recording (usually
record companies) for the manufacture and sale of individual CDs or albums.

and let's say that 10 percent of those people, let's say 20 percent actually, like country music. So that means that you've got, what, 6 million people globally listening to the MSN [Microsoft Network] country station today...you're in your car...so you determine on your computer, yes, I love these country standards and country oldies, but what about new country? Yes, I'd like to hear new country, and I'd like you to slip it in on this playlist because it's closest to this genre, give it to me every third song. So, you're cruising along in your car and you're hearing a song you've never heard before and you go, 'Oh that sucks!' and [you] hit the delete button, it's gone forever. If you're not sure, you let it play all the way through and if you don't hit the add button by the time it gets to the end of the song it's also gone forever. But, if you're liking it, you want to add it to your list on the fly...you hit the add button, boom! Now [that artist's] song is on your country playlist—that first day it comes out it's going to be heard by 6 million listeners, right. So, let's say you make a penny a piece, that's 6 million people, you made $60,000 today on that one play of that song....so today you made $60,000 on that one song on one network. Okay, let's say only 10 percent of the people who heard it liked it, and added it to their list, well that means that they're going to make $6,000 tomorrow. But, let's say they only get all the way around the list once every third day, so you're going to make $6,000 every third day which is like making $2,000 a day, so you've made $60,000 on the first day and then every third day, which you're going to have 100 of those in a year, that's 120 of those a year. 120 times $6,000, so you're going to make $720 grand a year, per penny per listen, on a [inaudible] basis, $720,000, so you've just made $780,000 on this thing. Realistically let's call it a tenth of a penny you're going to get paid, I have a hard time coming up with a smaller number than that, so you're going to make $78,000 on that one song this year. That creates a middle class of musicians, unknown to mankind, now that the home hobbyist can do his thing, on his $5,000 or $10,000 system...you've just made yourself at a tenth of a penny per listen you've made yourself $78,000 on one song [in a year]. Let's say that you do four of those in a year, you've made $312 grand that year, with just four songs. That's a really nice living for four songs and the public doesn't get the 10 shitty songs foisted on them on a CD anymore. (COO, MusicBroker.com, interview)

Significantly, this opened up the possibility of a middle class of professional musicians who, with the aid of home recording equipment, were able to produce music that would generate significant and regular sums of money. This group of musicians would bridge a gap in the currently highly polarized labour market, where the majority of artists are unsigned and making a meagre income (e.g. see Finnegan,

1989, and Chapter 7), but where a very small minority of artists have become fabulously wealthy. This vision also sketched out the business model of new services such as Pandora radio and streaming services like Spotify, which have the capacity to learn about a listener's preferences and tailor its service accordingly.

This vision of the music industry of the future is clearly based upon the business models of other media, such as television and radio. It envisages an arena of musical consumption where intermediaries such as CDs are no longer necessary because wireless devices will be permanently connected to ISP servers, with music available 'on demand' to all those able to pay the subscription fees required to gain access to such services (cf. Rifkin, 2000). Record companies, at least in their traditional form, become more or less redundant in this model. Not even their role in discovering, funding, and nurturing talent that has ambitions beyond home recording is secure; instead this becomes an opportunity for the venture capital industry, which will treat artists and bands as the equivalent of a business start-up:

> To get back to your earlier question, 'What about somebody that makes an expensive recording?'...let's say they spend a quarter of a million dollars. Where are they going to get it? [What about]...a band who [sic] doesn't have an income yet? They go out and get an investor...you'll get groups of investors.[22] I know this [happens] from being in the studio end of the business, [you] see anybody from dentists to lawyers to drug dealers investing in new artists because it's an ego trip and it's fun. So, if you get an artist that does one home recording, they come to [MusicBroker], they get the stamp of approval, say, 'Look we've already got the stamp of approval, would you like to back us on recording more material? And here's a business plan, here's our business model, we think we can do well, and we need a quarter of a million dollars'. Well, it's not a huge investment, then they can take some of that quarter of a million dollars and they can get themselves...an experienced label publicist to promote the fact that the band is going to tour the eastern seaboard, and they get a booking agent to book the shows, you do it all *à la carte*...That was the premise behind [MusicBroker, that] someday the industry was going to disintegrate and I wanted to be the guy who was going to be the arbiter of good taste because no matter what form it takes, they're only going to be downsizing and somebody is still going

---

[22] Again, this was a prescient prediction of the rise of funding sources such as Sellaband and Kickstarter (see Ch. 7).

to have to be the arbiter of good taste, if I do it for free, nobody can beat that! (COO, MusicBroker.com, interview)

The company's strategy, it emerged, was to just wait until this new musical world moved into view:

> after knowing these people for three years and living in this world since... 1991, I've come to realize that it's all a bunch of shit, it doesn't mean anything, and that it's just going to take its time and eventually we're going to end up with this subscription streaming service, and all I'm doing is sitting here biding my time but perfecting what we do and refining it and making it better and building our brands, so that when the day comes and somebody needs to step up and be the J. D. Power [of the music industry],[23] I'm there! (COO, MusicBroker.com, interview)

4.4. DISCUSSION

The case studies outlined in this chapter illuminate a number of central themes that were being played out within the music industry in the early twenty-first century. Thus, Global Records, which represented the strategic response of the major record companies, deployed a range of offensive and defensive strategies. The company sought to maintain its dominance within networks of creativity and reproduction, but to change the configuration of networks of distribution by shutting down P2P networks, replacing them with their own subscription and downloading services while, at the same time, maintaining their position within traditional, physical distribution networks.

In addition, the major companies moved into areas that formerly had been left to press agencies, agents, and the artists and their management teams. Thus, the record companies sought to control new revenue streams as traditional income sources were steadily eroded. Efforts were made to lock artists into deals where the record company could earn a share of artist-related merchandising.[24] It was a process

---

[23] J. D. Power & Associates undertakes consumer satisfaction surveys to provide quality recommendations for consumer products in the USA.
[24] e.g. in 2002 EMI signed a '360 degree' recording deal with Robbie Williams which guaranteed the record company 25% of earnings from the sale of merchandising such as T-shirts, posters, etc. (Sandall, 2003).

that signified one of the ways 'in which record companies learn[ed] to adapt to a world that loves their artists more than it loves buying their records' (Sandall, 2003: 30).

The major companies also stressed the importance of what they saw as their critical role in developing a product superior to anything that could be developed by artists without music industry intervention. Companies sought to make transparent the role of the producers, engineers, co-writers, artists, marketers, and new media departments. Companies such as Global Records emphasized the importance of marketing and promotion and the ability to reach a mass audience that, they insisted, was more difficult for online companies to achieve. Most of the product that is file-shared and pirated is product that was previously subject to a marketing campaign; indeed, that is why this material is in such demand. These elements, the large companies contend, lend credibility to the idea that the networks of creativity that surround them, and that are in some cases funded by them, are essential to the successful reproduction of the music industry.

Meanwhile, Online Music was a company that, as an autonomous subsidiary pursuing a subscription model, was located between the majors and the independent companies. The company's business model offered a possible reconciliation of the current crisis of the musical economy wherein subscription services provided content from both major and independent record labels. Its strategy was to navigate between existing networks of reproduction and distribution, and heralded a mode of operation that could be adopted by the music industry more generally.

Finally, MusicBroker, like Online Music, developed a business model that positioned it between labels and artists. Its mission was to obtain deals for artists with record, television, or film companies. Thus, MusicBroker was seeking to extract value from networks of creativity by providing services previously unavailable before the advent of the internet. But, over the longer term, MusicBroker was positioning itself for a more radical restructuring of the networks of the musical economy. Within networks of creativity MusicBroker represented an externalization or reintermediation of A&R functions, shifting the balance of power between artists and record companies and other entertainment companies. This model also assumed that extant networks of reproduction were reconfigured, with a greater focus on home recording (see Chapter 6). The company envisaged networks of distribution being replaced by pure digital distribution through

ISPs, subscription services, and mobile devices, be they phones or car stereos. The company positioned itself to take advantage of this proposition, which individuals in and around the company sought to talk into existence. For example, the CEO of MusicBroker was a member of a Los Angeles-based music industry think-tank that debated ideas surrounding the future of the music industry. This particular knowledge community was developing ideas in the hope that they would seep into practice, while at the same time abstracting from the new practices being pioneered by firms like MusicBroker to imagine a new musical economy.

For this particular version of practical virtualism (cf. Leyshon et al., 2005) to become significant was dependent on a sufficient critical mass of influential individuals and companies within the industry reaching the same conclusion and being able to mobilize the technological and cultural resources to switch the musical economy to a new mode of accumulation and reproduction. Clearly, of the three models discussed, MusicBroker's was both the most radical, but also the most marginal and fragile. A second 'tipping point'—one of reorganization and of new institutional and competitive logics—may be reached with the continued roll-out of broadband, the further financial problems of the major record companies, the continued growth of new companies able to provide new means of accessing music, and the emergence of sufficient music recommendation facilities that would substitute for traditional marketing tools. But, although some elements of this vision of the musical economy have moved into view, overall it remains just that at present, a vision.

4.5. CONCLUSION

In conclusion, the three companies profiled in this chapter provided examples of differing strategies in the face of the contemporary crisis of the musical economy. Major companies sought to adapt to the challenges of software formats and internet distribution systems through litigation, diversifying through multimedia, seeking to add new revenue streams (such as ring tones and merchandising) while promoting transparency so that people could see the value added by labels in the networks of the musical economy. Meanwhile, innovative business models, such as those instituted by Online Music and

MusicBroker, sought to reformulate the networks of the musical economy by reintermediating musical value chains. This included attempts to radically reconfigure expectations within the industry, for example, by challenging the concept of the 'album', which was later exploited more fully by iTunes, or the notion that an artist needs to be 'discovered' by a record label.

What was clear was that the problems surrounding the decline in sales and the difficulty of enforcing copyright against the backdrop of P2P meant that the musical economy became an arena within which a range of experiments were undertaken in an effort to develop new ways of generating income. They ranged from the highly organized, 'TV spectacular', where programmes such as *Pop Stars, Pop/American Idol*, and *X-Factor* showcased new talent to large media audiences, thereby generating large record sales for the record companies that underwrote such events, to the grassroots funding of formerly successful artists who were no longer able to secure record deals with major companies, in a process that Michael Lewis (2001) described as 'interest group economics'.[25]

All this is reminiscent of Erica Schoenberger's (1997) analysis of the crisis of US manufacturing in the 1970s and 1980s, whereby once-dominant US industrial organizations quickly became uncompetitive in the face of new international rivals. One of the key reasons for the failure of so many companies across a range of industries and sectors was the adoption of inappropriate strategies in the face of crisis. While the leaders of these companies realized that change was necessary, their management of change was compromised by the kinds of investments and interests they had in the organizations that employed them. Schoenberger observes that:

> although there is much talk these days of qualities of leadership and vision, there seems no particular reason to suppose that the problem was a lack of either. Leaders, as we know, can lead right over the edge of the cliff. And it seems far more likely that managers and strategists *did* have a vision: they envisioned preserving a social order that affirmed the value of their social and material assets and the basis of their social power, and they fought strenuously to make that vision a reality. In the

---

[25] Lewis gives the example of the band Marillion which utilized an enthusiastic but distributed fan base to raise cash to pay for tours and albums when traditional sources of funding for such activities within the industry had been denied to them (Lewis, 2001).

course of that struggle, it seems fair to say, the burden of loss fell disproportionately on people who did not have the power to propose and realize their own vision of the social order. (1997: 227)

Thus, the ways in which these companies responded to new competition were by intensifying and adjusting existing modes of operation, rather than seeking to move over to an entirely different business model.

The parallels with the musical economy of the early twenty-first century are striking. While it was clear from interviews with major record companies that there was a recognition that 'something must be done' that went beyond relatively limited defensive and offensive strategies, there was a reluctance to embrace the more radical organizational changes that might allow them to accommodate the impact of software formats and internet distribution systems. A key reason for this was the stakes that the leaders of the major record companies had in the preservation of the current social order of the musical economy. And, as in the case of the companies studied by Schoenberger, the major record companies resorted to classic strategies of corporate restructuring to tackle problems of declining sales and falling markets. Record companies cut capacity to match the shrinking rosters of artists, which meant that declining sales needed to be set against declining output, while at the same time making deep cuts in employment. In the decade to 2009, employment within UK record companies declined by more than a quarter, from 6,200 to just 4,582 (Wadsworth with Forde, 2011: 20).

Chapter 6 explores in more detail some of the responses to this crisis by one record company, EMI, as it sought to radically engineer its business model to reflect the more straitened times of the musical economy. However, the next chapter first looks at how the crisis around software formats has affected another part of the musical economy, and that is the professional recording studio sector.

5

The Software Slump?[1] Digital Music, the Democratization of Technology, and the Decline of the Recording Studio Sector within the Musical Economy

5.1. INTRODUCTION

The role that software plays within the economy is now widely acknowledged (Dodge and Kitchin, 2004, 2005a, 2005b, 2007; Lessig, 1999; Thrift and French, 2002; Wise, 1998). Software is recognized as a significant economic agent in at least three ways. First, the production of software constitutes an important industry in its own right. There is no clearer signal of this than the fact that Apple and Microsoft are among the world's largest companies, and that the software industry is a significant generator of income and profits the world over (Auletta, 2000; Hozic, 1999). Indeed, the industry is so large that it is able to remain highly profitable despite a chronic problem of copyright infringement in many countries, while it is also able to support the business model of open source which is based on the giving away and sharing of code between programmers and users (von Krogh et al., 2003; Weber, 2004; Zeitlyn, 2003). Second, the significance of software can be determined, ironically, by its taken-for-granted nature. Software and code have sunk into the business background (Leyshon et al., 2005a), and much of the economy would simply be unable to run without it—and all manner of procedures, conventions, and protocols are highly dependent on the

---

[1] The title of this chapter was inspired by *The Sophtware Slump* (2000) by Granddaddy (V2 Records).

unproblematic unfolding of software programs (Dodge and Kitchin, 2005b; Thrift and French, 2002). Moreover, within some industries software has been part of the business vernacular for decades, since at least the 1960s in some cases (e.g., Leyshon and Pollard, 2000). Third, and finally, software is seen as a catalyst for economic change. This view of software and code became particularly prevalent in the 1990s as part of the hyperbole that surrounded the unfolding of the New Economy. As the dot.com bubble burst in 2000, many people were equally quick to dismiss the significance of this software-fuelled era of rapid boom and bust (Henwood, 2003). However, while it is important to guard against the danger of technological determinism in explaining economic change, recent critical reflections on the New Economy have concluded that its legacies have been significant and enduring, with important geographical consequences (Leyshon et al., 2007; Martin, 2007; Pratt, 2007; Zook, 2007).

This chapter focuses upon the second and third aspects of software as an agent of economic change just outlined: that is, it explores the ways in which software may be seen to have been embedded in industries over often surprisingly long periods of time, and also how the utilization of software can be part of quite fundamental processes of sector-wide change. It does this through an analysis of the music industry which, as the foregoing chapters have outlined, has undergone significant changes as a result of software applications that have both enabled the internet and developed compression programs such as MP3 that tipped an already struggling industry into a full-blown crisis of reproduction (Fox, 2004; Jones, 2002; McCourt and Burkart, 2003; Power and Jansson, 2002). To date, this book has focused on the crisis of the music industry through an analysis of problems within distribution and sales, with attention inevitably aimed at the implications for record companies and the media conglomerates of which they are a part. This chapter goes beyond record companies and seeks to uncover the consequences of the crisis of the music industry within another set of institutions at the heart of the agglomerated musical economy: recording studios. However, the approach in this chapter needs to be qualified. It develops a historical geographical account of the recording studio sector, and of the role of socio-technical change in its evolution. The chapter seeks to place the emergence of software in context; software emerges as an agent of change at two particularly important periods—the late 1970s and from the mid-1990s onward—to change the trajectory and organization of the recording studio sector. Drawing on research undertaken in British recording studios, the chapter reveals an even deeper and transformative crisis at the heart of the musical economy which in part turns on the introduction of digital technology controlled by software.

The remainder of the chapter is organized as follows. Section 5.2 sets out the context for the analysis, and outlines the ways in which a combination of the internet and the development of software compression programs brought about fundamental change within the musical economy. Section 5.3 sets out an economic geography of recording studios, and outlines their role and function within the overall musical economy. Section 5.4 undertakes a socio-technical history of recording studios, looking at the 'analogue' and 'digital' eras in turn, and reveals how the privileged position of studios within the musical economy has been undermined through the incremental development of applications within the recording process, which has led to a growing democratization of technology.

5.2. COPYRIGHT CAPITALISM IN AN ERA OF DIGITAL REPRODUCTION

Since at least the 1990s a number of industrial sectors have been caught up in a crisis afflicting copyright capitalism in an era of digital reproduction (Lessig, 1999, 2001). Industries that produce commodities which rely on copyright legislation for their efficient commercial exploitation but that can also be rendered in digital form have been subject to significant processes of restructuring.

They include the motion picture, photographic, publishing, and software industries (Currah, 2003, 2006, 2007; Gluckler, 2005; Pratt, 2007; Vaidhyanathan, 2001). However, it was within the music industry that this digitally induced crisis of reproduction first came to prominence and arguably has developed most fully. The scale of the problem facing the music industry by the middle of the first decade of the twenty-first century can be gauged by comparing legitimate and illegitimate download services. Developed by Apple to provide a legal download site which would ensure that customers generated revenues for music that would flow through the music industry value chain, iTunes has undoubtedly been a very successful innovation. As illustrated in Chapter 1, by 2013 the site recorded its 40 billionth download, and the revenues from downloads reached more than $4 billion per quarter. Moreover, Apple was just one of a number of companies that ensured revenue flowed from downloads to record companies, publishing companies, and artists.

However, Chapter 1 also illustrated the scale of the problem facing the industry: infrastructure for legal downloading is dwarfed in scale and scope by systems that make it possible to download illegal or 'pirated' material. As long ago as 2003 the top-ten peer-to-peer (P2P) download programs—systems that facilitate the illegal downloading of music—had themselves been downloaded more than 640 million times, and it is estimated that 2.3 billion files were downloaded across these networks every month. For example, consider one of the most successful of these networks, Kazaa; by 2006 it had been downloaded more than 239 million times, commanded a user base of over 140 million computer users, which was more than double that of Napster at its peak, with as many as 4 million users simultaneously online at any time (BBC News, 2006).[2] The availability of so much copyrighted material on sites such as this, for which no fee is received, created an environment which poses a significant threat to the musical economy. As discussed in Chapter 4, unlike other 'piracy' cultures that have chronically beset the music industry since the first availability of consumer recording and playback technologies in the late 1960s and early 1970s, the free exchange of music in MP3 format has been a more intractable problem, given that MP3s produce a durable and near-perfect copy of the original recording, they are available in an insecure format that can be copied and recopied without any reduction in quality, and they are exchanged in an environment that is indifferent to intellectual property rights (Choi and Perez, 2007; Higgins, 2007; Higgins et al., 2007; Ouellet, 2007). By way of illustration, consider this following vignette. I used to give lectures on the economic geography of the music industry as part of an introductory first-year class on human geography. During the lecture I always conducted a straw poll to gain an indication of the number of students who downloaded music from P2P sites and their awareness of the illegality of their actions. Among the 200 or so students there was always a forest of arms raised in response to both questions, indicating

---

[2] Following a string of legal actions against it, the owner of Kazaa, Sharman Networks, announced in 2006 that it would convert to a legal music download site (BBC News, 2006).

that they were regular users of such sites, and that most were aware that what they were doing was illegal. However, as McCourt and Burkhart (2003) observed in their pioneering analysis of online file trading, most people calculated that their chances of being caught were remote and, in any case, they were only doing what everyone else was doing. To pay for commodities that one's peers were routinely obtaining for nothing, particularly when there were considerable constraints on the expenditure of students, meant that one must have a particularly strong moral compass. Indeed, it is probable that there is now a culture of expectation among many music consumers that the default position for obtaining music is that it should be free, an observation which is backed up by the figures recorded by internet consultancy Comscore, which analysed the outcome of the 2007 experiment by the band Radiohead who chose to make their *In Rainbows* album available online but allowed consumers to set their own value for the tracks. Over 60 per cent of consumers chose to pay nothing at all, apart from the obligatory 45 pence administration fee (Comscore, 2007).

The correlation between the rise of material available to be downloaded freely on P2P download sites, and the sharp fall in the volume of global music sales—a decline of at least 15 per cent between 2001 and 2004—unsurprisingly led many people within the music industry to argue that the rise of freely downloadable material was responsible. While it would be naive to suggest that the amount of material available online has had no implications for retail sales, research commissioned by the music industry itself suggested that the relationship was a little more complex and ambiguous than many industry insiders believed. The value of UK recorded music sales actually increased in real terms between 1978 and 2004 (see Table 5.1). Sales also increased between 1994 and 2004, while data on UK-based record companies' net invisible earnings between 1993 and 1998 reveal that this form of income peaked in 1995, going into decline before the MP3 gift economy broke out of the tightly defined groups of hackers and programmers to which it was formerly confined (Table 5.2). Therefore, as argued in the last chapter, internet piracy is better seen as a 'tipping point' in the development of the music industry, which was already struggling and on the verge of crisis. Internet piracy has legitimized the talk of a crisis of reproduction within the music industry, but, in truth, this crisis had been brewing for many years, as the recorded music increasingly had to compete

Table 5.1. Real value of UK recorded music sales, 1978–
2004 (£million: 2004 constant prices)

Year	£ million
1978	934.2
1984	688.8
1994	1,188.4
2004	1,214.1

Source: BPI.

Table 5.2. UK-based record companies net invisible earnings, 1993–1998

Year	£ million
1993	233.0
1994	225.4
1995	317.7
1996	280.0
1997	261.5
1998	207.7

Source: Dane et al., 1999.

for the under-24 'share of wallet' retail market with new objects of consumption such as computer games, mobile phones, and DVDs. Having seen the discourse of crisis become legitimized, those who ran the large record companies wasted little time in resorting to tried and tested practices of industrial restructuring. Rounds of job losses were followed by a series of contractual changes with artists, which involved the cancellation of contracts, as well as making surviving contracts broader in scope to include new potential revenue streams such as merchandising, etc.

One significant outcome of this process was a shrinking of artist rosters and, particularly significant in the context of this chapter, large reductions in the size of budgets for A&R, which includes the recording budgets that pay for producers, engineers, and studio time (discussed in more detail in section 5.4). Thus, the development of software has clearly had a material impact on the musical economy, at least as far as distribution and sales are concerned. In the remainder of the chapter the focus shifts to the process of musical creativity and to the recording studio sector.

5.3. THE ECONOMIC GEOGRAPHY OF THE RECORDING STUDIO SECTOR

The recorded music industry is, for the most part, an urban phenom-enon, and the realization of musical creativity is a spatially agglom-erated process. Like other creative industries, the music industry is rooted in communities of workers anchored to particular places which, once established, become 'magnets for talented individuals from other areas, who migrate to the centres in search of personal and professional fulfilment' (Scott, 2004a: 7). London has been an im-portant centre for the music industry since at least the 1960s, when the major US and European record labels increased their capacity in the city as British popular music become internationally significant in the wake of the success of The Beatles and the 'British invasion' of US popular culture. London was the headquarters of one of the trad-itional 'big four' music conglomerates—EMI—and has long been an incubator site for smaller and independent record labels.

The urban focus of the recorded music industry can be explained to a large extent by the concept of the musical network introduced in Chapter 2. To recap, there are four main types of musical network: cre-ativity, reproduction, distribution, and consumption. Each of these plays a distinct role in the value chain of the musical economy, and also has its own distinctive geography. Creativity, which involves prac-tices such as composition, performance, and recording—what Scott (2000) describes as the 'creative field'—is the network within which music is at its most unstable and volatile. It involves the participation of large numbers of actors with different skills and competencies from an array of different institutions. These actors and institutions tend towards agglomeration in an attempt to cope with spillovers, which are endemic where knowledge is volatile and in process (Bassett et al., 2002; Bathelt et al., 2004; Coe and Johns, 2004; Pinch et al., 2003; Scott, 2001, 2004b). To date, academic research on the functions that make up networks of creativity have mainly focused on the role of record companies (Negus, 1999a, 1999b), while those studies that have been concerned to determine the impacts of the current crisis on the musical economy have also tended to take the record company as their default institutional focus (see Chapters 4 and 6).

This chapter focuses instead on the role of recording studios within networks of musical creativity, and analyses the impact of the ongoing crisis of the musical economy upon them. It also identifies two critical moments in the history of the recording studio sector when software has helped to reconfigure the institutional and competitive structure of the industry.[3]

5.3.1. The Recording Studio Business

While the volume of geographical work on the music industry is limited, the amount of work on recording studios is scarce. The sole contribution to date is the study of recording studios undertaken by Gibson (2005) as part of a broader analysis of the relationship between music and urban landscapes. While this is a perceptive and valuable study, it touches only on the economic role of recording studios within the broader musical economy, although it does indicate a possible business model for economically failing studios that, nevertheless, have iconic status as a result of earlier achievements: that is, studios are able to convert themselves into urban heritage sites. Indeed, there is very little academic literature at all on the recording studio sector, and much of what does exist emanates from fields such as musicology, sociology, and science studies (Hennion, 1989; Horning, 2004; Kealy, 1979, 1982; Perlman, 2004; Porcello, 2004; Theberge, 2004). Moreover, very little of this material has taken a broader perspective of the economic role of recording studios within the contemporary musical economy.[4]

Perhaps one of the reasons for this is that there is actually very little background information on the economy of recording studios. Most of the information that does exist is in the form of estimates, and much of this is for the UK. For example, a report by the National Music Council (2002) estimates that in the early twenty-first century there were around 300 or so 'economically significant' recording studios in the UK (although what represents economically significant is never defined). A majority of these studios—nearly 200—were located in London. Taking a broad definition of the sector, the report estimates the number of employees engaged in the recording studio sector to be in excess of 1,000, and calculates the value added of the sector—that

---

[3] The chapter draws upon interviews with owners and employees of recording studios and management companies in the UK, as well as various freelance workers, generating over thirty hours of interview material. All interviews were transcribed and coded.

[4] More recently, Allan Watson has begun to undertake valuable work on the recording studio sector, but it post-dates the research being described here.

is, the sum of income from employment and self-employment, plus the gross trading profits of companies and the value of rent received— to be about the £50m per annum. In addition to this, the report estimates that there were around 350 full-time producers, who, combined, were responsible for generating £20m of value added to the economy. This report was an extension of an earlier study undertaken for the National Music Council by Dane et al. (1999) which provided a more detailed analysis of what might be described as the value chain of the musical economy. An analysis of value added per employee revealed that the average figure across the industry was £29,000. The highest contributions to value added per capita were made by composers, publishing companies, and record companies, whereas both recording studios and record producers fell well below this industry average at £22,000 and £18,000 value added per employee, respectively (see Table 5.3). This analysis revealed that the recording studio sector was not a particularly profitable or efficient part of the musical economy overall, particularly when compared with record companies and publishing companies, notwithstanding the recent deepening of the crisis of the music industry. Nevertheless, it is, or at least was, a crucial part of the overall value chain of the musical economy, producing commodities upon which large parts of the industry depend.

So, how are we to understand the role played by recording studios within the broader musical economy? One way is to outline the assets that they possess that enable them to generate business within the music industry. Studios may thus be seen as socio-technical spaces

Table 5.3. The value chain of the UK musical economy

	Value-added (£ million)	FTE Employment	Value-added per employee (£)
Composers	930	1,500	620,000
Publishing companies	96	1,275	75,000
Collection societies	26	913	28,000
Performers	350	46,000	8,000
Record companies	405	7,128	57,000
Record producers	14	750	19,000
Recording studios	15	660	22,000
Manufacturers	87	3,000	29,000
Distributors	86	2578	33000
Retail	279	16090	17000
Total	2228	79894	29000

Source: Dane et al., 1999.

that use, in combination, the following assets: space, time, technology, expertise, and 'emotional labour'. I will now deal briefly with each of these assets in turn. First, recording studios provided dedicated spaces for the recording of music, which vary from large orchestral rooms to smaller and more intimate spaces, but all of them have distinctive acoustic properties that have been created either by their original design or through subsequent iterative acts of tinkering, which make them suitable spaces for the performing and recording of music (Cogan and Clark, 2003; Cunningham, 1998). Second, studios sell time in these spaces, and are the sites for project-based work (Christopherson, 2002; Grabher, 2001, 2002a, 2002b, 2002c; Hertel et al., 2003; O'Mahony, 2003; O'Riain, 2000; von Krogh et al., 2003). This mode of work is common across the creative industries more generally (DeFillippi and Arthur, 1998; Jones, 1996), and recording studio projects can last from just a few days to many months. Third, studios provide dedicated technology that facilitates the recording of music, and to that end are the sites of considerable sunk costs that have accumulated over many years. Fourth, studios provide expertise in the operation of recording technology and, crucially, the ability to combine it with the relative skills, proficiencies, and musical ambitions of its clients. Fifth, and finally, recording studios provide what has become known as emotional labour: that is, interactive service work heavily loaded with feeling and affect that is part of the service being provided (Hochschild, 1983; Steinberg and Figart, 1999). Unlike the other four assets, the significance of emotional labour became obvious to me only after undertaking several interviews in studios and observing just how 'nice'—there is just no other word to describe it—everyone in recording studios seemed to be.[5] This contrasted strongly with the indifference and passive aggression that I perceived in my initial attempt to gain access to studios in the first place, which proved to be difficult, if not impossible, places to access

---

[5] I should emphasize that this observation is based on nearly thirty years of experience of undertaking corporate interviews. While interviewees in other sectors where I have researched have for the most part been polite and courteous, and often generous with their time and knowledge, the welcoming atmosphere within recording studios was markedly different. This, in part, may be a product of the fact that most recording studios are effectively small businesses, but it is also a product of their recruitment strategies and deliberate attempt to create an environment that is facilitative and supportive of creativity. However, that tangible sense of congeniality does not mask the often brutal power relations that frequently play out within recording studios.

without a personal referral or reference to an already known contact within the recording studio sector.[6] It became clear that an asset of what might be described as congeniality was deliberately cultivated and worked upon, and is a long-standing feature of studios, having been observed in studios as early as the 1970s (Kealy, 1979, 1982). Moreover, compared with other assets, the significance of emotional labour is not being eroded by broader forces of competition and technological change within the musical economy. Thus, while the demand for space, time, technology, and expertise is (increasingly) substitutable, emotional support and encouragement for the creative process is an asset that studios can actively cultivate and promote. Moreover, it becomes a reputational asset (Gluckler, 2007) that can be strongly linked to particular studio spaces and infrastructure.

Thus, in much the same way that Thrift (2005) has argued that the affective turn within capitalism more generally is really driven by a hard-edged concern for competitiveness and profitability, so the cultivation of congeniality within studios is a response to the fact that many of the other barriers to competition within the sector have been progressively lowered and eroded. Recording studios were once highly privileged sites that allowed only those with sufficient resources to gain access to their facilities; however, with the growing ubiquity of digital recording media, and the possibilities of open access distribution sites such as MySpace and YouTube, all manner of artists that might once have been prevented from finding an audience through the normal narrow channels of the music industry gained the opportunity to do so. This presented a significant challenge to the long-term

[6] Traditional modes of gaining access to elites within organizations proved ineffective in recording studios. Letters, e-mails, and telephone calls to identified individuals in recording studios were not returned and I was forced to change tack and negotiate access via the Association of Professional Recording Studios (APRS). Once I had successfully undertaken a couple of interviews that the APRS helped set up, I was able to use these names in approaches to other key gatekeepers which helped to gain wider access. Eventually, I was being approached by people within the industry who wanted to speak to me as they were curious about my research and wanted to contribute. This culminated in a presentation that I gave to the APRS. The problems of gaining access were revealed to be a result of the high number of approaches they receive from individuals seeking employment or intern experience at recording studios, so that most employ a 'don't call us we'll call you' policy. In addition, within the higher profile or 'top end' studios, there was an general unwillingness to engage with anyone wishing to write about recording studios, which was attributed to negative experiences with journalists in the past, but also to the need to protect the privacy of their often high-profile clients.

viability of recording studios, and the analysis in this chapter seeks to explain how this came about.

5.3.2. The Recording Studio Market and Business Models

The assets outlined were deployed by recording studios in a market that is characterized by oligopsony: that is, a market characterized by few buyers. The demand for the services of recording studios were driven by a relatively small coterie of record, motion picture, and television companies which, for the most part, provided the investment that enabled artists to use professional studios. As is typical of oligopsonies, the concentrated power of buyers encouraged intensive competition among suppliers, which brought about a significant deflation of studio fees.[7] It was widely reported during interviews that the rates for renting studio time in the 2000s were the same as in the 1980s, which, if one takes into account wage and price inflation over that time, represented a significant *de facto* deflation of the fees studios were able to charge. All studios had a set of declared 'day rates' for the hire of their studios, but it was admitted that it was very rare to be able to charge this as the representatives from the record companies in particular, which constitute the heaviest demand for studio time, were well aware of the level of competition between studios for business and expected discounts on the published rate. The APRS sought to resist the tendency towards rate discounting, and encouraged studios to hold the line on fees, arguing for a transparent market within which studios competed on their posted day rates. However, as a number of studio managers admitted in interviews, the tendency to cut a deal was difficult to resist in times of slack trading. Studio managers were all too aware that in a market of comparatively few buyers there were only so many clients who refused to pay the going rate for services that one could turn away. The problem of fee deflation was further exacerbated by the progressive lowering of the barriers to entry in the market, as the cost of technology fell and, in particular, the use of software to stand in for and replace acts of studio craft that were

---

[7] There is a sizeable economic literature on oligopsonies, which are particularly prominent in agricultural and natural resources sectors, where the retail end of the supply chain is often characterized by oligopsony (see Just and Chern, 1980; Lowry and Winfrey, 1974; Schroeter and Azzam, 1991; Sexton et al., 2007).

formerly embodied and tacit in nature. It was also exacerbated, at the margins, by the existence of so-called 'vanity projects', where wealthy individuals set up recording studios not based on coherent sustainable business models but more as glamorous ventures which created a space where it was possible to associate with (famous) musicians.

There are two main types of market in which recording studios operate. The first is the recording market, which is the *de novo* recording of material. This, in turn, is divided into two areas. On the one hand, there is the classical and film score market. On the other, there is the 'rock and pop'—popular music—market. The studio rates in the UK for these markets combined vary from £400 to £2,500 per day, with the higher rates largely being earned by studios that have large rooms which are used for orchestral recordings. Most studios charge by the day rather than by the hour, which became the standard way of costing studios from the 1970s onwards as new studios dedicated to a rock and pop market undermined the regime of union-regulated working hours that restricted sessions to three hours at a time. The 'days' that can be hired at studios are, in effect, twelve-hour days—which converts into hourly rates that vary from £33 to £200 based on the day rates reported above—and usually include the use of an in-house recording engineer and a 'tape-op' (or tape operator, a generally menial position or 'gofer' for the artist(s), producer, and engineer). As will be outlined in section 5.4, record producers used to be part of the package bought by users of recording studios, although from at least the 1950s onwards these increasingly became freelance employees (as now are engineers), and are hired by the company organizing the recording session. It is the producers who are given responsibility for the recording budget, and have a large choice over the studio and environment in which the work will take place.

In the UK at least, the institutional fabric of the recording studio market was characterized by a distinctive hierarchal division. At one extreme, there are the so-called 'top-end' studios that are large, often prestigious institutions which have large rooms capable of high-quality orchestral recording for classical and film score production. These include studios such as Abbey Road (formerly EMI studios) and AIR (formerly owned by George Martin, producer of The Beatles recordings). Just below this level was a set of smaller studios that mainly plied their trade in the established rock and pop market. Many of these studios were less than forty years old (see section 5.4). Below this level there was a long tail of small-budget studios (and increasingly home studios) which catered for those unable or unwilling to pay the rates demanded by the more established studios. There was, in addition, a fourth recording studio business model: that is, the residential studio, essentially a recording hotel, where artists both live and record for the duration of the project. They are normally located in rural areas—notable examples in the UK included Rockfield and Chapel Studios, located near Brecon and Lincoln, respectively—and often hired by record labels when they have a newly signed young band whom they wish to isolate from urban temptations in order to get music recorded.

The second type of market in which recording studios operate is the postproduction market. This covers a range of work on already recorded music and includes mixing, scoring to visual material, and the mastering of disks. The attraction of this work for studios is that the rates for studio space are higher than for recording, and there is a high demand for space for such projects, although the duration of the projects is shorter. For example, the process of mixing, which involves finalizing the balance of sound within recordings, usually takes about two days per track. For both mixing and music scoring, the fee covers the use of the technology and space only, as the producers and engineers are freelance. However, the third arm of the postproduction market, mastering, is unusual in that it is the last remnant of the traditional model of recording studio provision. The fees paid for mastering buy both the in-house engineer and the studio in which he (and it is invariably he) works. Mastering is the final act of the creative process, where the mix of the tracks is transferred onto a master disk which is then sent off to networks of production where the now stabilized cultural commodity is mass produced and distributed. This is a highly specialized and concentrated market, and the Anglo-American market was dominated by a handful of studios with a reputation for high-quality mastering, such as Sterling Sound in New York, Gateway Studios in Portland, Maine, and Abbey Road studios in London.

The chapter so far has placed the recording studio sector within the context of the musical economy as a whole, and outlined its market structures and some pressing imperatives. The next section sets the evolution of recording studios within a broader historical context, and charts their rise and fall in line with associated developments in the social organization of the musical economy and the development of technology and, in particular, software.

5.4. A SOCIO-TECHNICAL HISTORY OF RECORDING STUDIOS: AN ANATOMY OF DECLINE

Since the development of Edison's first recording device in the late nineteenth century, the musical economy has evolved in lockstep with technological innovation and development. Up until at least the 1940s the socio-technical evolution of the recording studio sector served to lock up expertise in studios, making them privileged sites of knowledge. But, beginning in the years after the Second World War, innovations in recording technologies have worked in the opposite direction, lowering both the cost and barriers to entry. Digital recording and the use of software are just the latest stage in this process.

5.4.1. The Analogue Era

A close relationship between the process of recording and technological development ensured that a laboratory-like regime persisted for decades within the recording studio sector. For example, consider the case of the studios built by EMI at 3 Abbey Road in north-west London. This purpose-built studio signalled a new development within the musical economy, and a move towards vertical integration that was already under way within the motion picture industry at the time (Christopherson and Storper, 1986). Opened in 1931, at the then not inconsiderable cost of £100,000, the EMI studios were the world's largest complex dedicated to gramophone recording (Southall, 1982). Thereafter, other large record companies—companies such as Pye and Decca in the UK, Warners, RCA, and Columbia in the US (Millard, 2005)—began to build their own dedicated recording studios which combined musical creativity and technological development within dedicated spaces. They became sites of innovation within which companies integrated activities all along the value chain of the musical economy. Thus, the equipment used in studios was often bespoke and available only within that company's studios. For EMI, this equipment was often developed in its manufacturing division located in Hayes, and would be tested in the Abbey Road studios which would have sole use of successful innovations. The laboratory-like status of studios of the early twentieth century was extended to the dress code expected of its employees, who were required to wear white coats at all times (see Figure 5.1), a practice which extended into the 1950s

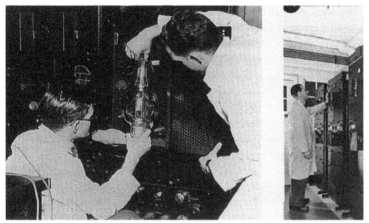

Fig. 5.1. The studio as laboratory: recording engineers (in obligatory white lab coats) at work in EMI studios, Abbey Road, 1930s.
Source: Southall, 1982.

(Southall, 1982). Technology was carefully guarded, as was a set of tacit skills and competencies developed by recording engineers, such as the placing of microphones in relation to the instruments being recorded, practices which, according to Horning (2004: 709), 'were considered in large recording companies to be proprietary information'. Indeed, at least until the 1960s, studios were highly regimented and bureaucratized institutions, which, in part, reflected the role they played within the large vertically integrated organizations to which they belonged. Campaigns by musicians' unions both in the US and in the UK against what was seen to be the threat to the livelihoods of performers from recorded music led to a series of accommodations between record companies and the labour that worked in their studios in the early twentieth century (Coleman, 2005). The unionization of both musicians and engineers within the studio environment saw the imposition of a maximum of three separate three-hour recording sessions per day maximum—normally 10.00–13.00, 14.00–17.00, and 19.00–22.00—and a clear demarcation of duties and responsibilities within both the studio and the control room, which Kealy (1979) describes as a regime of craft union regulation. An outcome of this system was the development of clearly defined technical career paths for engineers, and in Britain the large recording studios played the same role in inculcating a training labour force much in the way that the BBC did within the field of broadcasting.

The legacies of this more formal and rigorous approach to the production of sound lasted well after Abbey Road had abandoned the
obligatory white coats in the 1950s. A recording engineer who was
recruited by EMI in the early 1970s confirmed the strong links that
existed between the research and development arm of the companies'
manufacturing and technical division and the recording process in
the studio:

> There was a chief engineer who set technical standards in the studio, it
> was very much the technical off-shoot of the record company and they
> were used as an advisory centre…in those days there was a laboratory
> so we tested every bit of gear before it went into use and it was very
> much the technical department controlled what went on in studios.
> (Freelance engineer/former Abbey Road employee, interview)

This particular mode of development—where the leading studios
dominated the recording industry, were owned by major recording
companies, and were connected to their technical equipment divisions—created idiosyncratic studio spaces that were unique to each
organization. The space in each studio was different, and the acoustic
environment often developed incrementally and organically in relation to the nature of the materials used in its construction or to subsequent experiments with baffling and other materials introduced
to the studio fabric.[8] In addition to variations in acoustic environment, different studios often worked with a distinctive palate of
technologies. Although some of the equipment was generic, much
was specific and unique to the studio, having been produced by the
manufacturing division of the large company. Moreover, the ways
in which this equipment was deployed varied from studio to studio, and recording configurations often 'depended on experimentation, trial and error, and innovative thinking' (Horning, 2004: 707).
Moreover, distinctive employment cultures emerged within each

---

[8] The importance of the very fabric of the studios to the sound generated within
them has led studios to adopt cautious and conservative approaches to renovation.
For example, when the parquet wood flooring laid down in Studio 1 at Abbey Road
in 1931 eventually needed replacing because it had worn away, concerns about the
implications of the renovation for the resonance of the room meant that the studio
undertook the job in the most laborious way possible: block by block, overnight,
and stretching over a much longer period than if the studio had been closed for a
large-scale refurbishment.

studio; all producers and engineers were salaried employees of the studio, their regular employment guaranteed by the fact that, until at least the late 1960s, the studios were available only to artists signed to the record company that owned it. This contractual requirement locked artists into particular studios and guaranteed work. As a result, there were few knowledge spillovers between studios, as both staff and artists tended to be confined to the same space over relatively long periods of time. A particularly good illustration of this system in action is revealed by a vignette from the early recording career of Pink Floyd which is contained in the 1960s memoirs of promoter and producer Joe Boyd (Boyd, 2006). Having negotiated money from a management agency to pay for a recording session in one of the fledgling independent studios in London, which he produced, Boyd found that the band's manager used the resulting single—'Arnold Layne'—to negotiate a long recording contract with EMI. Despite his role in the initial success of the band, the deal meant the end of Boyd's role as the band's producer because EMI insisted that all future recordings would take place at Abbey Road under the control of one of its house producers.

Although this policy effectively meant that artists had producers and engineers imposed upon them, it produced creative opportunities in other ways. Because studios were constructed in part as technical laboratories, there was a very liberal attitude to the use of studio time by artists. As studios could be used only by artists signed to the record company, the studios were often not used to full capacity, and were certainly not seen as profit centres in their own right. Recounting the period in which he worked in Abbey Road in the early to mid-1970s, one engineer observed that the large Studio 1 at the complex was often at a standstill and available for other activities as it was not booked to full capacity:

> the number 1 studio is 90 feet by 40 odd or whatever, huge area, and if it wasn't busy we'd play badminton in there or there'd be someone maintaining a car...it was pretty laid back...(Freelance engineer/former Abbey Road employee, interview)

The loose and liberal organizational space of the studio came into its own for those artists who wanted time to experiment with new musical styles and technologies, and it was during the 1960s that the studio became a compositional tool in its own right, rather than simply a space for making natural-sounding recordings of music that could otherwise be performed live (Cunningham, 1998; Coleman, 2005).[9] In this respect, the studio system worked for the record companies, but it was an era that was already coming to an end. The decline of the record company-dominated studio system can be traced back as far as the immediate post-war period, and is related both to significant technological developments in sound recording, which increasingly democratized technology, and to the rising profile of 'star' producers and their attempts to break free from the restraints of bureaucratic careers. The immediate post-war period had a significant deflationary impact on the cost of equipment used in sound recording as surplus military technology found its way onto the open market (Cunningham, 1998). The barriers to entry to the sector were lowered still further by the development of tape as a recording medium, which made the process of recording much cheaper and easier than the traditional direct-to-disk method (Jones, 1992).[10] The development of this technology meant that the investment needed to establish a recording studio fell significantly, so decentralizing the capacity to make sound recordings, weakening the hold of the large vertically integrated record companies (Kealy, 1979). In the US, for example, the 1950s saw a growth in the number of recording studios linked to newly formed record labels, which were now able to compete with established companies as the post-war market for recorded music grew, particularly with the rapid growth in sales of popular music and linked, in part, to the rise of the sociological phenomenon of the teenager. Many of these new studios were owned by small and medium-sized record companies, who were often willing to rent out their other facilities to other record companies without studios, lowering the barriers to entry still further.

The growth of independent recording studios, and a greater capacity for knowledge to spread beyond the large established studios, was propelled further by an undermining of the bureaucratic culture

---

[9] Abbey Road was a particularly good illustration of this tendency. It was the studio at which both The Beatles and Pink Floyd, leading exponents in the use of the studio as a compositional tool in the late 1960s and early 1970s, recorded much of their musical output.

[10] This innovation was also a by-product of military investment in sound technology, as tape as a recording medium had been developed in Germany by AEG and IGFarben and utilized for the broadcast of propaganda. It was discovered by chance by Allied forces at the end of the war after raids on German radio stations (Coleman, 2005).

that had hitherto dominated employment relations. There was a clear imbalance between the money which the recordings made by 'star' producers and engineers earned for their employers and the relatively modest incomes they were offered in return. By trading in on their past successes and becoming self-employed, producers and engineers could pursue entrepreneurial careers with significantly larger incomes, based in large part on being remunerated by a share of the profits from the sales of the record they produced and engineered. However, even in the 1960s, the number of independent studios that would allow such freelancers to work was limited (Cunningham, 1998). A significant fracture in the traditional model of labour regulation in the UK came in the late 1960s when George Martin, the producer employed by EMI to manage the recording sessions of The Beatles, quit his job and first started up an independent management company and then established a recording studio. Thereafter, there was a shift of successful producers and engineers to freelance status and then, in the 1970s, a growth in the number of independent studios which provided the space for freelance producers to work beyond the studios of the record companies. Many of these studios were set up by producers, and their business models were, therefore, based more on producers' royalty income than on the efficient management of the studio assets themselves. In this regard, at least, independent studios were similar to the established record company studios.

5.4.2. The Digital Era

The rather casual approach to the use of studio assets came to an end in the late 1970s. For the traditional studios, it was often the result of the record companies of which they were a part being taken over by larger corporate bodies. For example, when EMI was taken over by the electronics conglomerate Thorn in 1979, financial discipline was imposed on the Abbey Road studio, which subsequently ran as a cost centre. This quickly saw the studio opened up to non-EMI artists and producers to maximize returns from the use of studio space. For the sector as a whole, it was the development of new digital recording consoles by UK technology companies such as Solid State Logic (SSL) and Neve, both established in the late 1960s and located in Oxford and Cambridge, respectively, within what would later be identified as the British high-fidelity cluster (May et al., 2001). These firms specialized in making recording consoles: that is, the control desks at which

engineers and producers work to craft recordings in studios. SSL
and Neve were responsible for the development of so-called 'in-line'
recording consoles, which gave engineers more control over the
various sounds and components that were recorded in the studios,
each microphone and effect having its own set of faders and controls
(see Figure 5.2). More importantly, from 1977 onwards, SSL began to
integrate computer software into recording consoles, which significantly increased the ease and flexibility of recording sessions. This
development was to further break the hold of the large studios over
the recording market and usher in a new wave of competition in the
sector. In particular, it was the development of a recording console
with 'Total Recall' that ensured their SL 4000 E desks transformed not
only the practice of studio management but also the market for studio
space, and Neve developed a similar system—the NECAM system—a
year later. By integrating software and memory into the operating of
desks, producers and engineers were able to easily re-establish the settings between recording sessions. Previously, detailed notation would
have to be made of the position of faders and other instruments. This
was not an insignificant task; during the 1960s, four-track recording
was the standard, although this had increased to sixteen tracks by the
early 1970s. By the end of the decade, thirty-two-track machines were
common. However, by simply saving the settings onto a floppy disk,

Fig. 5.2. A late 1970s–early 1980s in-line Solid State Logic (SSL) recording
console.
Source: SSL.

the producer or engineer could ensure that the settings were exactly the same from track to track, from session to session.

The integration of software into recording consoles ensured that the SSL and Neve machines became the desks of choice for producers and engineers. As a result, they became necessary investments for recording studios wishing to capture the work of leading producers and engineers, who were now almost invariably freelance, and were responsible for the choice of studio for their recording projects. Indeed, to use the terminology of actor-network theory, consoles integrated with software and with the capacity for memory became obligatory passage points for studios wishing to attract producers. This required significant investment, from record companies and independent studios alike. The SSL and Neve consoles cost between £250,000 and £300,000 each and, given that most establishments would need one for each of their constituent studios, this represented a considerable investment, particularly for the independent studios. Ironically, this very act of investment served to move power away from studios and towards producers, because it now became the consoles and not the studio spaces per se that were the most desirable assets in the recording process. The fact that in a very short period of time most recording studios installed similar consoles powered by software and with the capacity of memory eroded the technological gap between studios and made them far less idiosyncratic spaces. Through a floppy disk, work was now transferable between recording consoles, and therefore between studios, which improved producers' choice of workplace, but also increased the power of the record companies in leveraging rates for recording time by playing one studio off against another.

Therefore, it is from this period—the early 1980s onwards—that one can begin to see a new era of destructive competition pervade the recording studio sector. As the ubiquity of SSL and Neve consoles levelled the technological playing field, record companies and other buyers of studio time exploited their oligopsonistic power to progressively drive down the real cost of hiring studio time-space by encouraging studios to discount rates to secure business. As already indicated, studio rates were more or less stagnant from the mid-1980s onwards, which represented a significant decline in rents in real terms. This had beneficial impacts for those who paid to use these spaces, and the gradual deflation of rental costs in real terms opened up at least some of these spaces to artists who would otherwise have been priced out. However, heightened competition between studios began to have regressive effects on working conditions. It is from this time that the studios began to price hiring rates based on the 'lock out': that is, a day's booking would include the use of the studio for a twelve-hour shift, including the hire of an in-house engineer and usually a tape-op. This led not only to an effective devaluation of the price of studio time but also to a significant increase in the working hours endured by engineers. The move away from a profession characterized by a regime of craft union regulation was recognized as early as the 1970s by Kealy (1979, 1982), as the rise of less bureaucratic independent studios instilled more of a service ethic in the studio sector wherein the client's needs were valorized above all others.

The problem which confronted engineers was that, although some were still employed as salaried employees, many began to be classified as retained staff: that is, paid a small salary to be available to work for the studio, with pay increasing only when there was work to do, and which was funded out of the fees paid by the client. Moreover, engineers were expected to progress to freelance status before they reached the age of 30. To do so, they had to build up a reputation and portfolio of work that would enable them to pursue a more entrepreneurial career in the not too distant future. As a result, they submitted to an exhausting work regime:

> it's...24/7. You know, you feel guilty about asking for a Saturday off...in a month's time...if you were to leave a studio and go freelance you could probably earn in four days what you earn in a month as a retainer...[twelve-hour shifts] minimum...you leave home at nine and you get home at midnight, one o'clock and that's nearly every day, and if you have one day off, a Sunday, for instance, all you want to do is sleep, or do your washing. (Studio engineer, interview)

Thus, employment conditions within studios conformed to a familiar model of project-based work, found in other parts of the creative sector, of punishing overwork when studios are busy, but with little or no pay at other times (Christopherson, 2002). But, unlike in some other sectors, this resulted in relatively low salaries for engineers; in the mid-2000s the average starting salary for an engineer in central London was £12,000, which was about half national average annual earnings.

The collapse of craft union regulation brought about a casualization of training, with greater emphasis being placed on applicants' subjectivities rather than a set of formal skills. Indeed, there was a search for compliant employees with 'emotional intelligence'. One studio manager expressed a desire for what he described as 'translucent' staff: those who 'are there, but not there'. This was seen to be an important coping strategy for engineers in dealing with the often monstrous egos of artists (and some producers). When recruiting, he was looking for:

> People who have complementary personalities, and by that I mean not...sycophantic. They must be the kind of people that...are quite happy for their egos to be smashed and jumped on 50 times a day and get on with it and realize it's all part of the process of that artist [who] has to walk in and be the boss. [A]t times, yes, he [the client] is going to be goddam rude to you and the rest of it, make you feel like shit. (Studio manager, interview)

Thus, like other interactive service workers—but here over prolonged periods of time in the close proximity of a recording studio—engineers have to work out a way of balancing the conflicting needs of clients and the studio management, but also their own ego and self-esteem (cf. Leidner, 1993). Studios also look to recruit engineers who have the potential to become successful freelancers, as they may become future clients for the studio as producers/engineers, who might bring commissioned work back to the studio. In this way, studios seek to generate their own future demand through the labour market.

This era of destructive competition among recording studios ushered in during the 1980s, as the recording process incorporated software and digital technology, was mitigated for a decade by a boom in postproduction work. The advent first of CDs and then DVDs saw a marked increase in work that transferred sound from analogue master disks to digital media, which effectively masked and compensated for the more competitive market in *de novo* recording. However, from the mid-1990s onwards, clear signs of a looming economic crisis began to emerge within the recording studio sector. This was manifested in at least four ways. First, a new generation of software applications served to disrupt the recording studio sector. The large recording consoles—still for the most part supplied by SSL and Neve—were increasingly supplanted by more overtly software-based digital recording systems. The rise of systems such as Pro Tools, which was essentially a PC-based recording console, became the latest obligatory passage point for studios and necessitated another round of significant investment.[11] Although the recording rigs were considerably cheaper than the large recording consoles—at around only £30,000 per system, they were about a tenth of the price of the standard desk—their initial cost concealed significant recurring expenses in terms of software upgrades and new releases. The shift to digitally based recording also removed one important income stream for studios—the supply of tape for the recording process. Studios insisted on sourcing all their own tape and admitted placing considerable price markups upon it in costing studio time. However, direct recording to hard disk has made the use of tape superfluous. Moreover, the switch to digital recording has reduced the demand for space and time in the studio. The shift to software-enabled recording has significantly reduced the cost of entry-level equipment, which has improved the quality and capacity of home recording. This has encouraged many artists to do considerable amounts of pre-studio preparation work, which signalled a further fragmentation of project work to incorporate the space of the home or at least the home studio (Goodwin, 2006). In this regard, software and code made possible a regime of more distributed musical creativity, which represented a democratization of technology.

Second, there was a steady decline in the size of recording budgets, which reduced the volume of money circulating within the sector:

> it would be nice if you had…a budget of £100,000 to include some money for the producer in there. But we're…making albums for 20 grand…[a] lawyer was telling me this story, it was either Universal or Sony, the…recording budget was £85,000, it could never be less than that, that was written into their standard contract that they would offer all bands, £85,000, and you could argue a case for more, but you couldn't spend less. I'd be very happy with 85 grand on most projects these days. (Producer manager, interview)

Third, there was an increase in runaway production from London to cheaper locations, typically for orchestral work and film scoring, which had a disproportionate impact on the top-end studios. Traditionally, the large London studios benefited from runaway production for film score work from Los Angeles; the large Hollywood

---

[11] Pro Tools was originally released in 1991 by Digidesign based in Silicon Valley, which is now a subsidiary of Avid Technology, having been purchased in 1995.

studios negotiated deals with US entertainment unions to be able to outsource a proportion of film scoring work away from Los Angeles, which parallels the runaway production of other parts of the film-making process to places such as Vancouver (Coe, 2000a, 2000b, 2001; Scott, 2002). The relocation of film scoring work to London was a boon to the large recording studios, and provided something of a buffer to the trends mentioned. However, from the 1990s onwards there were signs of this runaway production bypassing London altogether for even cheaper locations in central Europe, such as Prague and Budapest, which were establishing their own satellite production clusters for the film and television industries more generally (Coe and Johns, 2004), but also had a strong orchestral tradition and a labour market of trained musicians familiar with the classical canon.

Fourth, studios also paid the cost of overestimating consumer demand for high-fidelity playback, and many invested heavily in equipment that would produce recordings in 5.1 format, which is suitable for home cinema 'surround sound'. However, the market for such recordings was slow to take off. Ironically, the growth in MP3 players and the use of PCs and laptops as home jukeboxes actually indicated the opposite trend and the embrace of relatively low-fidelity playback platforms. Fifth, and finally, the long-term failure of UK-based artists to break into established large markets and achieve popularity in the large US market had a negative effect on UK studios. Several informants told me that the international success of British acts between the 1960s and 1980s had beneficial effects on studios because it had positive reputational effects as international artists would be drawn back to the spaces of creativity of music they liked and admired.

5.5. CONCLUSIONS

This chapter has explored the impact of the crisis of the musical economy on the recording studio sector. Technological change is intimately bound up with the history of the industry more broadly but, as in the distribution and retail parts of the industry, software has had significant implications for the economic viability of recording studios. Indeed, software has played a significant, albeit unforeseen, role in the crisis that currently besets the recording studio sector, which is characterized by falling recording budgets, declining demand for studio space-time, deteriorating employment conditions, continuing erosion of barriers to entry, runaway production, and, increasingly, studio closures. One of the major outcomes of the crisis has been an accelerated vertical disintegration of production. This process has been under way since at least the 1970s, as the number of independent studios and equipment suppliers increased, and most record companies have either sold or closed their own studios.[12] However, the crisis deepened the process of vertical disintegration still further. Record companies devolved the responsibility—and cost—of delivering albums to management companies. Record companies scaled back their involvement in the A&R activities responsible for discovering and developing new talent as they have increasingly become brand-led marketing companies. Management companies responded to this growing reticence by becoming significant intermediaries within the musical economy and developing artists to pitch to record companies in the hope of securing long-term recording—but also significantly—marketing deals. The implications of this vertical disintegration of production served to embed the musical economy further into established musical agglomerations, which in the UK means a strengthening of the music industry's ties to London and the wider South-East region, which is now host to more institutionally diverse networks of creativity (albeit that some of these institutions have been thinned out).

The process of vertical disintegration could also be observed within the studios themselves. To cope with the dilemma of selling studio space-time in a falling market, and to respond to the ability to use smaller studio spaces to record and mix tracks, several studios created 'project rooms', small, self-contained recording spaces which studios rent on an annual basis to producers. The rooms were large enough to record all but acoustic instruments (these could be accommodated by hiring one of the studio's traditional recording spaces for the day). This strategy had the advantage of externalizing revenue risk to producers, while producers benefited by having their own studios and office within a city-based creative environment which provides the buzz (Storper and Venables, 2004) often missing from the isolation and solitude of the home studio. However, while studios externalized the risk of filling space in this way, they were unable to avoid it

---

[12] The major exception here is EMI, which retained ownership of the iconic Abbey Road studios. This relationship is examined in more detail in the next chapter.

altogether, and the turnover of producers in project rooms was high, as many found it difficult to generate sufficient work to justify the costs of the room over long periods of time.

In their efforts to survive the downturn in the musical economy, some studios considered converting the vertical disintegration of production to their advantage by utilizing their recording assets to become management companies or even production-publishing companies. Studios would use their specific assets and advantages— technology, labour, expertise, etc.—to help develop new talent and look to keep some rights to the product they sell on to record companies. However, the obstacle to such a strategy was that studios needed money to fund the identification and development of talent and, as was pointed out earlier, few recordings cover the costs of their production. That is why levels of capital concentration are so high among record companies, as they need to have deep pockets to cover the inherent riskiness of the business. Alternatively, studios could seek to exploit their buildings as part of the musical heritage, in the manner that Gibson has suggested (2005). However, in the studios I visited, this option was seen to be at odds with any attempt to maintain a working studio environment and was either not seen to be a viable option or the studios were insufficiently famous for such a strategy to be possible. In the meantime, as studios sought to work out strategies for survival in a business environment that has turned against them, recording studios continued to close in all the major musical agglomerations of the Anglo-American world, which will have important, but as yet unforeseen, implications for the geography of the musical economy.

6

A Social Experiment in the Musical Economy: Terra Firma, EMI, and Calling Creativity to Account

6.1. INTRODUCTION: ABBEY ROAD (NOT) FOR SALE

On 15 February 2010, the *Financial Times* newspaper broke the story that Abbey Road Recording Studios in North-West London were to be put up for sale by the EMI record company (Edgecliffe-Johnson and Davoudi, 2010a). It was anticipated that the sale of the property would raise as much as £30m (US$45m) for the financially troubled company. At one level, this news was hardly a surprise; the decision to sell the studios had been widely anticipated within the industry for several years, with the recording studio sector in decline (see Chapter 5), following a wave of closures that claimed some of the most iconic popular music studios.[1] The closures were part of a wider international process of contraction as a similar thinning out of institutional capacity was witnessed in other major recording centres such as New York and Los Angeles.

The rash of studio closures reflects two broader processes within the music industry that have been documented earlier in this book. First, the crisis within the musical economy caused a decline in revenues from the sale of recordings which reduced the amount of money circulating within recording centres as record labels cut

---

[1] In London, closures included Olympic Studios (where The Beatles recorded 'All You Need is Love', Procol Harum 'A Whiter Shade of Pale', and Led Zeppelin their first album); Wessex Studios (where The Clash recorded *London Calling*), as well as Mayfair and Eden Studios, both well regarded and established rock and pop studios.

the A&R budgets which pay for studio time. Second, there was a crisis of creativity, although this requires qualification; this does not mean a decline in the creativity of artists, but rather a change in the ways in which artists choose to stabilize their creativity through acts of recording. Artists no longer needed to access specialized—and expensive—socio-technical spaces such as recording studios in the ways that they once did, because so much could now be done on computer-based recording rigs using specialized software,[2] or, in the case of more established artists, using scaled-down mixing desks in home studios, marketed to clients by companies as suitable 'for your everyday creative process'.[3] As a result, studios often became places to finish recordings, to add a professional finish to raw material, where 'star' producers and/or engineers could sprinkle their 'fairy dust' to make music sound better, or to achieve acoustic effects in 'live rooms'. For recording studios that had business models based on selling time and space, developments that restricted the amount of time that artists needed to spend in studios were little short of catastrophic. Thus, studios were the victims of changes in both the consumption and production of music that have laid waste to the sector.

However, while the closure of major studios in London and elsewhere passed with barely any attention or comment, the announcement that Abbey Road was to close did catch the media's attention, at least in the UK. And the reasons for this were not hard to find. First opened in 1931, the studios were witness to historically important recordings from the likes of Edward Elgar, Pink Floyd, but most notably, of course, The Beatles, who recorded the bulk of their recorded output in Studio 2 and, short of any better ideas, named their 1969 album *Abbey Road*. The attraction of recording in the same spaces as such iconic artists remains strong, and working at the studio became a rite of passage for many acts once they achieved a certain level of success and so could afford the top-end day rates that the studio still charged for the use of its space and technology. Second, Abbey Road

---

[2] The most successful of which by far is a system known as Pro Tools.

[3] Which is the claim that Solid State Logic, a UK-based company which is the world's leading designer and manufacturer of audio consoles, makes for its compact, Matrix mixing desk (<http://www.solid-state-logic.com/music/matrix/index.asp>). These were not cheap, costing around £13,000 ($19,500), but they were a lot cheaper than the desks residing in large recording studios, new editions of which started at around £130,000 ($195,000), although many of those in use cost upwards of £250,000 ($375,000).

studios were highly unusual in that they were still owned by a record company, EMI, and it was late in its history that the complex officially changed its name from EMI Recording Studios to the more vernacular Abbey Road. As Chapter 5 revealed, recording studios were once part of vertically integrated companies and their role was to provide recording facilities for contracted artists, but from the 1950s onwards such facilities were challenged by the rise of independent studios, and in the last twenty years or so they have been sold off to the highest bidder. EMI's ownership of its own studio was very much an anachronism in the industry. Third, and finally, EMI achieved a relatively high public profile in the UK; it was the country's one remaining major record label, and the UK's music industry has tended to punch above its weight given the size of the national economy. The company tended to generate considerable coverage in the financial press, not least because the artists contracted to it brought celebrity and stardom to financial stories that would otherwise be absent (Southall, 2009). But a new interest in the company began in 2007 when EMI was purchased for £4.2bn by private equity firm Terra Firma, not least because its ownership cast doubt on the survival of both EMI and Terra Firma and, and as will be illustrated later, brought into sharp focus the rather different modes of economic calculation within the financial and musical economies.

In catching the attention of the media, the proposed sale of the studio also drew the attention of the public. Alarmed by concerns about the potential loss of a key piece of popular music heritage, and championed by broadcasters on national radio shows in the UK, the National Trust—a charity that protects and preserves historic buildings, gardens, and monuments—was petitioned to save the building for the nation. The National Trust responded enthusiastically to what it described as 'An astonishing outpouring of public emotion'[4] at the possibility of the studios being sold and perhaps closed.

---

[4] National Trust website: <http://www.nationaltrust.org.uk/main/w-global/w-news/w-latest_news/w-news-should-national-trust-save-abbey-road-studios.htm>. A spokesperson for the charity commented that 'It is not often that the public spontaneously suggests that the National Trust should acquire a famous building...However, Abbey Road Studios appears to be very dear to the nation's heart—to the extent that we will take soundings as to whether a campaign is desirable or even feasible' (Edgecliffe-Johnson and Davoudi, 2010b). A poll on the Trust's website indicated that 95 per cent of those who participated supported such a campaign, and if it had purchased Abbey Road the Trust would have added it to its stock of Beatles-related properties, having already taken into ownership two Merseyside

However, less than a week after the story broke, EMI announced that it was abandoning its plans to sell Abbey Road (Fenton, 2010). The reason for this volte-face was explained by an EMI representative who claimed that, "The scale of the outcry has brought it home to everyone what a core asset it is' (Fenton, 2010). Exactly how EMI would exploit this asset was never made clear, although hints could be found later in the statement which revealed that the company had been in discussion with potential partners that could fund renovations, with a view to 'providing access to artists and, where possible, members of the public' (quoted in Fenton, 2010). Thus, an Abbey Road 'museum with tour', to capitalize on the public's affection for the site, appeared to be on the agenda, although whether this could ever be compatible with retaining the site as a working studio was doubtful.[5]

6.2. DANCING TO THE MUSIC OF 'THE SUITS': TERRA FIRMA AS A SOCIAL EXPERIMENT IN THE MUSICAL ECONOMY

So, on the face of it, this story might appear to be something of a mere footnote, one in which a record company announces the sale of a studio one week, only to withdraw the plan the next in the face of public opposition, realizing that it has possession of a much revered asset from which they may, after all, be able to make more money from its use (albeit in a new way) rather than through its sale. Perhaps, but this episode also reveals something more about the contemporary musical economy, and the implications that it has for networks of creativity. There had long been doubts about the profitability of the Abbey Road complex, but the figures had never been separately identified within the financial returns for the company as a whole. However, in initially justifying their decision to sell Abbey Road, EMI finally revealed that

suburban houses, 20 Forthlin Road and Mendips, which were the childhood homes of Paul McCartney and John Lennon, respectively.

[5] Nor should it be assumed that The Beatles management would cooperate with EMI in the use of their image rights in any museum, as Apple Computers have found to their cost over the tortuous and protracted negotiations over the use of the Apple name and logo or being permitted to add The Beatles to the iTunes catalogue.

the studio had been losing money for years. More importantly, there was a widespread feeling within the recording community that if EMI were to give up on Abbey Road, which it apparently did, albeit just for a week, then it would signal the end of London as a major recording centre. As a former employee of Abbey Road put it:

> Imagine a property like that in the middle of St John's Wood, the tempta-tion's always there for top brass to say 'Ooh, £20 million there we could do with that this year'...Very sad because a one off injection of 20 mil-lion is almost nothing to a company like EMI, really, and it'll be gone forever...And the message it would send out to the industry it would be pretty negative I think, it would be an absolute last resort. If you saw Abbey Road for sale I think that would be [it]. (Freelance engineer, interview)

There was also a sense in the industry that if EMI decided to sell the studio then that would indicate the company was indeed in serious trouble, in that it was prepared to face the public backlash from pro-posing to sell an institution held in high affection by the general public for its role in popular music history. Discussing the possibilities of the sale of Abbey Road, another former employee commented that:

> the thing that jumped to my mind is Rolls Royce and Bentley...when that was sold to Volkswagen...you've got this great British company that has...heritage and vocation in the UK for ... many years and, I think, there is definitely an element of that with EMI and Abbey Road...there is that intertwined affection for Abbey Road as a gem...having said that...people like Terra Firma aren't going to fall for that kind of romantic rubbish. (Freelance recording consultant, interview)

Which brings us to the second reason why the abortive sale of Abbey Road is significant; it draws attention to what, thanks to Terra Firma, can be seen as something akin to *a social experiment within the musical economy*, and which throws light on the tension between economy and creativity that exists within it. In their purchase of EMI Terra Firma, like all private equity companies, were on a mission to restructure and transform a failing company in order to extract value by reselling the company at a future date. At the time of its purchase of EMI in 2007, Terra Firma had been in existence for five years, hav-ing been formed by financier Guy Hands, a Goldman Sachs alumnus, who had begun working on leveraged buyouts for Japanese bank Nomura in the 1990s. By 2007, Terra Firma had become the largest owner of property in Germany, as well as the biggest cinema operator and supplier of waste-generated energy in Europe (Wark, 2007).

Private equity is a form of financial engineering that emerged during the 1980s, which was then described as leveraged buyouts (Froud et al., 2008). Private equity firms attract funds to them from entities such as pension funds and other institutional investors with the promise of returns that are in excess of those that can be obtained through normal stock market investment. The shift to a global macroeconomic environment characterized by low inflation and low interest rates in the 1990s and 2000s—the so-called 'NICE decade' of Non-Inflationary Continuous Expansion—enabled private equity funds to attract significant volumes of money, and collectively these firms generated a compound annual growth of 18.5 per cent between 1985 and 2005 (Froud and Williams, 2007: 4). The *modus operandi* of private equity funds has been succinctly summarized by Julie Froud and Karel Williams:

> The fund is…typically invested by purchasing between 10 or 20 companies or divisions as operating businesses. The purchase…is highly leveraged so that on the standard deal of the 2000s some 70 per cent of the cost of purchase is funded by debt, which reverses the usual capital structure of a publically held firm…Each individual company would normally be disposed of by trade sale or flotation after three to five years and the fund as a whole would be wound up within seven to ten years, with capital returned as and when investments are sold.

Attempts to theoretically justify the process of private equity have been made by financial and business economists, arguing that taking companies into private ownership overcomes the so-called 'agency problem' in capitalism, where the incentives of owners and managers may become unaligned. Private equity, its supporters claim, realigns ownership with control (Froud et al., 2008).

Having bought the company, private equity firms then have to act to extract value from it so that they can meet the repayment conditions they offer to their investors. According to Froud and Williams (2007), this value can be extracted in at least three ways. First, value may be produced simply through a process that can be described as *arbitrage*, in that market conditions may change which may enable the private equity firm to sell the company for more than it was purchased. Second, value can be constructed through *financial engineering*; by loading a company with debt it may become more tax efficient, and value may be extracted simply through a reduction in the tax burden. Another common method of value extraction through financial engineering is sale and lease-back, where assets (such as property and other assets, for example) are sold to realize a capital gain and then leased back by the company for a fee that has to be paid out of revenues. The third and final process is perhaps the most difficult, and requires that private equity firms improve profit margins through *corporate restructuring* which changes product lines and/or processes, reduces labour costs, and/or improves revenues and sales.

Which of these strategies Terra Firma actually had in mind for EMI when it purchased the company in August 2007 was never entirely clear. However, almost from the moment Terra Firma took control of EMI things began to go wrong. The first challenge was the tightening of credit conditions in the period running up to the bid, followed by the breaking of the global financial crisis in 2008 and the subsequent recession. Indeed, as the credit crunch began to bite, Terra Firma's bid for EMI was reliant upon a loan from Citibank to fund the deal as money from other investors was not forthcoming (Osborne, 2007). This deal established set repayment conditions for Terra Firma that would subsequently prove highly problematic in its attempts not just to turn EMI around, but to retain ownership. The second challenge was the manner in which Terra Firma intended to extract value from EMI, a struggling company in a floundering industry. It should be emphasized that Terra Firma was not the only organization that believed that additional value could be realized through the purchase of EMI, as Terra Firma became involved in a bidding war for the company, mainly with Warner Music but also with some other private equity companies. For Warner Music, the logic of buying EMI was fairly straightforward, with traditional processes of capital centralization and concentration yielding efficiency gains through merging activities in similar markets and driving down costs by rationalizing support and administration services.[6]

Whatever Terra Firma's intended private equity strategy for EMI, the room for manoeuvre was quickly constrained by macroeconomic circumstances. Given the turmoil in financial markets, and the deterioration of economic conditions that saw all asset classes sharply

---

[6] Whether Warner Music was really in a bidding war became the subject of a legal case brought by Terra Firma against Citibank in 2010. Terra Firma argued that Citibank had exaggerated Warner's interest in EMI, to encourage them to close the deal and overbid, so drawing down more money from Citibank to fund the transaction. It also emerged that Terra Firma was holding a large amount of cash which it had raised to buy Alliance Boots but had lost out and EMI became an alternative outlet for these funds.

decline in value from the middle of 2007 onwards, it quickly became apparent that Terra Firma would not be able to extract value as a result of arbitrage; assets almost universally lost value after 2007. A sale would generate much less than was paid for it. There was scope for financial engineering, but much relied upon the ability to demonstrate that it would be possible to identify reliable income streams that could be capitalized through securitization (cf. Leyshon and Thrift, 2007). Such reliable income streams still exist in the music industry, but tend to be delivered through publishing divisions, which collect royalty income from the use of recorded music in media such as radio, television, and film (Caves, 2000: 311; Southall, 2009: 216; Vogel, 2001). This part of the business is highly amenable to securitization, given that it produces steady if unspectacular earnings. However, by purchasing the company as the financial crisis began to break, Terra Firma found that its ability to break up the business and sell off its income streams to investors was severely curtailed, and it also meant that Terra Firma was unable to unload its debt burden by selling on its loan from Citibank. Moreover, the other part of the music industry, the recorded music division, was far more problematic, given that the chances of recovering the money invested in artists has always been low—but which is compensated for the low marginal costs of reproducing the output of those artists that are successful, which cross-subsidizes the majority of the roster—while the problems of internet piracy made this even more difficult (Barfe, 2004; Jaisingh, 2007; Shiga, 2007; Johns, 2009). The difficulty of making money in this part of the business was partly due to the fickle nature of markets and taste, but also because of the problem of successfully managing the creative process. It is here that Terra Firma quickly came to the conclusion that the existing music industry business model was broken, and new ways of thinking were needed. The existing management of EMI were fired and three new executives were appointed, one of which was given the title of Director of Business Transformation (Southall, 2009).

6.3. 'GETTING TO NO'

Although it took a while for Terra Firma to announce what the new business model for EMI might actually be, this did not stop artists, their managers, and other industry commentators rushing to judgement. The broad conclusion seemed to be that the entry of a private equity company into the music industry was likely to end in disappointment; for Terra Firma, for the artists and their entourages, or, in all likelihood, just about everyone. These concerns arose due to an appraisal of where value still lay in the music industry and where a company like Terra Firma might look to extract it most easily. For a number of observers, the economically logical choice was to abandon any attempt to even try and manage the creative process and extract the maximum value out of the back catalogue and publishing. One City-based financial analyst observed that:

> It's the first time that [Hands] or a private equity company has taken on a talent business. There's always an intangible reason, but with Hands he would have looked at the publishing business and seen it almost an annuity while the recorded music he probably saw as a punt, and if the worst came to the worst he could always sell it on. (Hilton, quoted in Southall, 2009: 214)

A similar line of thought was expressed by at least two other experienced managers of popular music artists:

> you are dealing [in Terra Firma] with people purely interested in making money, and someone might just tell Guy Hands that if he goes into liquidation and sells off the catalogue in the right way and to the right people, he would suddenly find that he didn't have to pay any more royalties. That I think is the really scary thing knocking around—that they could take the record company into liquidation. (Jenner, quoted in Southall, 2009: 213)

> If Terra Firma was just thinking about making a profit, they should dump all new releases, reduce overheads to a minimum and just resell back catalogue. It wouldn't be exciting but it would be much more profitable. (Bicknell, quoted in Southall, 2009: 232)

However, not all music industry commentary on Terra Firma's foray into the field was as considered and temperate as this. The company, and in particular the figure of Guy Hands, were the target of abuse and scorn, mainly, it would seem, because there was an assumption that a company dedicated first and foremost to the production of profit and the extraction of value would be unable to create an environment that would be sufficiently supportive and nurturing of the creative process necessary for making music. Managers looked at Terra Firma's existing roster of companies under management, and drew withering comparisons: 'He's not dealing with motorway cafes in Germany or pubs.

I don't think he understands the artistic process' (Summers, quoted in Southall, 2009: 224). Other commentators, such as music journalist Neil McCormick, took a more personal line, arguing that Guy Hands' physical appearance betrayed a lack of interest in creativity:

> I don't understand how someone can have that much money and look that bad, and how a guy can be in the music business and he can't even get a decent haircut, Hands' haircut tells me that he does not trust creative people because if he can't even trust his hairdresser—who is about the least creative person he's ever going to meet—how can he trust some 20 year old artist? (Quoted in Southall, 2009: 234)[7]

EMI artists were keen to offer up their thoughts on the Terra Firma experiment. Some, such as Damon Albarn, were temperate although damning: 'I'm not sure the people who own [EMI] now are interested in [the music]. I think they love money. Money and music are not necessarily a good mix. EMI has lost some of its humanity' (quoted in Southall, 2009: 253). Others, such as Lily Allen, were simply damning: 'I hate Terra Firma. They're wankers and they don't know what they are doing' (quoted in Southall, 2009: 247).

Eventually, after digging into the EMI books and accounts, Terra Firma began to announce what their new business model might look like. Or rather, they made it clear what the business model wouldn't look like: and that was the traditional way in which record labels had managed their artists. In flat contradiction of the advice of the business book staple, *Getting to Yes* (Fisher et al., 2003), Terra Firma's new injunction to EMI management in dealing with the demands of its artists, and in particular their managers, was simply getting them to say no:

> One of the concerns voiced by the new EMI management was aimed directly at the manner in which staffers dealt with the creative community. Apparently they were concerned about an on-going tendency to agree, at all times, with the artists and managers. It seemed to the team who had taken over that in face-to-face meetings, managers and artists were told how wonderful they were by EMI contacts before later

---

[7] Hands' hair style could perhaps best be described as unkempt. McCormack was not alone in thinking that a haircut might provide an insight into how connected the person wearing it might be with the creative zeitgeist: in *The Rise of the Creative Class*, Richard Florida (2002: 76–7) reflected on the creativity of his hairdresser: 'The person who cuts my hair is a very creative stylist much in demand, and drives a new BMW...Both my hairdresser and my housekeeper have taken up their lines of work to get away from the regimentation of large organizations; both of them relish creative pursuits.' In addition, see Thrift (2008).

being stabbed in the back. The new maxim the management wanted to put in place was for their people to tell the creative community to their faces if they thought a record, a campaign or an album cover was crap. (Southall, 2009: 227)

At the same time, Terra Firma began to leak to the media some of the excesses they claimed to have found at the record company, to illustrate the kind of mismanagement they had to correct. The revelations of extravagance approaching the bacchanalian certainly suggested business practices that one might think a tad unusual and indulgent, such as the £20,000 spent on candles to decorate a Los Angeles apartment used to entertain clients, and a £200,000 annual budget for fruit and flowers (Sabbagh, 2007). However, in leaking this information, Terra Firma's forensic accountants only confirmed to music industry insiders how little they knew about its mores and practices: fruit and flowers were accounting codes for spending on prostitution and drugs, and described as such so that they could be run through the company's books as legitimate business expenses to satisfy the needs and desires of its artists, presumably to help them in their musical creativity. Undeterred, Terra Firma continued digging into the accounts and it emerged that EMI had spent over £700,000 on taxis in London alone in the year to March 2008 and that almost 90 per cent of its artists failed to return an income for the company (Southall, 2009: 250).

As a result, part of the solution for EMI was to disempower the irresponsible 'creatives', and impose financial discipline. At a financial conference in February 2008, Hands set out his approach as follows:

What we are doing is taking the power away from the A&R guys and putting it with the suits—the men who have to work out how to sell music... We had labels at EMI that were spending five times as much on marketing as their gross revenues. We told them you could stick a £50 note on the cover of a CD and have the same effect and we also wouldn't have to pay them. (Quoted in Southall, 2009: 237)

6.4. THE DEATH OF THE STUDIO AS A CREATIVE SPACE?

The fact that EMI deemed it necessary to stem the flow of money to the creative part of the business hardly boded well for the recording studio sector. Studios were already struggling before EMI turned off the tap, and it was not only studios that suffered from the new financial discipline: presumably the taxi, candle-making, vice, and narcotics industries must also have felt the pinch too. While EMI were not the only funders of creative activity within the UK musical economy, it was perhaps no coincidence that the rate of studio closure in Britain accelerated after Terra Firma's purchase of EMI, given that EMI's artist roster tended to favour UK-based artists.

In one sense, the entry of Terra Firma into the musical economy may be seen as an amplification of a tendency for it to become financialized that has developed over a number of years, with a much greater focus on profits and losses. This much is reflected in some of the observations made in interviews conducted with informants within the recorded studio sector. As one studio manager remarked:

> more and more I think the record industry is being run by accountants, it's moneymen and they just want to see profits and sales and they're not in it for the music. It used to be that record companies were people who truly loved music, truly wanted to support artists, signed artists because they thought they were great, had commitment to the artist if the artist didn't sell the first record, wasn't a huge success, they'd carry on with them...And now it's all about...the bottom line. (Studio manager, London, interview)

This same manager argued that this was having a negative impact on creativity, as successful artists responded badly to the requirement that they keep producing revenue for the company:

> they're a big cash cow so they're put under a lot of pressure to...keep on making money and I think that...when people who are artistic are pressed into doing something, they're never going to come up with the goods,...it's not a science, it's...an art form and if you feel pressurized or whatever then you're probably not going to perform as well. (Studio manager, London, interview)

These financial pressures were also reducing the amount of time artists had to be creative in studios, which have been a key part of the compositional process since at least the 1960s:

> It's really changed, it's changed radically in the time that I've been doing it...in the 80s people would probably book about three months...you might get a booking and they would be in for months and months; I'm a producer...and it took me nine months to produce, all in studio time...And that doesn't happen anymore. (Studio manager, London, interview)

The long durations of time in the studio were seen by many to be a key part of the creative process within the popular music industry:

> That's sort of partly the enjoyment of it, I think. For the artists getting into the studio to record something is just one of the things they love most, and if it takes a little bit longer, they don't mind, they're really enjoying it, and a lot are perfectionists so they want to make it even better all the time, until someone kicks them out . . . But if you're making an album, you know, it's a big creative deal. (Director, technology manufacturer, Oxfordshire, interview)

However, in all this, one has to guard against a kind of romantic nostalgia, and the assumption that long-term bookings of studio time are necessary for creative and commercial success. As some participants in the studio sector observed, some artists and their managers deliberately obfuscated the nature of the creative process which enabled them to extract more money than was really needed from their record companies for acts of creativity:

> I think some people took advantage of the fact that record companies didn't really [understand], it was a black art as far as the up and coming [bands] were concerned and they just let them get on with it. I think they understand how it is now . . . record companies don't mind if U2 take a long time, or Coldplay take a long time making their record, because it's their money now. [But] when it's 'Baby Band' who hasn't sold a record it can't take long! And theoretically they should have the energy and the drive and the ambition and whatever to crack it down pretty sharpish. (Producer/manager, London, interview)

Moreover, studio managers and engineers who are required to serve studios during long and incessant sessions were also quick to puncture the romantic myth that having large expanses of time for acts of creativity is strictly necessary or indeed helpful:

> I did work in post-production for a couple of years at the end of my career, where it is completely different: 'We've got to get this done in the next two hours and then we're on to something else', and the whole attitude to doing work is completely different. (Director, technology manufacturer, Oxfordshire, interview)

> I suppose people are aware that there's only so many hours in the day and thereafter they're being charged extra, but it never ceases to amaze me how much faffing goes on and the fact that people will be in the studio for god knows how long and they don't really achieve that much at the end of the day. I mean, why do they work such ridiculous days? . . . on

band sessions it's always a 12 hour day minimum...I don't know why they don't start work at 10, finish about 7, I'm sure they'd get just as much done if they concentrated a little bit harder during that time, but no. (Studio manager, London, interview)

...if you get the sound right then I think it's really *boring* because you might sit there 12 hours doing one song and the bloke can't play it properly. And then you've got to sit there for another 12 hours while he puts his vocal on and he can't sing it properly. It's such a *boring* job; it's why I could never do it very much because it's so *boring*. And the engineers I know can't do it, film and sort of orchestral engineers can't stand sitting—even [with] the best band in the world, they fall asleep. (Studio manager/producer/engineer, London, interview; emphasis added)

6.5. DISCUSSION

In light of comments such as these, if the new frugalities of the musical economy are making the use of time in studios more urgent, and through necessity driving much other activity into bedrooms and home studios, then this may not necessarily be seen as altogether a bad thing, although it has had a negative impact on the careers and livelihoods of those working in a support function within networks of creativity within the musical economy. The criticisms aimed at Terra Firma by artists and their managers conform to what Thomas Osborne has identified as an uncritical and unexamined doctrine of creativity, where creative work is seen in essence to be an 'heroic affair' (2003: 519; original emphasis). The relentless focus on the bottom line by companies such as EMI and Terra Firma was implicitly assumed within the industry to be philistine, refusing to fund the time and resources that artists need to be creative. However, as Osborne (2003: 516) has argued, it might be preferable for 'the description of what is creative...[to] await the onset of the [product] itself not its concept'. Despite its problems, there would seem to be little evidence to suggest the changes in the musical economy have meant that it has become less creative or that the flow of new music has been held up. Indeed, quite the contrary; due to the democratization of recording technologies and of the means of distribution through the internet, artists are no longer so reliant on the traditional institutions of the music industry to be productive. Certainly, aspiring artists need to become more resourceful, and of necessity to embrace a more expanded and diverse understanding of economy than what would otherwise be defined simply by wage labour for capitalist firms like EMI and Terra Firma (Gibson-Graham, 2006) (see Chapter 7).

During one interview with a leading Los Angeles-based record company executive about how his company might transform its business model to deal with the problems of internet piracy, my informant became exasperated with my line of questioning: the music industry, he said, 'was never meant to be a big business. If I was in business to be in business I wouldn't be in this business' (Senior VP for New Media, Global Records, interview). Indeed, the growth in revenues enjoyed by the industry between the early 1980s and the late 1990s meant that during this period record company executives could afford to be a little blasé about any marginal gains or losses that might accrue from changes in business practices and processes. By purging EMI of executives such as this, Terra Firma was actually on the way to establishing a sustainable business model within the musical economy, because it was actually turning around EMI's financial position. By reducing the funds that it disbursed into the musical economy and laying off around 20 per cent of its workforce EMI took £200m per annum out of its cost base (Reece, 2010). This dramatically improved parts of the balance sheet; in the year to March 2009, EMI's recorded music division recorded an operating profit of over £160m, which was predicted to rise to over £200m by the end of March 2010, outperforming rivals such as Sony BMG and Warner Music. Unfortunately, interest costs in 2008–9 were £223m, and overall costs, including value write-downs, totalled more than £1bn, so that the organization lost £1.75bn as a whole for that financial year (Cardew and Williams, 2010). As a result, it became increasingly clear that Terra Firma was unlikely to benefit from its paring down of the music industry business model.

6.6. CODA

On 11 November 2011, one day short of the eightieth anniversary of the opening of the EMI Recording Studios, EMI was sold by Citicorp for £2.6bn. The bank had taken control of the company from Terra Firma in February that year after it had failed to make repayments on the loan provided to buy EMI in 2007. Citibank thereafter wrote down its loans to the company from £3.4bn to £1.2bn, and as a result anticipated at least breaking even and perhaps even profiting from the sale. The publishing division was to be sold to Sony for £1.4bn, while the recorded music division was to be sold to Universal Music for £1.2bn, pending competition law approval. To make the deal financially viable, Universal announced that it would be making divestments of around €500m. However, the Abbey Studio complex would not be part of this. Speaking during a Vivendi conference call to financial analysts on 11 November 2011, Universal Music Group chairman and CEO Lucian Grainge commented: 'It's very much our intention to keep the Abbey Road studios. It is a symbol of EMI, it is a symbol of British culture. I think it's a symbol for the creative community about exactly what the company is, and I think it's very important that we are also part of it.' However, this will in all likelihood only be until financial conditions in the music industry deteriorate to the point that it isn't, and it will be back on the market and the cycle will begin again.

7

Afterword

As I was completing this book I was intrigued by an interview undertaken by the music journalist Alex Petridis with members of a new and relatively obscure UK band called Hookworms on the release of their first album.[1] Amid the usual music interview staples such as how the band formed, the nature of their musical style, and their main influences, the discussion moved on to the band's relationship with the recording industry. More specifically, Petridis was keen to explore why it was that the band seemed to be embarking on a professional career without a recording contract which, in the past, would have been an essential staging point for musicians, given the cost of funding studio time and the investment required to pay for promoting, marketing, and advertising recorded output. One member of the band, who also held down a day job as an engineer in a recording studio, pointed out that their rejection of the traditional path was influenced by his first-hand experience of witnessing just how rapidly new bands were cycled through his studio by record labels, only to be then discarded within a short period of time, the reasons for which, having got this far into the book, should by now be well known:

> Bands get picked up really quick[ly], make an average record and get dumped just as quick[ly], and [then] they're really jaded. And I didn't really want that to happen to us because I enjoy playing music with everyone [in the band].[2]

The increasingly precarious and volatile nature of recording contracts, combined with the fact that the members of Hookworms

---

[1] *Guardian*, Music Weekly, 4 Apr. 2013, <http://www.guardian.co.uk/music/audio/2013/apr/04/music-weekly-hookworms-charli-xcx>.
[2] *Guardian*, 4 Apr. 2013.

enjoyed some economic security from the regular income they received from their 'day jobs', had clearly prompted them to temper any unrealistic ambitions of seeing music as a route to untold riches, and to turn down offers from record companies that would have provided (recoupable) advances to secure their services:

> We've all got jobs and fairly comfortable with our lives as they are. We don't have any interest in being aspirational rock musicians. We're happy... two of us work in schools, so we kind of tour in [the school] holidays, we're just really not that interested in it. We play music because we enjoy it. And I think people say that a lot, and so it's gonna [*sic*] sound clichéd for me to say it, but it is genuine.

To which, Petridis responded sympathetically, asking rhetorically, 'When did becoming a member of a band mean earning a deposit for a mortgage?'

However, Petridis' attempt to draw a division between art, musical integrity, and the intrinsic value of music on the one hand and commerce, financial literacy, and extrinsic motivations on the other, and his implicit placing of Hookworms firmly on the art/musical integrity side of this dichotomy, may, in fact, have been somewhat wide of the mark. While the members of Hookworms may have rejected the traditional route to a remunerative career by passing up the chance to sign a record contract, given the nature of the musical economy as they encountered it, a do-it-yourself strategy might actually have been one that made for a longer term and more secure professional career in music. The fact that one of their members was a recording engineer was clearly advantageous in this strategy, and meant that the band had ready access not only to professional recording equipment but also to his expertise and knowledge of using different recording and production techniques. Moreover, the band recognized the value of live performance as a means to producing, or at least supplementing, an income. Later in the interview another member of the band commented on the traditional use of the word 'gig' to refer to paid work of *any* kind: in that sense they saw live performance as a form of paid employment that could deliver additional earnings that would enable them to carry on as a band while supplementing the income from their non-musical careers. In this sense, the band aligned itself with the broader changes in the industry, which had shifted in favour of live performance. Thus, rather than take the speculative route to success that might be achieved through a recording contract, where the chances of being successful over a long period of time are low, as indicated by the high turnover of artists on the rosters of record companies, the band chose to embark upon a steadier and low-key approach to career development that was more reliant upon performance.

I found this vignette fascinating, because it gave a further insight into just how far the received understanding of how a sustainable career might be pursued in the music industry had changed as a result of it being reformatted by software. Thus, the way in which Hookworms set out on their career, and in particular their rejection of a record contract, should not necessarily be interpreted as indicating a lack of ambition. Rather, it might be better seen as realistic and pragmatic. Indeed, it strongly echoes the argument developed in Chapter 4 which predicted the end of the highly bifurcated career trajectory produced by the traditional music industry, in which a relatively small group of fabulously wealthy professional musicians are surrounded by a much larger group of lower paid and/or indebted counterparts, who are either on the verge of being released from their record label contracts because they have failed to recoup their advances due to poor sales, or already have been released. Bands such as Hookworms were emblematic of the rise of an intermediate stratum of professional musician where music is fitted around other sources of employment to which professional musicianship is an addition or supplement. That artists still cleave to the traditional model is clear from the observations of Hookworms' recording engineer of how rapidly bands transited through both his studio and recording contracts, but his own band's recourse to a career path in which performance is central has, necessarily, become increasingly common.

Hookworms and artists like them embody an important transformation in the received understanding of the music industry business model. When sales and profits of recorded music were high, live performance was a means of promoting new recordings. However, as revenues from record sales declined, so the industry began to reconsider live performance. As Frith (2007: 5) has argued:

> The conventional argument in rock analysis has been that live concerts exist courtesy of the record industry: their function is to promote records, to which they are subordinate (and for which purpose they are subsidised). But this argument no longer seems valid.

Indeed, income from live performance has surpassed that of recorded music since at least 2008 in the UK (Table 7.1), and since at least 2010

Table 7.1. UK music industry income, 2008–2011 (£million)

	2008	2009	2010	2011
Recorded	1309 (49%)	1343 (46%)	1151 (45%)	1112 (40%)
Live	1391 (51%)	1589 (54%)	1418 (55%)	1624 (60%)
	2700 (100%)	2932 (100%)	2569 (100%)	2736 (100%)

Source: PRS, 2008, 2009, 2010, 2011.

globally (PwC, 2013). For many artists recorded music increasingly became a way of promoting live performance. This itself is being further encouraged by developments in the live music production process, where elements from recorded performances are blended into the live mix through the use of digital inserts, or 'stems' (Gander, 2011). This not only improved the sound quality of live performance but also blurred the boundary between live and recorded music performances. It is no doubt for all these reasons that many artists chose to simply give music away as free downloads on their websites or as podcast downloads provided by radio stations.[3]

Mathew David (2010) claims that this 'shift back' to performance and the inversion of the traditional model only really disadvantages the capital-intensive part of the music *industry*, and not the production of *music* in total. The traditional music industry business model was configured in ways that required significant volumes of capital investment for acts of creativity to reach their market. Money was required for artist development, but in particular the costs of recording, marketing, and distribution. However, as software reformatted the music industry, so that music could be both made and moved for a fraction of its previous cost, and the role of record companies became ever more problematic, bringing into question their role and why artists would ever consider signing away the rights to so much of their potential earnings. As David suggests, the record contract is a legal arrangement that has been designed to strongly favour capital over labour, partly in order to ensure that the investments made in networks of production are recovered:

[3] Such as e.g. the daily free downloads provided by US radio stations, KCRW and KEXP.

why [would] any musician or band... sign a contract with a record company. If the signature on a deal requires that you hand over eighty-five
per cent of the sale value of your recorded music to that company, while
undertaking to cover the cost of your production and promotion from
the remaining few per cent, in addition to paying the cost of management and lawyers and others from such royalties—and this tends to
leave you in debt to the very company that is taking such a large percentage, while you struggle to make a basic living —why would anyone
pick up the pen? (David, 2010: 130)

As Passman (2012) points out, the structure of traditional recording
contracts means that even records that sell in high volumes generate
relatively meagre financial returns for artists, representing only a relatively small share of gross sales. According to Passman's calculations, an
album that sold 500,000 copies at wholesale price of $9 would generate
gross earnings of $4,500,000. However, on a typical 14 per cent roy-
alty rate, from which the costs of recording, promotion, video, and tour
support were also usually subtracted, only $170,250 would be paid in
income to the artists (or, in other words, less than 4 per cent of the gross
income) (Passman, 2012: 101–12). Record companies continue to insist that 'Talent needs capital investment to reach its potential' and that
as such capital investment 'is an essential part of the creative process'
(David, 2010: 131). However, while capital investment is clearly still important, given that popular music requires instruments and recording
equipment, the costs of the latter in particular have fallen markedly
over time, thanks largely to software, so that the requirement for large
investments is much less important than it was. And while the growth
of live performance as a way of making money has been a welcome re-
lief for the industry as a whole, this form of income generation has been
perennially an important source of income for musicians, and one that
traditionally 'has benefitted artists more significantly than any loss in
what were likely to be trivial royalties' (David, 2010: 143).

As the balance of earnings has shifted towards live performance,
one of the arguments developed earlier in the book does seem to
be moving into view; in a world where recorded music has become cheaper or even costless for many consumers of music, what
becomes revalued and considered worth paying for is the unrepeat-
able, embodied, affect-rich, place-based experience of performance.
Live performance has been revalued (Connolly and Kruger, 2005;
Krueger, 2005). In his analysis of the rapid growth in ticket prices for
live performance in the US after 1997, Krueger attributes the largest

causal factor to the 'Bowie theory', referring to an interview David Bowie gave in the early 2000s in which he accurately predicted a transformation in the ways in which artists would have to generate revenue, arguing that in the near future music was to become akin to a utility like water or electricity and that artists should 'be prepared for doing a lot of touring because that's really the only unique situation that's going to be left' (David Bowie, interview with Pareles, in Krueger, 2005: 26). In particular, Krueger argues that in the past record sales and concerts were complementary products, with the former more important than the latter, so concert prices were kept down in order not to jeopardize record sales. However, as record sales have declined in importance, 'artists and their managers do not…feel as constrained when they set concert prices' (2005: 26). So not only have ticket prices increased but there has been a marked growth in the opportunity to see live acts, which is demonstrated most strongly by the size of the festival circuit (Frith, 2007). For example, in the summer of 2013, there were over 160 popular music festivals in the UK (Figure 7.1), and a further seventy organized in mainland Europe.

The growth of live performance has reinvigorated those parts of networks of creativity that are associated with it, with the growth of rehearsal and performance spaces, and cities like London have become key points in the emergence of a global live performance industry (Garrahan, 2013). The growing importance of live music has been accompanied by the growth of increasingly powerful institutions that were once focused exclusively on the organization and administration of live events, but which have now expanded into areas formerly the preserve of record labels. For example, Live Nation Entertainment, a Los Angeles based concert promoter, used the growing importance of live revenues to sign deals with artists that not only included securing exclusive rights over the promotion of live performances but also recording contract deals, enabling promoters to extend their influence into new areas of the music industry value chain. As David (2010: 153) argues, the logic of artists signing with promoters rather than record labels is also a product of the shift of revenues away from recorded music and towards performance:

> Why sign over a share of performance rights to a recording company which cannot secure its profits by what it allegedly does best, when you might rather sign over a proportion of your recording rights to a live performance promoter who can at least make their side of the business pay?

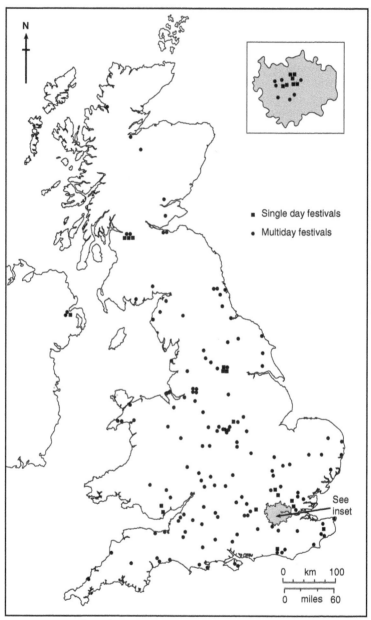

Fig. 7.1. Festivals in the UK, 2013.

The rise of new competitors such as Live Nation has compounded the problems faced by the traditional institutional anchors of networks of creativity, record companies. As Chapter 6 illustrated through the example of EMI, record companies have fared badly in the new musical economy. While the demise of EMI as an independent company has reduced competition, the steady decline in sales of physical product has reduced the power and capacity of the four remaining large recording companies. For not only have such companies lost sales to file sharing, even the emergence of new legitimate forms of digital music distribution has led to lower rates of royalty payment than hitherto. Thus, as outlined in Chapters 2 and 3, the hesitation within the industry during the 1990s in the face of the emergence of MP3 allowed new competitors to develop business models that enabled the holders of intellectual property rights to earn income on their copyrights, but in ways that began to make the royalty rate returned to record labels more problematic. This was a notoriously complicated and byzantine part of the traditional music industry at best, and the advent of new music formats presents an opportunity for record companies and artists to engage in struggle over the appropriate rate of return on intellectual property rights (Passman, 2012). While existing CD royalty rate agreements were more or less adopted for digital downloads, the advent of streaming services—such as Spotify, Deezer, Last.fm, etc.—resulted in a reduction in effective royalty rates, as income is paid as a proportion of subscription or advertising revenue. Spotify, for example, reportedly pays 0.4 pence per stream and has been criticized by a series of artists for being more appropriate to topping up the incomes of already established artists rather than cultivating the careers of emerging talent (Mance, 2013).[4] However, while record companies have sought to maintain their share of intellectual property income flowing from such services—not least by taking ownership shares in such companies as a hedging-cum-diversification strategy—there is at least evidence that they have sought to inflate their share of their income at the expense of their artists, prompting

---

[4] Indeed, some established artists refused to allow their material to be available on the streaming service, Spotify, in protest against the meagre royalty rates paid. Nigel Godrich, the highly successful producer of Radiohead and member of band Atoms for Peace, claimed in an interview with Harriet Gibsone (2013) that current streaming models were 'a land grab being carried out by "the same people who sold you your record collection again for £20 on CD" (i.e. major labels who have bought up shares in services such as Spotify)'.

some performers to take legal action against their record companies for the reduced payment terms being offered on electronic transmission income (Passman, 2012).

The continued financial difficulties faced by record companies, and their greater sensitivity to costs and tendency towards parsimony on the length and terms of contracts, as well as concerns about the revenue models of streaming services like Spotify, mean that other economic actors have emerged as increasingly important within networks of creativity, to provide the money and knowledge that enables new acts to become established. Thus, as was argued in Chapter 5, artist management companies have increasing taken on A&R roles formerly provided by record companies, supplying the initial capital to allow artists to develop before they sign a record contract.[5] The internet's ability to mobilize 'long tails' (Anderson, 2006) has been put to use through the rise of a series of new crowd sourcing solutions to the funding of musical creativity, such as Sellaband and Kickstarter. Both sites seek to mobilize the interest and passion of fans of artists to supply the capital investment needed to allow creative projects to unfold. Sellaband and Kickstarter differ in the ways in which they frame the motivations of fans and followers in their contributions to the start-up fund.

Sellaband, which began in Amsterdam in 2006, used crowd funding, making it possible for funders to act more as investors in the manner of A&R departments at record companies, spotting and helping to facilitate talent development. Investors were also able to take a profit share in the output of projects if such terms were offered by the artist in their funding appeal. Unlike Kickstarter, which takes an open approach to artists' creativity, Sellaband is focused on music and the usual project aim was to raise the funds required to record an album. By 2013 more than eighty artists or acts had had their recording projects funded by fans through this method. As a result, over US$4m had been invested in the development of new bands, while existing artists also used the crowd funding capacity of the site, including Public Enemy, which raised US$75,000 to fund the recording of a new album in 2010.

---

[5] Indeed, so successful have some management companies been in exploiting new revenue streams for artists that some record companies have even considered reversing the trend towards vertical disintegration by reabsorbing artist management within their activities (Wadsworth with Forde, 2011: 6).

Kickstarter, established in New York in 2009, and which expanded its operations into the UK in 2012, allowed artists of all kinds to make appeals for money to fund their 'projects', with the donor's reward being the successful completion of a project to which supporters were committed or at least interested in seeing bear fruit and even— although this is not obligatory—obtaining a copy of the output of the project or, in the case of performance art, for example, participation in it. An examination of the music section of Kickstarter quickly establishes that the kinds of activities for which artists are appealing for funding are those formerly undertaken by record companies across all the four musical networks. These include the recording, mixing, and mastering of new songs, album artwork design, the manufacturing and printing of CDs, promotion and publicity, and website design. The amount of money requested varies, from relatively modest amounts to levels of investment that even record companies at the height of their financial powers may have hesitated to approve. For example, a former member of the band Dresden Dolls, Amanda Palmer, used Kickstarter in a bid to raise $100,000 so that she could record her first solo album (Lindvall, 2012). However, although the appeal period for all artists is strictly limited—if artists do not raise the target fund in a maximum of 60 days all investments are returned to supporters—Palmer managed to earn more than ten times her target figure, generating a total fund of $1.2million. The ability of artists like Palmer to leverage the affect and loyalty of fans into investment capital was particularly impressive given that she was seen as having only a relatively narrow market appeal. However, she successfully monetized the demand for fans to experience unique and distinctive performances:

> Her previous album only sold about 36,000 copies and she tours small clubs and theatres. The money Palmer raised on Kickstarter came from 24,883 fans who pledged anything from $1 for a download of the album (4,744 pledgers) to $10,000 or more for an 'art-sitting' and dinner with her (bought by two fans). Many tiers focused on her attending house parties, tickets for exhibition openings, custom painted turntables or her art book, while the music itself was the lowest pledge tier. (Lindvall, 2012)

The funding was used to record the album, which sold enough copies in its first week to make the Billboard Top 10. Helpfully, as Lindvall points out, Palmer provided a detailed breakdown to her supporters of how the $1.2m was to be divested:

She said she would use $250,000 to 'pay off the lovely debt—stacks of bills and loans and the like—associated with readying all of the stuff that had to happen before I brought this project to Kickstarter'. She also cited $105,000 for '7,000+ high-end CD books & thank you cards', $80,000 for art books, $15,000 to $20,000 for the visual artists, $150,000 for her manager, lawyer and other staff, $80,000 for music videos, $75,000 to $100,000 for Kickstarter and Amazon's credit card processing, and so on. 'If we keep our expenses down, and keep the tour pretty practical and the video budget way down, I could probably put $100k of this in the bank personally, which would be great,' she wrote—although she said she would be equally happy if she broke even as it would show her model can work. (Lindvall, 2012)

Palmer's use of Kickstarter was a good illustration of what Hracs et al. (2013) have identified as a turn to exclusivity by artists in response to the 'dilemma of democratization'. Digital technology has lowered barriers to entry in the creative industries, with the consequence that the market has filled up, making it difficult for individual producers to make a living from their output.

This move to crowd sourcing and pursuit of a more independent career was prefigured by one of the studio managers I interviewed, who noticed the change in the focus of artists and bands as they responded to the gradual withdrawal of record labels from the micro-management of careers:

I have to say I'm very impressed by a lot of the young musicians who come in here, how...serious they are about what they do; this isn't a joke, this is not something they're doing for fun, they're doing it because they really want to do it and they want to be successful and they want to make a good record...if you start a band now you've got to be proficient at website design, you've got to know about setting up a fan club and fan bases...when bands are here they're on [the internet] all the time, they're looking at their website, they're answering questions for people, you know. Nowadays if you're going to make a living out of being in a band...you've got to get out there, you've got to play, you've got to earn money in lots of different ways, merchandising, websites, this is the new world we live in...And they're savvy to that and they're getting on with it. Endlessly I'm coming down here [to the studio] and I find they're having meetings, discussing 'how we're going to do this', 'how we're going to do that'. But I think you've *got* to be like that now...(Interview, studio manager/owner)

This respondent later compared new bands to small businesses, as they required a higher degree of organizational capability and planning than was the case when artists were more dependent upon the guidance and direction provided by record labels. To be successful in such an environment, artists required the traditional combinations of talent and drive, but also entrepreneurial ability and a way of sustaining themselves through periods when income is liable to be minimal, volatile, or indeed both.

But, as Hracs and his colleagues have noted through their research into the musical economy in Canada, while operating outside the traditional record label model is now the norm—95 per cent of Canadian musicians are not associated with major or independent record companies (Hracs and Leslie, 2013)—developing a career is both time-consuming and precarious (Hracs, 2012a, 2012b; Hracs et al., 2011, 2013). While the idea of operating outside the control of a record company was appealing for many artists, in that they were offered artistic freedom, it also meant a collapse of the traditional division of labour which saw musicians take on series of non-creative roles that otherwise would not get done. This sometimes resulted in self-exploitation, as artists sought to 'outwork the competition' (Hracs, 2012b: 17), or suboptimal decision-making because among musicians there tended to be 'an abundance of creative capacity' but also 'a general lack of business skills' (Hracs, 2012b: 15). It was for this reason that, as observed in the case of London and the South-East of England in Chapter 4, management companies were increasingly being sought out by musicians to provide the organization and coordination functions to artists that were formerly the preserve of large record companies. And, as in the UK, this reconfiguration of the musical economy in Canada had similar agglomerative tendencies: management companies could only operate effectively through realizing economies of scale and scope, by taking on large numbers of clients within large Canadian urban agglomerations like Toronto, Montreal, and Vancouver (Hracs et al., 2011; Hracs, 2012b).

One of the key reasons that artists in Hrac's sample felt the need to hire managerial services was the amount of time they needed to dedicate to non-creative activities, which in turn reduced the amount of time spent on creative tasks, including composing, rehearsing, and performing. This was problematic not only because many musicians were holding down other jobs to supplement the income they earned from music, but also as securing sufficient live performances was increasingly complex and time-consuming, not least because the competition between acts had intensified. Thus, although live performance had become more important as a source of income within the musical economy, the share of total income enjoyed by musicians was in decline. According to Hracs et al. (2011), musicians in Toronto saw their annual incomes fall by over a quarter between 2001 and 2006 alone.

This more competitive market for performance, which is a logical outcome of the shift in revenues towards live performance and away from recordings, tempers the more enthusiastic embrace of this transformation in the musical economy by commentators such as David (2010). Live performance may produce more earnings than royalties for most musicians over time; it is just that those earnings are, on average, quite low.[6] In this light, the traditional music industry recording contract at least had the merit of providing a guaranteed income to artists over a fixed period of time, through the advance, which in the majority of cases was non-returnable to the record company, even if sales did not cover (recoup) the value of this investment (Passman, 2012). Given that even before the music industry crisis over 90 per cent of acts did not recoup the investment made in them, it is perhaps not surprising that deals were structured so strongly in favour of copyright holders, because the small proportion of acts that did recover their investment were supporting the majority of acts that did not. In this sense, the recording industry provided a financial platform that supported *all* the acts on its roster, albeit for fixed periods of time. This form of pooling equilibrium operated well enough in an environment characterized by high levels of information asymmetry, where unpredictability was a chronic state of affairs, and which precluded 'picking winners'. However, gaining access to this form of financial support is now both more difficult and more short-term, as rosters have shrunk and are turned over more quickly. To be sure, record labels are still the most important source of investment in the musical economy, which in the UK in 2010 was estimated to be annually around £200m per year for recording budgets and £170m for marketing and promotion (Wadsworth with Forde, 2011: 30). However,

---

[6] Although, here too, the traditional hierarchies of the musical economy persist, so earning power varies. Neil McCormack argues that genuinely superstar acts such as Paul McCartney can charge up to £4m per festival appearance. Headline acts for the (normally) annual Glastonbury festival in the UK are generally paid £200,000. An indication of the earning power of live performance for such acts is indicated by the fact that the Rolling Stones Bigger Bang tour in the late 2000s generated gross earnings of £558m, surpassed only by that of U2's 360 Degree tour, which grossed $736m (McCormack, 2013).

these budgets were much reduced compared to those available at the dawn of the 2000s. In this new environment, emerging artists need to be more resourceful and be able to mobilize whatever social, cultural, and financial assets they have to hand, and which is why the burdens of entrepreneurialism and management have fallen upon them.

And it is here that it is interesting to refer to commentary that, in the UK at least, has claimed that the popular music industry has increasingly become dominated by artists who had been privately educated. Writing in the magazine *Word*, Simon Price (2010) argued that a comparison of the backgrounds of the British artists with records in the Top 40 during the same week in 1990 and 2010 revealed the growing influence of fee-paying schools. Drawing on some admittedly flimsy research, that seemed to mainly consist of Google and Wikipedia searches, Price argued that in 1990 only one of the twenty-one UK acts in the charts was privately educated (5 per cent), compared to seven out of seventeen in 2010 (41 per cent). Price was suggesting that a private education was becoming as much an advantage in the musical economy as it clearly was in gaining access to elite universities and to graduate careers in the private and state sectors. Given the rudimentary nature of the research undertaken by Price, which was mainly undertaken as fodder for a fairly inflammatory and intemperate article on class, his argument might be easily dismissed. Far more careful research on this matter conducted by the Sutton Trust (2012) explored the educational backgrounds of over 8,000 people in leading positions and revealed that only the Police Service had a lower proportion of leading practitioners that had been independently educated (13 per cent) than did the category of Pop Music (19 per cent) (Table 7.2). Given that only 7 per cent of the UK population is privately educated it would seem that even in popular music an independent education makes a difference (although Pop Music did have the highest proportion of profession leaders with a state school background). The domination of the professions by privately educated individuals is normally explained by the ability of such schools to generate higher examination results, all other things being equal, which helps individuals obtain access to the best universities and the highest possible academic credentials. But why would there be a similar bias towards private education in a field that, on the face of it, would appear to be democratic, meritocratic, and open, based on talent and creativity, where the skills and techniques required can be self-taught or obtained for relatively low levels of investment?

Table 7.2. Schools attended by leading people in each profession, UK, 2012: five professions with lowest percentage with independent school background

Profession	Type of School				
	Independent	Direct Grant	Grammar	Other (state)	Number
Police	13	3	57	27	60
Pop Music	19	3	24	54	408
Sport	26	3	18	53	613
Education	34	11	46	9	302
Science	34	12	43	11	203
All professions	45	8	27	21	8,503

Source: Sutton Trust, 2012.

In the immediate reaction to Price's article, one explanation proffered by those on the right of the political spectrum was to blame the demise of the successful state-educated musician on the comprehensive education system, and the lack of investment in music. For example, the *Daily Mail* enthusiastically picked on Price's report to reveal the school backgrounds of a host of privately educated artists, while arguing that investment in music provision by the local authorities that controlled school funding had declined by 50 per cent since 1990, and that some schools spent as little as £1.15 per child per annum on music (Thomas, 2010). While it is impossible to dismiss this as a discriminating factor, nor that private schools because of their greater resources are able to give those with musical talent greater support and opportunity to fulfil their potential, the disproportionate success of privately educated musicians may have less to do with educational opportunity and academic credentials than to do with uneven access to, and possession of, reserves of social and cultural capital. As the large record companies have withdrawn from the development of talent and as the welfare role they played has reduced, so artists have to be more resourceful both in spotting opportunity and being able to survive on relatively little money as they establish their careers. This is more likely where artists come from backgrounds where there are plentiful reserves of social, cultural, *and* financial capital, so that advice and support can be offered at appropriate times and occasions.

And here we can see the dialectical process that Angela McRobbie identified as emerging more generally within the cultural industries, which consists of an intensification of individualization within the context of a greater reliance on and the importance of network sociality. Record companies have reduced the extent to which they subsidize creativity by cutting the number of recording contracts which support artists through the advance. This, in Britain at least, followed the earlier withdrawal of state support for creativity which had been established in the 1980s through the Enterprise Allowance scheme, which paid a guaranteed income to unemployed people who set up their own business.[7] Such an environment, McRobbie argued, favours those who practise what she describes as a 'kind of middle class "ducking and diving"' (2002: 525), where well educated individuals, skilled in the art and practice of working networks, are able to mobilize their social and cultural capital in an environment where 'the individual becomes his or her own enterprise' (2002: 519). This is perhaps why private education is important here, because not only are individuals from such backgrounds more likely to be able to access financial resources to fall back on in times of hardship—significant amounts of disposable income were mobilized to enable them to opt out of the state system in the first place after all—but such schools are particularly good at getting their students admitted to leading universities:

> Universities and colleges become key sites for developing the social skills for the network... so, for the 45% of young people who at present do not enjoy three years of higher education, this is a further absence of opportunity... It is also unlikely that... mature students who are concentrated in poorer universities are in the position to immerse themselves in the hedonistic and expensive culture of networking. (McRobbie, 2002: 526–7)

This ability to network and to pursue an entrepreneurial project of the self will no doubt become increasingly important as the musical economy continues to change and be reformatted by the socio-technical changes that have ripped through it since the 1990s. The music industry has always been complex and transactional in nature, but the industry has been made more complex still as incumbents and new entrants experiment with new business models and ways of making a living, meaning that it is a difficult terrain to navigate successfully (Wadsworth and Forde, 2011). Thus, it should come

---

[7] Although in early 2013 the government introduced a facsimile of this scheme, called New Enterprise Allowance, that would pay £65 per week for thirteen weeks, and then £33 per week for a further twenty-three weeks, plus access to a loan to cover start-up costs.

as no surprise to learn that the band that I used at the start of this chapter to illustrate an alternative route through the musical economy formed while the majority of the band members were at university in Leeds, and now combine careers in secondary education in the city in tandem with their musical careers.[8]

It is interesting in this regard that one of the leading gurus of creativity in place, Richard Florida, has recently begun to publish work on the geography of the musical economy as part of his on-going project on the rise of the creative class (Florida, 2013; Florida and Jackson, 2010; Florida et al., 2010; cf. Florida, 2002). This work provides some empirical evidence to support the arguments made earlier in the book that the reformatting of the musical economy has led to the consolidation of existing musical centres like New York and Los Angeles, albeit identifying signs of new musical scenes in relatively remote locations in the US Midwest (Florida and Jackson, 2010; cf. Zook, 2005). Like Attali before him (see Chapter 2), Florida clearly believes that musical creativity is a kind of bellwether for broader social, economic, and political forces, and as Jamie Peck (2005) points out, in a piece Florida wrote for popular magazine *Washington Monthly*, he referred positively to what he described as the 'Eminem economy', one based on the kind of spontaneous creativity that emerges from low-income and socially disadvantaged urban areas of cities, which can generate unexpected and highly lucrative social and economic trajectories. But, as Peck points out, while encouraging such creativity through urban policy is all very well, it would still have to go a long way to counteract the way in which life chances are conferred upon those from more privileged backgrounds—even in what might appear to be an open and merito-cratic field such as music—who have the time and space to express their creativity that may not necessarily be available to those who are more concerned about how they might survive in an era where both money and welfare are in short supply. And in that sense, at least, the musical economy may indeed be seen as a bellwether, in that while artists are free to pursue a life of musical creativity if they so desire, at a time when their ability to produce music is more affordable than ever before, with a decline in the real cost of technology to erode craft skills that were normally the preserve of technical experts, the

---

[8] Hookworms, personal communication, 25 July 2013.

ability of musicians to both be creative and to make a living remains a challenge. Indeed, for those from more disadvantaged backgrounds it may be even more of a challenge, as the social welfare function performed by record companies, in the form of non-returnable advances as part of record contracts, become shorter, less valuable, and harder to obtain. Quite what long-term impacts these combinations of inclusionary and exclusionary processes will have for the long-term future of the music industry remain to be seen.

Bibliography

Adorno, T. (1976) *Introduction to the Sociology of Music* (New York: Seabury Press).

Alderman, J. (2001) *Sonic Boom: Napster, P2P and the Battle for the Future of Music* (London: HarperCollins).

Alexander, P. J. (1994) 'Entry Barriers, Release Behaviour, and Multi-Product Firms in the Music Recording Industry', *Review of Industrial Organization*, 9: 85–98.

Andersen, B., James, V., Kozul, Z., and Wright, R. K. (2000) *Copyrights and Competition: Towards Policy Implications for Music Business Development*, DP33 (Manchester: Centre for Research on Innovation and Competition, University of Manchester).

Anderson, C. (2006) *The Long Tail: How Endless Choice is Creating Unlimited Demand* (New York: Random House).

Anderson, D. (2001) 'SETI@home', in A. Oram (ed.), *Peer-to-Peer: Harnessing the Power of Disruptive Technologies* (Sebastopol, CA: O'Reilly), 67–76.

Attali, J. (1984) *Noise: The Political Economy of Music* (Minneapolis: Minnesota University Press).

Auletta, K. (2000) *World War 3.0: Microsoft and its Enemies* (London: Profile Books).

Barbrook, R. (1998) 'The Hi-Tech Gift Economy', *First Monday*, 3: 1–13.

Barbrook, R. (1999) 'Cyber-Communism: How the Americans are Superseding Capitalism in Cyberspace', <http://amsterdam.nettime.org/Lists-Archives/nettime-l-9909/msg00046.html>.

Barbrook, R., and Cameron, A. (1996). *The Californian Ideology*, <http://www.hrc.wmin.ac.uk/ theory-californianideology.html>.

Barfe, T. (2004) *Where Have All the Good Times Gone? The Rise and Fall of the Record Industry* (London: Atlantic Books).

Bassett, K., Griffiths, R., and Smith, I. (2002) 'Cultural Industries, Cultural Clusters and the City: The Example of Natural History Film-Making in Bristol', *Geoforum*, 33: 165–77.

Bathelt, H., Malmberg, A., and Maskell, P. (2004) 'Clusters and Knowledge: Local Buzz, Global Pipelines and the Process of Knowledge Creation', *Progress in Human Geography*, 28: 31–56.

Bauman, Z. (2000) *Liquid Modernity* (Cambridge: Polity Press).

BBC News (2006) 'Kazaa Becomes a Legal Service', 27 July, <http://news.bbc.co.uk/1/hi/5220406.stm>.

Berners-Lee, T., and Fischetti, M. (2000) *Weaving the Web: The Past, Present and Future of the World Wide Web by its Inventor* (London: Texere).

Bettig, R. V. (1996) *Copyrighting Culture: The Political Economy of Intellectual Property* (Boulder, CO: Westview Press).

Beuscart, J. S. (2002) 'Putting Napster to Use: Between a Community and a Body of Customers: The Construction and Regulation of a Sociotechnical Group', *Sociologie du Travail*, 44(4): 461–80.

Bloch, M., and Parry, J. (1989) 'Introduction: Money and the Morality of Exchange', in J. Parry and M. Bloch (eds), *Money and the Morality of Exchange* (Cambridge: Cambridge University Press), 1–32.

Borland, J. (2000a) 'Court Adjourns without Decision in Napster Case', *CNET News.com*, <http://news.cnet.com/news/0-1005-200-2895878.html?tag=st.ne.ni.rnbot.rn.ni>.

Borland, J. (2000b) 'Band Posts Songs as Apology for Napster Ban', *CNET News.com*, 15 Dec., <http://news.cnet.com/news/0-1005-200-4165683.html>.

Borland, J. (2001) 'RIAA Says Online Piracy Shot up', *CNET News.com*, 9 May, <http://news.cnet.com/news/0-1005-200-5879583.html>.

Borland, J. (2003) 'Judge: File-Swapping Tools are Legal', *CNET News.com*, 10 June, <http://news.com.com/2100-1027-998363.html>.

Boshoff, A. (1998). 'CD "Pirates" on Internet Pose Risk to Pop Industry', *Electronic Telegraph*, 28 May, <http://www.telegraph.co.uk>.

Bourdieu, P. (1997) 'Marginalia: Some Additional Notes on the Gift', in A. D. Schrift (ed.), *The Logic of the Gift: Toward an Ethic of Generosity* (London: Routledge), 231–41.

Boyd, J. (2006) *White Bicycles: Making Music in the 1960s* (London: Serpent's Tail).

Boyle, J. (1996) *Shamans, Software and Spleens: Law and the Construction of the Information Society* (Cambridge, MA: Harvard University Press).

Boyle, J. (2000) 'Britney Spears and Online Music Fears', *Financial Times*, 23 May, <http://ft.com>.

Breen, M. (1995) 'The End of the World as we Know it: Popular Music's Cultural Mobility', *Cultural Studies*, 9(3): 486–504.

Brindley, P. (2000a) *New Musical Entrepreneurs* (London: Institute for Public Policy Research).

Brindley, P. (2000b) 'All the Web's a Stage', *Guardian.co.uk*, 1 June: 2–3.

Callon, M. (1998) 'Introduction: The Embeddedness of Economic Markets in Economics', in M. Callon (ed.), *Laws of the Markets* (Oxford: Blackwell), 1–57.

Cardew, B., and Williams, P. (2010) 'Time Running out for Terra Firma?', *Music Week*, 13 Feb.: 1.

Carey, M., and Wall, D. (2001) 'MP3: The Beat Bytes Back', *International Review of Law Computers*, 15: 35–58.

Carrier, J. (1991) 'Gifts, Commodities, and Social-Relations: A Maussian View of Exchange', *Sociological Forum*, 6: 119–36.

Carrier, J. (1994) *Gifts and Commodities* (London: Routledge).

Cassidy, J. (2002) *Dot.Con: The Greatest Story Ever Sold* (London: Allen Lane).

Caves, R. (2000) *Creative Industries: Contracts between Art and Commerce* (Cambridge, MA: Harvard University Press).

Chappel, S., and Garofalo, R. (1977) *Rock 'n' Roll is Here to Pay: The History and Politics of the Music Industry* (Chicago: Nelson-Hall).

Choi, D. Y., and Perez, A. (2007) 'Online Piracy, Innovation, and Legitimate Business Models', *Technovation*, 27: 168–78.

Christensen, C. (1997). *The Innovator's Dilemma* (Boston, MA: Harvard Business School Press).

Christopherson, S. (2002) 'Project Work in Context: Regulatory Change and the New Geography of Media', *Environment and Planning A*, 34: 2003–15.

Christopherson, S., and Storper, M. (1986) 'The City as Studio; the World as Back Lot: The Impact of Vertical Disintegration on the Location of the Motion Picture Industry', *Environment and Planning D: Society and Space*, 4: 305–20.

Clarke, I., Hong, T. W., Miller, S. G., Sandberg, O., and Wiley, B. (2002) 'Protecting Free Expression Online with Freenet', *IEEE Internet Computing*, 6(1): 40–9.

Clarke, T., and Clegg, S. (1998) *Changing Paradigms: The Transformation of Management Knowledge for the 21st Century* (London: HarperCollins).

Coe, N. M. (2000a) 'On Location: American Capital and the Local Labour Market in the Vancouver Film Industry', *International Journal of Urban and Regional Research*, 24: 79–94.

Coe, N. M. (2000b) 'The View from out West: Embeddedness, Inter-Personal Relations and the Development of an Indigenous Film Industry in Vancouver', *Geoforum*, 31: 391–407.

Coe, N. M. (2001) 'A Hybrid Agglomeration? The Development of a Satellite-Marshallian Industrial District in Vancouver's Film Industry', *Urban Studies*, 38: 1753–75.

Coe, N., and Johns, J. (2004) 'Beyond Production Clusters: Towards a Critical Political Economy of Networks in the Film and Television Industries', in D. Power and A. J. Scott (eds), *The Cultural Industries and the Production of Culture* (London: Routledge), 188–204.

Cogan, J., and Clark, W. (2003) *Temples of Sound: Inside the Great Recording Studios* (San Francisco, CA: Chronicle Books).

Coleman, M. (2005) *Playback: From the Victrola to MP3: 100 Years of Music, Machines and Money* (Cambridge, MA: Da Capo).

Comscore (2007) 'For Radiohead Fans, does "True" + "Download" = "Freeload"?', <http://www.comscore.compressrelease.asp?press=1883>.

Connolly, M., and Krueger, A. B. (2005) *Rockonomics: The Economics of Popular Music*, NBER Working Paper, 11282, <http://www.irs.princeton.edu/pubs/pdfs/499.pdf>.

Cooper, J., and Harrison, D. M. (2001) 'The Social Organization of Audio Piracy on the Internet', *Media, Culture and Society*, 23: 71–89.

Corradi, A., Cremonini, M., Montanari, R., and Stefanelli, C. (1999) 'Mobile Agents Integrity for Electronic Commerce Applications', *Information Systems*, 24: 519–33.

Cunningham, M. (1998) *Good Vibrations: A History of Record Production* (London: Sanctuary).

Currah, A. (2003) 'Digital Effects in the Spatial Economy of Film: Towards a Research Agenda', *Area*, 35: 64–73.

Currah, A. (2006) 'Hollywood versus the Internet: The Media and Entertainment Industries in a Digital and Networked Economy', *Journal of Economic Geography*, 6: 439–68.

Currah, A. (2007) 'Managing Creativity: The Tensions between Commodities and Gifts in a Digital Networked Environment', *Economy and Society*, 36: 467–94.

Curry, G. (1999) 'Markets, Social Embeddedness and Precapitalist Societies: The Case of Village Tradestores in Papua New Guinea', *Geoforum*, 30: 285–98.

Curry, M. (1996) *Digital Places* (London: Routledge).

Dane, C., Feist, A., and Manton, K. (1999) *A Sound Performance: The Economic Value of Music to the United Kingdom* (London: National Music Council).

Daniels, E., and Klimis, G. M. (1999) 'The Impact of Electronic Commerce on Market Structure', *European Management Journal*, 17: 318–25.

Daniels, P., Bryson, J., Henry, N., and Pollard, J. (eds) (2000) *Knowledge, Space, Economy* (London: Routledge).

Daniels, P., Leyshon, A., Bradshaw, M., and Beaverstock, J. (eds) (2007) *Geographies of the New Economy: Critical Reflections* (London: Routledge).

David, M. (2010) *Peer to Peer and the Music Industry: The Criminalization of Sharing* (London: Sage).

DeFillippi, R. J., and Arthur, M. B. (1998) 'Paradox in Project-Based Enterprise: The Case of Film Making', *California Management Review*, 40: 1225–38.

De Gusta, M. (2011) 'The REAL Death of the Music Industry', *Business Insider*, 18 Feb., <http://www.businessinsider.com/these-charts-explain-the-real-death-of-the-music-industry-2011-2>.

Dempsey, M. (1999) 'MP3 Heralds the Birth of a New Sector for IT Industry', *Financial Times FT-IT Review*, 3 Nov.: 6.

DeNora, T., and Belcher, S. (2000) ' "When you're Trying Something on you Picture Yourself in a Place Where they are Playing This Kind of Music": Musically Sponsored Agency in the British Clothing Retail Sector', *Sociological Review*, 48(1): 80–101.

DiBona, C., and Ockman, S. (1999) *Open Source* (London: O Reilly).

DiBona, C., Ockman, S., and Stone, M. (eds) (1999) *Open Sources: Voices from the Open Source Revolution* (Sebastopol, CA: O'Reilly).

Dodge, M., and Kitchin, R. (2004) 'Flying through Code/Space: The Real Virtuality of Air Travel', *Environment and Planning A*, 36: 195–211.

Dodge, M., and Kitchin, R. (2005a) 'Code and the Transduction of Space', *Annals of the Association of American Geographers*, 95: 162–80.

Dodge, M., and Kitchin, R. (2005b) 'Codes of Life: Identification Codes and the Machine-Readable World', *Environment and Planning D: Society and Space*, 23: 851–81.

Dodge, M., and Kitchin, R. (2007) 'The Automatic Management of Drivers and Driving Spaces', *Geoforum*, 38: 264–75.

Douglas, M. (1990) 'Foreword: No Free Gifts', in M. Mauss, *The Gift: The Form and Reason for Exchange in Archaic Societies* (London: Routledge).

du Gay, P. (1996) *Consumption and Identity at Work* (London: Sage).

du Gay, P., and Negus, K. (1994) 'The Changing Sites of Sound: Music Retailing and the Composition of Consumers', *Media, Culture and Society*, 16: 395–413.

Edgecliffe-Johnson, A., and Davoudi, S. (2010a) 'EMI's Long and Winding Road Leads to Abbey Road Sale Sign', *Financial Times*, 15 Feb., <http://www.ft.com/cms/s/0/889e63f0-1a70-11df-a2e3-00144feab49a.html>.

Edgecliffe-Johnson, A., and Davoudi, S. (2010b) 'National Trust could Bid for Abbey Road', *Financial Times*, 17 Feb., <http://www.ft.com/cms/s/0/9aae17c6-1bf5-11df-a5e1-00144feab49a.html>.

Evans, P. B., and Wurster, T. S. (1997) 'Strategy and the New Economics of Information', *Harvard Business Review* (Sept.–Oct.): 71–82.

Evans, P. B., and Wurster, T. S. (1999) *Blown to Bits: How the Economics of Information Transforms Strategy* (Boston, MA: Harvard Business School Press).

Farrell, G. (1998) 'The Early Days of the Gramophone Industry in India: Historical, Social and Musical Perspectives', in A. Leyshon, D. Matless, and G. Revill (eds), *The Place of Music* (New York: Guilford), 57–82.

Feng, H. Y., Froud, J., Johal, S., Haslam, C., and Williams, K. (2001) 'A New Business Model? The Capital Market and the New Economy', *Economy and Society*, 30: 467–503.

Fenton, B. (2010) 'EMI Suspends Plan to Sell Abbey Road', *Financial Times*, 21 Feb., <http://www.ft.com/cms/s/0/6a50e4c8-1f24-11df-9584-00144feab49a.html>.

Finnegan, R. (1989) *The Hidden Musicians: Music-Making in an English Town* (Cambridge: Cambridge University Press).

Fisher, R., Ury, W., and Patton, B. (2003) *Getting to Yes: Negotiating an Agreement without Giving in* (New York: Random House).

Florida, R. (2002) *The Rise of the Creative Class* (London: Random House).

Florida, R. (2013) 'The Geography of America's Pop Music/ Entertainment Complex', *Atlantic*, 28 May, <http:// www.theatlanticcities.com/arts-and-lifestyle/2013/05/ geography-americas-pop-musicentertainment-complex/5219>.

Florida, R., and Jackson, S. (2010) 'Sonic City: The Evolving Economic Geography of the Music Industry', *Journal of Planning Education and Research*, 29(3): 310–21.

Florida, R., Mellander, C., and Stolarick, K. (2010) 'Music Scenes to Music Clusters: The Economic Geography of Music in the US, 1970–2000', *Environment and Planning A*, 42(4): 785–804.

Fox, B. (2001) 'Free Speech, Liberty, Pornography', *New Scientist*, 169: 32.

Fox, M. (2004) 'E-Commerce Business Models for the Music Industry', *Popular Music and Society*, 27: 201–20.

Frank, T. (2000) *One Market under God: Extreme Capitalism, Market Populism and the End of Economic Democracy* (London: Secker & Warburg).

French, S., and Leyshon, A. (2004) 'The New, New Financial System: Towards a Conceptualisation of Financial Reintermediation', *Review of International Political Economy*, 11: 263–88.

Freud, J. (1999) 'Listen up', *Wired* (Mar.), <http://www.wired.com/wired/ archive/7.03/chuckd.html>.

Frith S. (1987a) 'Copyright and the Music Business', *Popular Music*, 7: 57–75.

Frith, S. (1987b) 'The Making of the British Record Industry, 1920–64', in J. Curran, A. Smith, and P. Wingate (eds), *Impacts and Influences* (London: Methuen), 278–80.

Frith, S. (1988) *Music for Pleasure: Essays in the Sociology of Pop* (Cambridge: Polity Press).

Frith, S. (2007) 'Live Music Matters', *Scottish Music Review*, 1(1): 1–17.

Froud, J., Johal, S., Leaver, A., and Williams, K. (2008) *Ownership Matters: Private Equity and the Political Division of Ownership*, CRESC Working Paper Series, 61 (Manchester: University of Manchester).

Froud, J., and Williams, K. (2007) *Private Equity and the Culture of Value Extraction*. CRESC Working Paper Series, 31 (Manchester: University of Manchester).

Gander, J. M. (2011) 'Performing Music Production: Making Music Product', unpublished Ph.D. thesis, King's College London.

Garofalo, R. (1999) 'From Music Publishing to MP3: Music and Industry in the 20th Century', *American Music*, 17: 318–53.

Garrahan, M. (2013) 'Live Nation Revels as Clamour for Gigs Reaches Crescendo', *Financial Times*, 21 June, <http://www.ft.com/cms/s/0/ a60b03fa-d73f-11e2-a26a-00144feab7de.html#axzz2XDpWEejF>.

Gelder, K., and Thornton, S. (eds) (1996) *The Subcultures Reader* (London: Routledge).

Gibson, C. (2005) 'Recording Studios: Relational Spaces of Creativity in the City', *Built Environment*, 31: 192–207.

Gibson-Graham, J. K. (2006) *A Postcapitalist Politics* (Minneapolis: University of Minnesota Press).

Gibsone, H. (2013) 'Streaming into the Abyss', *Guardian*, 23 Aug., G2: 14–15.

Gladwell, M. (2000) *The Tipping Point: How Little Things Can Make a Big Difference* (London: Abacus).

Gluckler, J. (2005) 'Digitalisierung und das Paradox informatorischer Reichweite in der Agentturfotografie', *Geographische Zeitschrift*, 93: 100–20.

Gluckler, J. (2007) 'Geography of Reputation: The City as the Locus of Business Opportunity', *Regional Studies*, 41: 949–61.

Goodwin, A. (2006) 'Rationalization and Democratization in the New Technologies of Popular Music', in A. Bennett, B. Shank, and J. Toynbee (eds), *The Popular Music Studies Reader* (London: Routledge), 276–82.

Grabher, G. (2001) 'Locating Economic Action: Projects, Networks, Localities, Institutions', *Environment and Planning A*, 33: 1329–31.

Grabher, G. (2002a) 'Cool Projects, Boring Institutions: Temporary Collaboration in Social Context', *Regional Studies*, 36: 205–14.

Grabher, G. (2002b) 'Fragile Sector, Robust Practice: Project Ecologies in New Media', *Environment and Planning A*, 34: 1911–26.

Grabher, G. (2002c) 'The Project Ecology of Advertising: Tasks, Talents and Teams', *Regional Studies*, 36: 245–62.

Gregory, C. (1982) *Gifts and Commodities* (London: Academic Press).

Hagel, J., and Armstrong, A. G. (1997) *Net Gain: Expanding Markets through Virtual Communities* (Boston, MA: Harvard Business School Press).

Hagel, J., and Singer, M. (1999) *Net Worth: Shaping Markets When Customers Make the Rules* (Boston, MA: Harvard Business School Press).

Harding, J., and Hargreaves, D. (2000) 'Music Mergers Concessions on Offer', *Financial Times*, 19 Sept.: 25.

Hedtke, J. (1999) *MP3 and the Digital Music Revolution* (Lakewood, CO: Top Floor).

Hennion, A. (1989) 'An Intermediary between Production and Consumption: The Production of Popular Music', *Science, Technology and Human Values*, 14: 400–24.

Henwood, D. (2003) *After the New Economy* (New York: New Press).

Hertel, G., Niedner, S., and Herrmann, S. (2003) 'Motivation of Software Developers in Open Source Projects: An Internet-Based Survey of Contributors to the Linux Kernel', *Research Policy*, 32: 1159–77.

Hesmondhalgh, D. (1998) 'The British Dance Music Industry: A Case Study of Independent Cultural Production', *British Journal of Sociology*, 49(2): 234–51.

Heylin, C. (2003) *Bootleg! The Rise and Fall of the Secret Recording Industry* (London: Omnibus Press).

Higgins, G. E. (2007) 'Digital Piracy: An Examination of Low Self-Control and Motivation Using Short-Term Longitudinal Data', *Cyberpsychology and Behavior*, 10: 523–29.

Higgins, G. E., Fell, B. D., and Wilson, A. L. (2007) 'Low Self-Control and Social Learning in Understanding Students' Intentions to Pirate Movies in the United States', *Social Science Computer Review*, 25: 339–57.

Himanen, P. (2001) *The Hacker Ethic and the Spirit of the Information Age* (London: Secker & Warburg).

Hochschild, A. R. (1983) *The Managed Heart: Commercialization of Human Feeling* (Berkeley, CA: University of California Press).

Horning, S. S. (2004) 'Engineering the Performance: Recording Engineers, Tacit Knowledge and the Art of Controlling Sound', *Social Studies of Science*, 34: 703–31.

Hozic, A. A. (1999) 'Uncle Sam Goes to Siliwood: Of Landscapes, Spielberg and Hegemony', *Review of International Political Economy*, 6: 289–312.

Hracs, B. J. (2012a) 'A Creative Industry in Transition: The Rise of Digitally Driven Independent Music Production', *Growth and Change*, 43(3): 442–61.

Hracs, B. J. (2012b) *Management Matters*, Martin Prosperity Institute Working Paper, University of Toronto, Mar., 2012-MPIWP-007.

Hracs, B., and Leslie, D. (2013) *Living under the Lights: The Intensification and Extensification of Aesthetic Labour for Independent Musicians in Toronto*, Martin Prosperity Institute Working Paper, University of Toronto, Mar., 2013-MPIWP-007.

Hracs, B. J., Grant, J. L., Haggett, J., and Morton, J. (2011) 'A Tale of Two Scenes: Civic Capital and Retaining Musical Talent in Toronto and Halifax', *Canadian Geographer-Geographe Canadien*, 55(3): 365–82.

Hracs, B., Jakob, D., and Hauge, A. (2013) 'Standing out in the Crowd: The Rise of Exclusivity-Based Strategies to Compete in the Contemporary Marketplace for Music and Fashion', *Environment and Planning A*, 45, 1144–61.

Hu, J. (2000) 'MP3.com Pays $53.4 Million to End Copyright Suit', *CNET News.com*, 14 Nov., <http://news.cnet.com/news/0-1005-200-3681102.html>

Hudson, A. (2000) 'Offshoreness, Globalization and Sovereignty: A Postmodern Geo-Political Economy', *Transactions of the Institute of British Geographers*, ns 25: 269–83.

International Federation of Phonographic Industries (2002) *Piracy Report*, <http://www.ifpi.org/site-content/antipiracy/piracy2002.html>.

International Federation of Phonographic Industries (2013) *IFPI Digital Music Report 2013: Engine of a Digital World*, <http://www.ifpi.org/content/library/DMR2013.pdf>.

ISO (1999) 'Introduction to ISO', <http://iso.ch/infoe/intro.html>.

Jaisingh, J. (2007) 'Piracy on File-Sharing Networks: Strategies for Recording Companies', *Journal of Organizational Computing and Electronic Commerce*, 17: 329–48.

Johns, A. (2009) *Piracy: The Intellectual Property Wars from Gutenberg to Gates* (Chicago: University of Chicago Press).

Johnson, J. (2002) *Who Needs Classical Music? Cultural Choice and Musical Values* (Oxford: Oxford University Press).

Jones, C. (1996) 'Careers in Project Networks: The Case of the Film Industry', in M. Arthur and B. Rousseau (eds), *The Boundaryless Career* (New York: Oxford University Press), 58–75.

Jones, G. (2009) *Last Shop Standing: Whatever Happened to Record Shops?* (London: Sage).

Jones, S. (1992) *Rock Formation: Music, Technology and Mass Communication* (Newbury Park, CA: Sage).

Jones, S. (2002) 'Music that Moves: Popular Music, Distribution and Network Technologies', *Cultural Studies*, 16(2): 213–32.

Just, R. E., and Chern, W. S. (1980) 'Tomatoes, Technology, and Oligopsony', *Bell Journal of Economics*, 11: 584–602.

Kan, G. (2001) 'Gnutella', in A. Oram (ed.), *Peer-to-Peer: Harnessing the Power of Disruptive Technologies* (Sebastopol, CA: O'Reilly), 94–122.

Kealy, E. R. (1979) 'From Craft to Art: The Case of Sound Mixers and Popular Music', *Sociology of Work and Occupations*, 6: 3–29.

Kealy, E. R. (1982) 'Conventions and the Production of the Popular-Music Aesthetic', *Journal of Popular Culture*, 16: 100–15.

Kenny, M., and Florida, R. (2000) 'Venture Capital in Silicon Valley: Fueling New Firm Formation', in M. Kenney (ed.), *Understanding Silicon Valley: The Anatomy of an Entrepreneurial Region* (Stanford, CA: Stanford University Press), 98–123.

Kittler, F. (1999) *Gramophone, Film, Typewriter* (Stanford, CA: Stanford University Press).

Klein, N. (2000) *No Logo* (London: Flamingo).

Knopper, S. (2009) *Appetite for Self-Destruction: The Spectacular Crash of the Record Industry in the Digital Age* (London: Simon & Schuster).

Kozinets, R. V. (1998) 'E-Tribalized Marketing? The Strategic Implications of Virtual Communities of Consumption', *European Management Journal*, 17: 252–64.

Krueger, A. B. (2005) 'The Economics of Real Superstars: The Market for Rock Concerts in the Material World', *Journal of Labor Economics*, 23(1): 1–30.

Lanza, J. (1995) *Elevator Music: A Surreal History of Muzak, Easy-Listening, and Other Moodsong* (New York: Quartet).

Latour, B. (1987) *Science in Action: How to Follow Scientists and Engineers through Society* (Cambridge, MA: Harvard University Press).

Latour, B. (1999) 'On Recalling ANT', in J. Law and J. Hassard (eds), *Actor Network Theory and After* (Oxford: Blackwell), 15–25.

Latour, B., and Woolgar, S. (1986). *Laboratory Life: The Construction of Scientific Facts* (Princeton: Princeton University Press).

Learmonth, M. (2001a) 'Pressplay Puts MP3.com to Work', *The Industry Standard*, 31 July, <http://www.thestandard.com>.

Learmonth, M. (2001b) 'Freenet's Ian Clarke Heads to California: The Man Who Calls Copyright Law "Unenforceable" is Bringing a Powerful File-Sharing Application across the Pond', *The Industry Standard*, 6 Feb., <http://www.thestandard.com>.

Leidner, R. (1993) *Fast Food, Fast Talk* (Berkeley, CA: University of California Press).

Leslie, D., and Reimer, S. (1999) 'Spatializing Commodity Chains', *Progress in Human Geography*, 23: 401–20.

Lessig, L. (1999) *Code: And Other Laws of Cyberspace* (New York: Basic Books).

Lessig, L. (2001) *The Future of Ideas: The Fate of the Commons in a Connected World* (New York: Random House).

Lessig, L. (2005) *Free Culture: The Nature and Future of Creativity* (London: Penguin).

Lessig, L. (2008) *Remix: Making Art and Commerce Thrive in the Hybrid Economy* (London: Penguin).

Levy, P. (1997) *Collective Intelligence: Mankind's Emerging World in Cyberspace,* tr. R. Bononno (Cambridge, MA: Perseus).

Lewis, M. (1999) *The New New Thing: A Silicon Valley Story* (London: Coronet).

Lewis, M. (2001) *The Future Just Happened* (London: Hodder & Stoughton).

Leyshon, A., and Pollard, J. (2000) 'Geographies of Industrial Convergence: The Case of Retail Banking', *Transactions of the Institute of British Geographers*, 25(2): 203–20.

Leyshon, A., and Thrift, N. (1997) *Money/Space: Geographies of Monetary Transformation* (London: Routledge).

Leyshon, A., and Thrift, N. (1999) 'Lists Come Alive: Electronic Systems of Knowledge and the Rise of Credit-Scoring in Retail Banking', *Economy and Society*, 28: 434–66.

Leyshon, A., and Thrift, N. (2007) 'The Capitalization of Almost Everything: The Future of Finance and Capitalism', *Theory, Culture and Society*, 24: 97–115.

Leyshon, A., Bradshaw, M., Daniels, P., and Beaverstock, J. (2007) 'Geographies of the New Economy: An Introduction', in P. Daniels, A. Leyshon, M. Bradshaw, and J. Beaverstock (eds), *Geographies of the New Economy: Critical Reflections* (London: Routledge), 1–14.

Leyshon, A., French, S., Thrift, N., Crewe, L., and Webb, P. (2005) 'Accounting for E-Commerce: Abstractions, Virtualism and the Cultural Circuit of Capital', *Economy and Society*, 34: 428–50.

Leyshon, A., Lee, R., and Williams, C. C. (eds) (2003) *Alternative Economic Spaces* (London: Sage).

Leyshon, A., Matless, D., and Revill, G. (1995) 'The Place of Music', *Transactions of the Institute of British Geographers*, 20(4): 423–33.

Leyshon, A., Matless, D., and Revill, G. (1998) *The Place of Music* (New York: Guilford).

Lindvall, H. (2012) 'Amanda Palmer Raised $1.2m, But is she Really "the Future of Music"', *Guardian*, 26 Sept., <http://www.guardian.co.uk/media/2012/sep/26/amanda-palmer-future-of-music>.

Lovering, J. (1998) 'The Global Music Industry: Contradictions in the Commodification of the Sublime', in A. Leyshon, D. Matless, and G. Revill (eds), *The Place of Music* (New York: Guilford), 31–56.

Lowry, S. T., and Winfrey, J. C. (1974) 'Kinked Cost Curve and Dual Resource Base under Oligopsony in Pulp and Paper Industry', *Land Economics*, 50: 185–92.

Luening, E. (2000) 'MP3.com Reopens Service for Free, and for Fee', *CNET News.com*, 5 Dec., <http://news.cnet.com/news/0-1005-200-4001419.html>.

Luke, T. W. (1998) 'Kanban Capitalism: Power, Identity, and Exchange in Cyberspace', paper presented at the annual meeting of the International Studies Association, 18–21 Mar.

Lury, C. (1993) *Cultural Rights: Technology, Legality and Personality* (London: Routledge).

McCormack, N. (2013) 'Glastonbury 2013: The Rolling Stones Road to Glastonbury', *Daily Telegraph*, 27 June, <http://www.telegraph.co.uk/culture/music/10118960/Glastonbury-2013-The-Rolling-Stoness-road-to-Glastonbury.html>.

McCourt, T., and Burkart, P. (2003) 'When Creators, Corporations and Consumers Collide: Napster and the Development of On-line Music Distribution', *Media, Culture and Society*, 25(3): 333–50.

McIntosh, N. (1999) 'The Singing Spy', *Guardian*, 4 Nov.: 4.

McRobbie, A. (2002) 'Clubs to Companies: Notes on the Decline of Political Culture in Speeded up Creative Worlds', *Cultural Studies*, 16(4): 516–31.

Malbon, B. (1999) *Clubbing: Dancing, Ecstasy and Vitality* (London: Routledge).

Malone, T., Yates, J., and Benjamin, R. (1987) 'Electronic Markets and Electronic Hierarchies', *Communications of the ACM*, 30: 484–97.

Mance, H. (2013) 'Spotify versus Thom Yorke: Streaming with Tears', *Financial Times*, 15 July, <blogs.ft.com/tech-blog/2013/07/spotify-versus-thom-yorke-streaming-with-tears>.

Marks, J. (1998) *Gilles Deleuze: Vitalism and Multiplicity* (London: Pluto Press).

Martin, R. (2007) 'Making Sense of the New Economy? Realities, Myths and Geographies', in P. Daniels, A. Leyshon, M. Bradshaw, and J. Beaverstock (eds), *Geographies of the New Economy: Critical Reflections* (London: Routledge), 15–48.

Marx, K., and Engels, F. (1977) *Manifesto of the Communist Party* (Moscow: Progress Publishers; first publ. in 1848).

Mauss, M. (1990) *The Gift: The Form and Reason for Exchange in Archaic Societies,* tr. W. D. Halls (London: Routledge; first publ. in 1950).

May, W., Mason, C., and Pinch, S. (2001) 'Explaining Industrial Agglomeration: The Case of the British High-Fidelity Industry', *Geoforum,* 32: 363–76.

Micklethwait, J., and Wooldridge, A. (1997) *The Witch Doctors: What the Management Gurus are Saying, Why it Matters and How to Make Sense of it* (London: Mandarin).

Millard, A. (2005) *America on Record: A History of Recorded Sound,* 2nd edn (Cambridge: Cambridge University Press).

Miller, D. (1995) 'Consumption as the Vanguard of History: A Polemic by Way of an Introduction', in D. Miller (ed.), *Acknowledging Consumption: A Review of New Studies* (London: Routledge), 1–57.

Miller, D. (2000) 'Virtualism: The Culture of Political Economy', in I. Cook, D. Crouch, S. Naylor, and J. R. Ryan (eds), *Cultural Turns/Geographical Turns: Perspectives on Cultural Geography* (Harlow: Prentice Hall), 196–213.

Miller, D. (2002) 'Turning Callon the Right Way up', *Economy and Society,* 31: 218–33.

Minar, N., Hedlund, M., and Power, P. (2001) 'A Network of Peers: Peer-to-Peer Models through the History of the Internet', in A. Oram (ed.), *Peer-to-Peer: Harnessing the Power of Disruptive Technologies* (Sebastopol, CA: O'Reilly), 3–20.

MMC (1994) *The Supply of Recorded Music: A Report on the Supply in the UK of Pre-Recorded Compact Discs, Vinyl Discs and Tapes Containing Music,* Cm2542, Monopolies and Mergers Commission (London: HMSO).

Monbiot, G. (2000) *Captive State: The Corporate Takeover of Britain* (London: Macmillan).

Moody, G. (1999) 'MP3', *New Scientist,* 19 June: 32–6.

Moody, G. (2001) *Rebel Code: Linux and the Open Source Revolution* (London: Allen Lane).

MusicMetric (2012) *Digital Music Index,* <http://static.semetric.com/dmi/2012.09.17/Musicmetric_DMI_Extended_Summary_2012.pdf>.

National Music Council (2002) *Counting the Notes: The Economic Contribution of the UK Music Business* (London: National Music Council).

Naughton, J. (2001) 'Why Microsoft is Fighting a Free and Open Exchange', *Guardian Unlimited,* 2 Aug., <http://www.guardian.co.uk/Archive>.

Negroponte, N. (1995) *Being Digital* (London: Coronet).

Negus, K. (1992) *Producing Pop: Culture and Conflict in the Popular Music Industry* (London: Edward Arnold).

Negus, K. (1995) 'When the Mystical Meets the Market: Creativity and Consumption in the Production of Popular Music', *Sociological Review*, 43: 316–41.

Negus, K. (1999a) 'The Music Business and Rap: Between the Street and the Executive Suit', *Cultural Studies*, 13: 488–508.

Negus, K. (1999b) *Music Genres and Corporate Cultures* (London: Routledge).

O'Mahony, S. (2003) 'Guarding the Commons: How Community Managed Software Projects Protect their Work', *Research Policy*, 32: 1179–98.

Oram, A. (2001) 'Preface', in A. Oram (ed.), *Peer-to-Peer: Harnessing the Power of Disruptive Technologies* (Sebastopol, CA: O'Reilly), pp. vii–xv.

O'Riain, S. (2000) 'Net-Working for a Living: Irish Software Developers in the Global Workplace', in M. Burawoy, J. A. Blum, G. Sheba, Z. Gille, T. Gowan, L. Haney, M. Klawiter, S. H. Lopez, S. O'Riain, and M. Thayer (eds), *Global Ethnography: Forces, Connections, and Imaginations in a Postmodern World* (Berkeley, CA: University of California Press), 175–202.

Osborne, A. (2007) 'EMI: The Good, the Bad, and the Ugly', *Daily Telegraph*, 2 Aug., City section: 3.

Osborne, T. (2003) 'Against "Creativity": A Philistine Rant', *Economy and Society*, 32: 507–25.

O'Shea, J., and Madigan, C. (1997) *Dangerous Company* (London: Nicholas Brealey).

Ouellet, J. F. (2007) 'The Purchase versus Illegal Download of Music by Consumers: The Influence of Consumer Response towards the Artist and Music', *Canadian Journal of Administrative Sciences: Revue Canadienne des Sciences de l'Administration*, 24: 107–19.

Parry, J. (1989) 'On the Moral Perils of Exchange', in J. Parry and M. Bloch (eds), *Money and the Morality of Exchange* (Cambridge: Cambridge University Press), 64–93.

Parry, J., and Bloch, M. (eds) (1989) *Money and the Morality of Exchange* (Cambridge: Cambridge University Press).

Passman, D. S. (2012) *All you Need to Know about the Music Business*, 8th edn (New York: Free Press).

Peck, J. (2005) 'Struggling with the Creative Class', *International Journal of Urban and Regional Research*, 29(4): 740–70.

Perlman, M. (2004) 'Golden Ears and Meter Readers: The Contest for Epistemic Authority in Audiophilia', *Social Studies of Science*, 34: 783–807.

Pinch, S., Henry, N., Jenkins, M., and Tallman, S. (2003) 'From "Industrial Districts" to "Knowledge Clusters": A Model of Knowledge Dissemination and Competitive Advantage in Industrial Agglomerations', *Journal of Economic Geography*, 3: 373–88.

Porcello, T. (2004) 'Speaking of Sound: Language and the Professionalization of Sound-Recording Engineers', *Social Studies of Science*, 34: 733–58.

Power, D., and Hallencreutz, D. (2002) 'Profiting from Creativity? The Music Industry in Stockholm, Sweden and Kingston, Jamaica', *Environment and Planning A*, 34: 1833–54.

Power, D., and Jansson, J. (2002) 'The Emergence of a Post-Industrial Music Economy? Music and ICT Synergies in Stockholm, Sweden', *Geoforum*, 35: 425–39.

Pratt, A. (1997) 'Production Values: From Cultural Industries to the Governance of Culture', *Environment and Planning A*, 29: 1911–17.

Pratt, A. (2000) 'New Media, the New Economy and New Spaces', *Geoforum*, 31: 425–36.

Pratt, A. C. (2001) *Intellectual Property Rights in the Age of Digital Reproduction: Implications for the Arts* (London: Arts Council of England).

Pratt, A. C. (2007) 'The New Economy: Or Emperor's New Clothes', in P. Daniels, A. Leyshon, M. Bradshaw, and J. Beaverstock (eds), *Geographies of the New Economy: Critical Reflections* (London: Routledge), 71–86.

Price, S. (2010) 'Education: The Low Spark of Well Heeled Boys', *Word Magazine* (Dec.): 33–4.

PwC (2013) *Global Entertainment Media Outlook*, <http://www.pwc.com/gx/en/global-entertainment-media-outlook/segment-insights/music.jhtml>.

Raymond, E. (1999) *The Cathedral and the Bazaar: Musings on Linux and Open Software by an Accidental Revolutionary* (Sebastopol, CA: O'Reilly).

Reece, D. (2010) 'Terra Firma Investors Would Rather Not Feel the Pain of Acquiring EMI', *Daily Telegraph*, 11 Mar., Business: 2.

Reuters (2000) 'Bertelsmann Attempts to Sell Napster Deal to Labels', *CNET News.com*, 27 Nov., <http://news.cnet.com/news/0-1005-200-3876053.html>.

Reuters (2001) Napster Use Affected by File Blocking', *CNET News.com*, 26 Apr., http://news.cnet.com/news/0-1005-200-5741252.html>.

Rifkin, J. (2000) *The Age of Access: How the Shift from Ownership to Access is Transforming Capitalism* (Harmondsworth: Penguin Books).

Robins, K., and Webster, F. (1999) *Times of the Technoculture: From the Information Society to the Virtual Life* (London: Routledge).

Rose, M. (1993) *Authors and Owners: The Invention of Copyright* (Cambridge, MA: Harvard University Press).

Rosen, H. (2000) 'Open letter from RIAA to MP3.com CEO Michael Robertson, MP3.com', 23 January, <http://www.riaa.com/news/newsletter/press2000/012100.asp>.

Rowe, H. (1998) 'Electronic Commerce: Legal Implications of Consumer-Orientated Electronic Commerce', *Computer Law and Security Report*, 14: 232–42.

Ryan, M. P. (1998) *Knowledge Diplomacy: Global Competition and the Politics of Intellectual Property* (Washington, DC: Brookings Institution).

Sabbagh, D. (2007) 'Guy Hands Aims to Snuff Out Excesses that Cost EMI £100m a Year', *The Times*, 29 Nov., <http://business.timesonline.co.uk/tol/business/industry_sectors/media/article2963629.ece>.

Sadler, D. (1997) 'The Global Music Business as an Information Industry: Reinterpreting Economies of Culture', *Environment and Planning A*, 29: 1919–36.

Sandall, R. (2003) 'The Day the Music Industry Died', *Sunday Times Magazine*, 16 Feb.: 24–30.

Sanghera, S. (2002) 'Rock 'n' Roll Suicide: How Napster, TV-Created Pop and a Dearth of Talent are Killing the Record Industry', *Financial Times*, 15 Nov.: 19.

Sanjek, R. (1988) *American Popular Music and its Business*, ii. *1909–1984* (New York: Oxford University Press).

Sassen, S. (2000) 'Digital Networks and the State: Some Governance Questions', *Theory, Culture and Society*, 17: 19–33.

Schoenberger, E. (1997) *The Cultural Crisis of the Firm* (Oxford: Blackwell).

Schrift, A. D. (ed.) (1997a) *The Logic of the Gift: Towards an Ethic of Generosity* (London: Routledge).

Schrift, A. D. (1997b) 'Introduction: Why Gift?', in A. D. Schrit (ed.), *The Logic of the Gift: Towards an Ethic of Generosity* (London: Routledge), 1–22.

Schroeter, J., and Azzam, A. (1991) 'Marketing Margins, Market Power, and Price Uncertainty', *American Journal of Agricultural Economics*, 73: 990–9.

Scott, A. (1999a) 'The US Recorded Music Industry: On the Relations between Organisation, Location, and Creativity in the Cultural Economy', *Environment and Planning A*, 31: 1965–84.

Scott, A. (1999b) 'The Cultural Economy: Geography and the Creative Field', *Media Culture and Society*, 21: 807–17.

Scott, A. J. (2000) *The Cultural Economy of Cities: Essays on the Geography of Image-Producing Industries* (London: Sage).

Scott, A. J. (2001) 'Capitalism, Cities, and the Production of Symbolic Forms', *Transactions of the Institute of British Geographers*, NS 26: 11–23.

Scott, A. J. (2002) 'A New Map of Hollywood: The Production and Distribution of American Motion Pictures', *Regional Studies*, 36: 957–75.

Scott, A. J. (2004a) *On Hollywood* (Princeton: Princeton University Press).

Scott, A. J. (2004b) 'Cultural-Products Industries and Urban Economic Development: Prospects for Growth and Market Contestation in Global Context', *Urban Affairs Review*, 39: 461–90.

Sexton, R. J., Sheldon, I., McCorriston, S., and Wang, H. M. (2007) 'Agricultural Trade Liberalization and Economic Development: The Role of Downstream Market Power', *Agricultural Economics*, 36: 253–70.

Shank, B. (1994) *Dissident Identities: The Rock 'n' Roll Scene in Austin, Texas* (Hanover, NH: Wesleyan University Press).

Shiga, J. (2007) 'Copy-and-Persist: The Logic of Mash-up Culture', *Critical Studies in Media Communication*, 24: 93–114.

Shirky, C. (2001) 'Listening to Napster', in A. Oram (ed.), *Peer-to-Peer: Harnessing the Benefits of a Disruptive Technology* (Sebastopol, CA: O'Reilly), 21–37.

Showcase (2000) *Showcase International Music Book 2000: The International Music Production Guide*, 32nd edn (London: Showcase).

Simpson, D. (2000) 'Back to the Factory', *Guardian*, 12 Jan., <http://www.guardianunlimited.co.uk>.

Sivadas, E., Grewal, R., and Kellaris, J. (1998) 'The Internet as a Micro Marketing Tool: Targeting Consumers through Preferences Revealed in Music Newsgroup Usage', *Journal of Business Research*, 41: 179–86.

Slater, D. (2000) 'Consumption without Scarcity: Exchange and Normativity in an Internet Setting', in P. Jackson, M. Lowe, D. Miller, and F. Mort (eds), *Commercial Cultures: Economies, Practices, Spaces* (Oxford: Berg), 123–42.

Southall, B. (1982) *Abbey Road: The Story of the World's Most Famous Recording Studios* (Cambridge: Patrick Stephens).

Southall, B. (2009) *The Rise and Fall of EMI Records* (London: Omnibus Press).

Stallman, R. (2001) 'Community versus Copyright in the Age of Digital Networks' The Arts Council of England, 30 July, <http://www.artsonline.com/servlet/ContentServer?pagename=AceOnline/MediaFile/Article&cid=1053079963625>.

Steinberg, R. J., and Figart, D. M. (1999) 'Emotional Labor since *The Managed Heart*', *Annals of the American Academy of Political and Social Science*, 561(1): 8–26.

Storper, M., and Salais, R. (1997) *Worlds of Production: The Action Frameworks of the Economy* (Cambridge, MA: Harvard University Press).

Storper, M., and Venables, A. J. (2004) 'Buzz: Face-to-Face Contact and the Urban Economy', *Journal of Economic Geography*, 4: 351–70.

Strader, T. J., and Shaw, M. J. (1997) 'Characteristics of Electronic Markets', *Decision Support Systems*, 21: 185–98.

Straw, W. (1991) 'Systems of Articulation, Logics of Change: Communities and Scenes in Popular Music', *Cultural Studies*, 6: 368–88.

Sutton Trust (2012) *The Educational Backgrounds of the Nation's Leading People*, <http://www.suttontrust.com/public/document/1leading-people-report-6-.pdf>.

Talacko, P. (2001) 'A Sound Marketing Idea for Web-Site Musicians', *Financial Times*, 11 July: 14.

Tamm, E. (1995) *Brian Eno: His Music and the Vertical Colour of Sound* (New York: Da Capo Press).

Tehranian, J. (2003) *Optimizing Piracy: The Uses and Limits of Intellectual Property Enforcement in the Cyberage* (mimeograph: available from author at S. J. Quinney College of Law, University of Utah).

Thèberge, P. (1997) *Any Sound you Can Imagine: Making Music/Consuming Technology* (Hanover, NH: Wesleyan University Press).

Thèberge, P. (2004) 'The Network Studio: Historical and Technological Paths to a New Ideal in Musicmaking', *Social Studies of Science*, 34: 759–81.

The Economist (1999) 'The Big Five Hit the Web', 8 May, <http://www.economist.com>.

The Economist (2000) 'Shopping around the Web: A Survey of E-Commerce', 26 Feb., survey supplement.

The Economist (2003a) 'Lights! Camera! No Profits!', 16 Jan., <http://www.economist.com>.

The Economist (2003b) 'How to Manage a Dream Factory', 16 Jan., <http://www.economist.com>.

The Economist (2003c) 'Unexpected Harmony', 23 Jan., <http://www.economist.com>.

The Economist (2003d) 'In a Spin', 27 Feb., <http://www.economist.com>.

Thomas, L. (2010) 'Public School Singers Take over the Pop Charts: 60% of Acts are Now Privately Educated', *Daily Mail*, 5 Dec. <http://www.dailymail.co.uk/tvshowbiz/article-1335880/Public-school-singers-pop-charts-60-acts-privately-educated.html>.

Thornton, S. (1995) *Club Cultures: Music, Media and Subcultural Capital* (Cambridge: Polity).

Thrift, N. (1994) 'On the Social and Cultural Determinants of International Financial Centres: The Case of the City of London', in S. Corbridge, N. Thrift, and R. Martin (eds), *Money, Power and Space* (Oxford: Blackwell), 327–55.

Thrift, N. (2001) ' "It's the Romance, Not the Finance, that Makes the Business Worth Pursuing": Disclosing a New Market Culture', *Economy and Society*, 30: 375–80.

Thrift, N. (2005) *Knowing Capitalism* (London: Sage).

Thrift, N. (2008) 'The Material Practices of Glamour', *Journal of Cultural Economy*, 1: 9–23.

Thrift, N., and Dewsbury, J. D. (2000) 'Dead Geographies—and How to Make them Live', *Environment and Planning D: Society and Space*, 18: 411–32.

Thrift, N., and French, S. (2002) 'The Automatic Production of Space', *Transactions of the Institute of British Geographers*, NS 27: 309–35.

Thurow, L. C. (1997) 'Needed: A New System of Intellectual Property Rights', *Harvard Business Review*, 75: 95–103.

Vaidhyanathan, S. (2001) *Copyrights and Copywrongs: The Rise of Intellectual Property and How it Threatens Creativity* (New York: New York University Press).

Vogel, H. L. (2001) *Entertainment Industry Economics: A Guide for Financial Analysis*, 5th edn (Cambridge: Cambridge University Press).

von Krogh, G., Spaeth, S., and Lakhani, K. R. (2003) 'Community, Joining, and Specialization in Open Source Software Innovation: A Case Study', *Research Policy*, 32: 1217–41.

Wadsworth, T., with Forde, E. (2011) *Remake, Remodel: The Evolution of the Record Label*, A MusicTank Report (London: MusicTank).

Waldman, S. (1999) 'What's the Story, Multimedia Glory', *Guardian*, 26 Nov., G2: 4–5.

Wallis, R., Kretschmer, M., and Klimis, G. M. (1999) *Globalisation, Technology and Creativity: Current Trends in the Music Industry*, Final Report to the

Economic and Social Research Council Programme, Media Economics and Media Culture; available at <http://www.city.ac.uk/rvs1392/finale4.html>.

Ward, A. (2000) 'Virgin: Company Threatens to Pull out of Music Retailing', *Financial Times*, 26 Jan., <http://www.ft.com>.

Wark, P. (2007) 'Record Deal-Maker', *The Times*, 3 Aug.: 2.

Wayner, P. (2000) *Free for All: How Linux and the Free Software Movement Undercut the High-Tech Titans* (New York: HarperCollins).

Weber, S. (2004) *The Success of Open Source* (Cambridge, MA: Harvard University Press).

Williams, K. (2001) 'Business as Usual', *Economy and Society*, 30: 399–411.

Wise, J. M. (1997) *Exploring Technology and Social Space* (Thousand Oaks, CA: Sage).

Wise, J. M. (1998) 'Intelligent Agency', *Cultural Studies*, 12: 410–28

Zeitlyn, D. (2003) 'Gift Economies in the Development of Open Source Software: Anthropological Reflections', *Research Policy*, 32: 1287–91.

Zetner, A. (2008) 'Online Sales, Internet Use, File Sharing, and the Decline of Retail Music Speciality Stores', *Information Economics and Policy*, 20: 288–300.

Zook, M. (2003) 'Underground Globalization: Mapping the Space of Flows of the Internet Adult Industry', *Environment and Planning A*, 35(7): 1261–86.

Zook, M. (2005) *The Geography of the Internet Industry: Venture Capital, Dot-coms and Local Knowledge* (Oxford: Blackwell).

Zook, M. (2007) 'The New Old Thing: E-Commerce Geographies After the Dot.Com Boom', in P. Daniels, A. Leyshon, M. Bradshaw, and J. Beaverstock (eds), *Geographies of the New Economy: Critical Reflections* (London: Routledge), 87–110.

Websites

AtomicPop.com http://atomicpop.com

Electronic Telegraph (*Daily Telegraph* e-edition) http://www.telegraph.co.uk

Financial Times http://www.ft.com http://www.telegraph.co.uk

International Organization for Standardization (ISO) http://iso.ch/infoe/intro.html

MP3.com Mhttp://MP3.com

Napster http://www.napster.com

Record Industry Association of America (RIAA) http://www.riaa.com

Secure Digital Music Initiative (SDMI) http://www.sdmi.org

The Economist http://www.economist.com

Wired http://www.wired.com

Index

Note: 'n' after a page reference indicates a footnote